STEP BY STEP

DIY

First Published in 1998

This edition Published in 1998 by
Brockhampton Press,
a member of Hodder Headline PLC Group,
20 Bloomsbury Street,
London WC1 B3QA

Specialist Authors:	David Holloway
	Mike Lawrence
	Martyn Hocking
	Diane Carr
Photographer:	Chris Allen
Illustrators:	Jane Pickering
	David Cook
	Clive Spong
Editors:	Martin Hocking
	Mary Morton
Colour Separation:	GA Graphics

Printed in Singapore by Imago

Title: STEP BY STEP DIY
ISBN: 1-86019-404-4

IMPORTANT NOTICE:
Every effort has been made to ensure that the information contained in STEP BY STEP DIY is accurate. However a book of this kind cannot replace the specialist advice concerning building regulations, planning, local by laws and related matters which are neither static nor simple. Therefore no responsibility can be accepted by the publishers, copyright holders or the authors for any loss, injury or damage caused by reliance upon the accuracy of such information.

STEP BY STEP DIY

A step by step guide to the essential elements of D.I.Y. in and around the home.

BROCKHAMPTON PRESS

CONTENTS

CONTENTS

INTRODUCTION

A house is not a home until it is organised, arranged and decorated to your own personal taste. Active participation in cost saving tasks and projects enhances a feeling of 'home' and quality of lifestyle, while often adding value to the property.
Until recently specialist tools and materials were the prerogatives of the professional trades due to limited availability. More and more these items are now available at retail stores making it possible for all of us, with the inclination, to undertake a multitude of projects around the home.

This book has been written by experts in their field, to make complicated tasks easy by using simple instructions and clear illustrations throughout. It will make completion of selected tasks as simple as possible. It does not endorse activities that are dangerous but concentrates on overcoming potentially difficult projects with tried and tested solutions.

This book is dedicated to all those who wish to have a go, but need 'expert knowledge' prepared in a manner that is simple, in order to aid them on the way to successful D.I.Y.

Right: A well used and cared for selection of D.I.Y tools.

PLUMBING

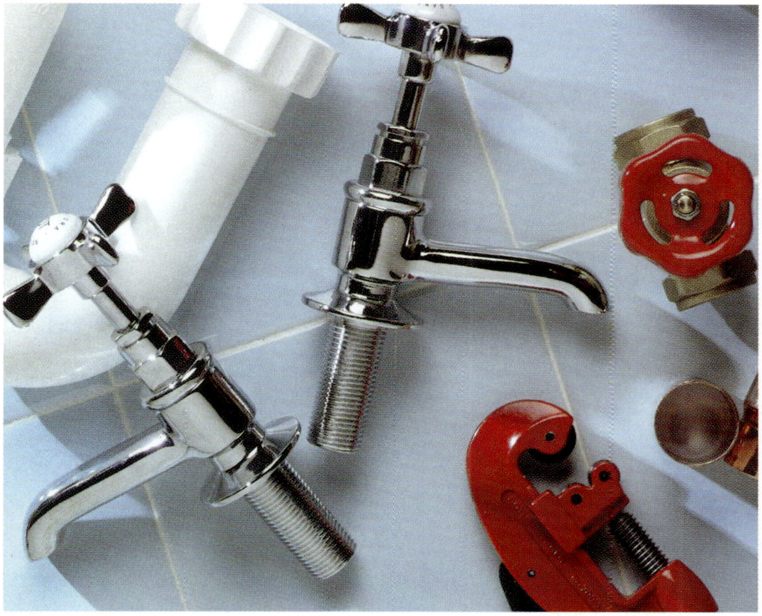

PLUMBING BASICS

To many people plumbing is a mystery. Turn the taps on and cold water comes out of one and hot out of the other; pull the plug out or flush the loo and water disappears. Everything is fine – until, that is, something goes wrong.

Understanding how your plumbing system works, learning about the tools, techniques and materials that you need, will help you to prevent problems, and cope with problems as they occur. It will also allow you to make additions and alterations to your plumbing system to improve and upgrade them.

For the amateur, plumbing has never been easier. For a start, the tools, materials and equipment you need are now widely accessible with the growth of the do-it-yourself superstores. Advances in the materials, especially with the advent of plastic pipe and push-fit fittings, have made the actual joining of pipe much easier. No longer is there a need to be able to work with lead supply pipe (the word 'plumber' comes from the Latin *plumbum* meaning 'lead'); nor is there a need to work with cast iron for outside soil pipes.

RULES AND REGULATIONS

The main rules affecting plumbing work in the home are the Water Bylaws issued by your local water company. Apart from some minor local differences, these are standard.

Bylaws are to prevent waste, undue consumption, misuse or contamination of the mains water supply. Many of the regulations are regarding back-syphonage – to prevent water from your house returning to the mains supply. You are required by law to give notice of five working days to your Water Company if you intend to fit a bidet, a flushing cistern, a hose union tap or any appliance through which water could contaminate the mains supply.

Prosecutions are rare but the penalties for contravening the water bylaws can be steep and will mount daily until you correct the fault. Bylaws represent good plumbing practice and you should get a copy from your local Water Company (they are usually free).

Water Bylaws cover only the supply side of plumbing; the waste and soil is covered by the Building Regulations administered by your local council. You should find out something about what the Regulations say in order that you do not contravene them.

Minor alterations and replacements are not affected, but to do work which will affect the underground drains, you should inform the Building Control Department of your local council.

Installing gas central heating is covered by the Gas Safety (Installation and Use) Regulations which make it illegal to do any of the gas-fitting work yourself. Only a gas fitter or plumber registered with CORGI (Council for Registered Gas Installers) may do the work.

Any electrical work is covered by the IEE Wiring Regulations, incorporated in British Standard BS 7671. Although not mandatory in England and Wales, in Scotland, they are part of the Building Regulations and have the force of the law.

THE WATER SUPPLY

There is just one water supply to the home – cold water from the Water Company mains.

Somewhere inside the house, there will be a system for heating the water to provide the domestic hot water (DHW) which comes out of the taps and often another system for heating water for radiators to provide central heating.

A system of pipes carries cold water, hot water, and central heating water around the house. Another system of (larger) pipes carries the waste water away from basins, sinks, baths and WCs. These are connected to the soil system which runs into underground drains.

1: Direct System

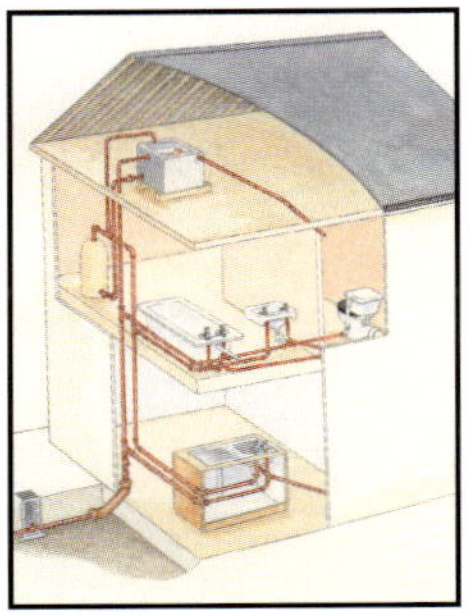

2: Indirect System

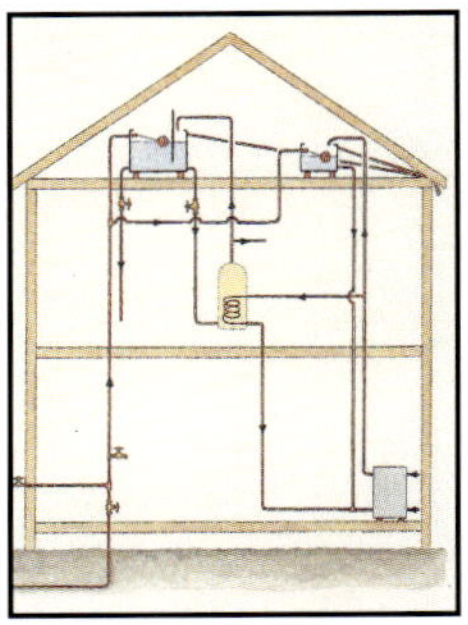

3: Cold Water Cistern

COLD WATER SYSTEMS

In all homes connected to mains water, the supply comes via a branch pipe from the water main in the street. Just outside the property boundary there is a stopcock under a metal cover, so that the Water Company can isolate the supply. From there the service pipe runs into the house under the floorboards to the householder's stopcock, usually situated under the kitchen sink or, in older houses, just inside the front door.

A pipe, called the rising main, runs through the house from the householder's stopcock with a branch pipe leading to the kitchen sink cold tap – to provide fresh water for drinking and cooking – and a draincock just above the stopcock – for draining down the system.

1: DIRECT SYSTEM

All the other cold taps in the house – usually the bathroom basin and bath – plus the WC are fed directly from this rising main.

2: INDIRECT SYSTEM

The rising main feeds a large (50 gallons/227 litres) cold water cistern (3) in the loft which in turn feeds the cold taps and WCs.

The flow of water into the cistern is controlled by a ballvalve – which shuts off when the water reaches a certain level – and an overflow pipe which leads to the outside and drains off excess water, if it rises too high or the ballvalve fails. A gate-valve on the pipe leading out of the cistern allows the cold taps and WC to be isolated for maintenance without having to drain the cistern down.

The original idea of the cold water cistern was to provide cold water storage for the home in the event of mains failure. Prolonged mains failure is rare these days and having a cistern has many disadvantages. The water inside can become contaminated or it can freeze (particularly now that loft spaces are well insulated), which could be disastrous.

HOT WATER SYSTEMS

The most common system for heating domestic hot water is a hot water cylinder. It is usually made of copper and contains around 26 gallons/120 litres of water.

An indirect cylinder (4) is fed from the main cold water cistern or, where the cold water system is 'direct', by its own mains-fed cold water cistern, mounted either in the loft or above the hot water cylinder.

The cold feed pipe to the cylinder enters at the bottom, while the pipe which feeds the hot water taps emerges from the top of the cylinder, because hot water rises. A third pipe – the safety open vent – is attached to the pipe leading out of the top of the cylinder and loops back to the cistern, and is twisted into a downwards-pointing position. This allows air and steam to escape should the system overheat – water expands as it heats up affecting the cold feed pipe.

A hot water cylinder can be heated either by an electric immersion heater or by a sealed, coiled pipe which carries water heated by the boiler. Except in very old (now outmoded) systems, the water from the boiler and the water inside the cylinder do not mix.

An alternative method of heating the hot water is to have a gas-fired multipoint heater. Cold water passes through this and is heated almost instantly by a gas burner. It then circulates to all the hot water taps in the house. A recent development is the combination boiler which combines the function of a multipoint heater and a central heating boiler. The advantages of both are that there is a constant supply of hot water and that it is possible to get rid of the cold water cistern in the loft (provided the cold water supply is direct); the disadvantage is that the water flow rate is generally slower than a cistern-fed system, meaning that baths take longer to fill.

The latest type of hot water system is the un-vented hot water storage system, in which a special hot water cylinder is fed direct from the rising main. An expansion vessel allows for expansion and safety valves allow air and steam to escape. This type of system can only be installed by a suitably qualified plumber.

4: Indirect Cylinder

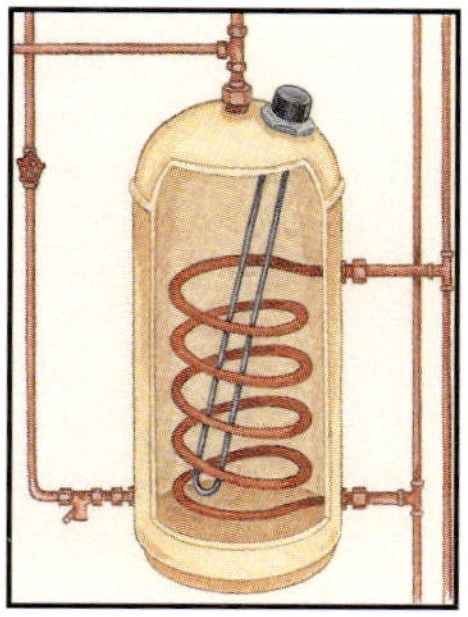

1: Modern System

3: Septic Tank

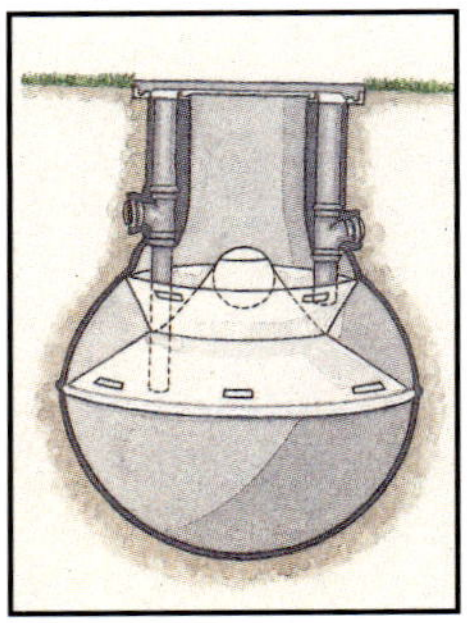

WASTE SYSTEMS

The dirty water from baths, basins and sinks is taken away by waste pipes, which lead to the main soil pipe. All these pipes must be fitted with a water-filled trap – fitted immediately after the bath, basin or sink – which prevents smells from the drains getting back into the house. There are different designs of trap, but they all perform the same job.

In older houses, the waste from the bath and basins is fed into a hopper head connected to the top of the soil pipe. This leads into the gully into which the waste pipe from the kitchen sink also runs. The gully leads to the underground drains.

A WC or bidet must also contain a water-filled trap (built into the WC pan) and the waste pipe goes directly to the soil pipe. In older (two-pipe) systems WCs have their own soil pipe which is separate from the soil pipe for baths and basins.

1: A MODERN SYSTEM

A single-stack with WC and bidet waste fed into the same pipe as the bath and basin wastes; the layout ensures the two wastes are kept separate until they are safely inside the pipe. Many modern single-stack systems may have the main soil pipe inside the house, but this is no longer a requirement of the Building Regulations.

Underground, the wastes from the soil pipes and kitchen sink gully are removed by the drains either to the main sewer or, in rural properties, to a cesspool or a septic tank.

2: A CESSPOOL

This is simply a storage tank which needs to be emptied regularly.

3: A SEPTIC TANK

A miniature sewage works, in which bacteriological action separates the waste into a harmless liquid and a sludge. The sludge needs removing about once a year. When working well, septic tanks are very effective, but you need to be careful to keep them clean. Special care must be taken when using bleach, disinfectant and detergents, which can kill the bacteria.

PLUMBING MATERIALS

Lead was the main material used in plumbing but new concepts and regulations have led to the introduction of new materials and techniques.

In some houses, you may need to join the older 'imperial' sizes of pipe to the now current metric sizes. To do this you will need the appropriate adaptor which can usually only be supplied by specialist plumbing suppliers.

For making capillary fittings you will need an adaptor when joining 22mm pipe to old ¾in pipe, or with 15mm pipe to old ½in pipe, and with 28mm pipe to 1in pipe.

When using compression fittings you do not need an adaptor for joining 15mm to 12in or 28mm to 1in pipe.

PIPES AND FITTINGS

For hot and cold water supply pipes, the most common material is copper.

There are two main pipe sizes. For pipes under mains pressure, and the final feed pipes to basins, WCs and radiators, 15mm is used.

The supply pipes to bath taps, the cold supply pipe to the hot water cylinder, the open vent pipe and the main central heating pipe runs use 22mm.

Copper pipe is mainly joined in one of two ways.

1: COMPRESSION FITTINGS

Nuts on the ends of the fittings compress flat brass rings – 'olives' – to make a seal. Compression fittings have the advantage that they allow some adjustment of the pipe within the fitting by loosening the nut which is helpful when making complicated pipe runs with lots of corners.

Below:

1: Compression fittings

2: Capillary fittings 'Yorkshire'

3: Capillary fittings 'End-feed'

4: Olives

5: Copper tube 15 mm

6: Copper tube 22 mm

7: Solder

1: Compression Fittings

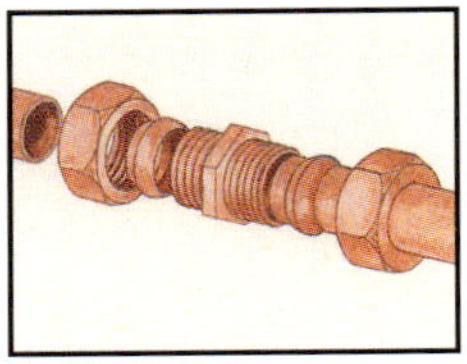

2: Capillary Fittings

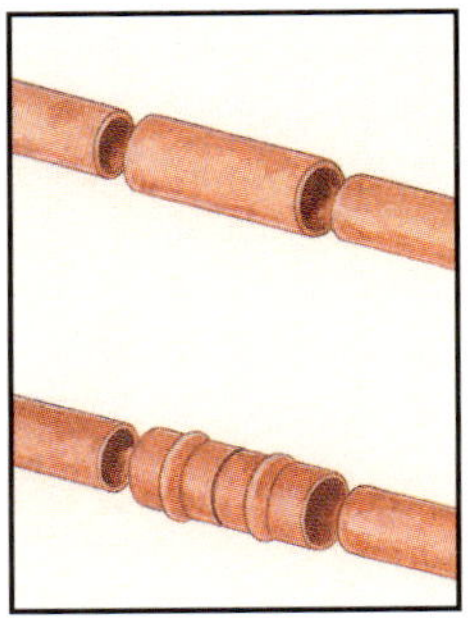

3: Push-fit Plastic Fittings

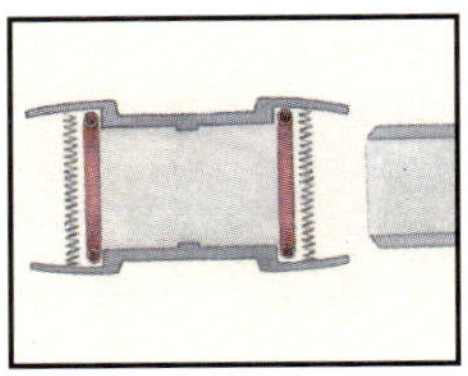

2: CAPILLARY FITTINGS

Solder is heated to flow between the pipe and the fitting to make the seal. There are two types of capillary fitting.

End-feed fittings need to have the solder added as the fitting is heated up.

Solder-ring or 'Yorkshire' fittings have solder contained within the end bulge of the fitting. Capillary fittings are cheaper and neater, but there is a skill required to make the join – which can be difficult to achieve.

3: PUSH-FIT PLASTIC FITTINGS

These are used largely for various drainage pipe systems and overflows. Some have to be made using a solvent adhesive although increasingly many drainage systems use built-in rubber seals. These can be expensive but are the easiest of all to make and allow the pipe to be turned inside the fitting even after the joint has been made.

Plastic has been the main material used for drainage services for some time and is increasingly used for supply plumbing. Some joins have to be made using a solvent adhesive although increasingly many drainage systems use built-in rubber seals.

Rigid plastic pipes and fittings used for supply services are very cheap, but they are not easy to make as the pipes have to be 'solvent-welded'.

Plastic pipes have the advantage that they come in long lengths, allowing pipe runs to be made with virtually no fittings and the pipe can be run through holes cut in the centre of joists rather than through notches cut in the top edge. However, they need to be fitted with adequate space for expansion, especially if used for, or near to, hot water or central heating, as plastic pipe tends to sag.

Below: Modern plastic fittings and pipe.

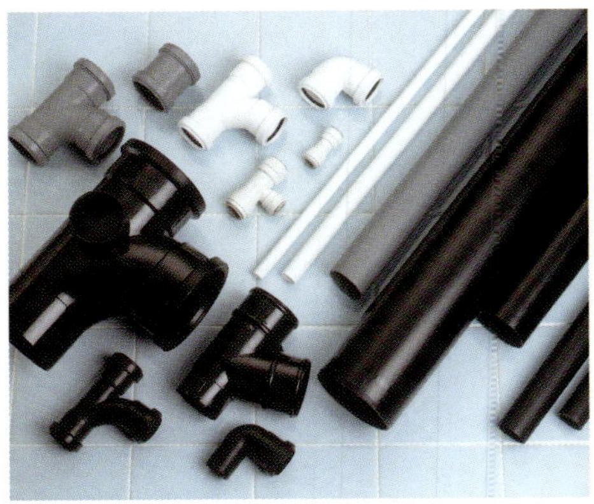

PLUMBING TOOLS AND TECHNIQUES

The main techniques needed are how to cut, bend and join pipes and how to make screwed connections.

You must also be able to do basic building work – lifting floorboards, making small, medium and large holes in walls, cutting notches and holes in joists, making good damage to plaster – and have the right tools for these jobs.

CUTTING PIPE

1 Semi-flexible plastic pipe is easy to cut. All you need is a pair of secateurs – either special or garden secateurs.

2 Rigid plastic piping including waste pipe is cut with a fine-toothed hacksaw. On large pipes, wrap a piece of paper around the pipe to ensure the cut remains square.

3 For copper pipe, the best tool to use is a pipe cutter which has a hardened steel wheel which is progressively advanced into the pipe. Small circular versions can be used close to walls, but sometimes you will need to use a hacksaw.

BENDING PIPE

Sometimes it is necessary to bend copper pipe in a gentle curve to go around corners or to fit round another pipe.

Semi-flexible plastic pipe can be bent without the use of tools – rigid plastic pipe cannot be bent at all.

TO BEND SMALL BORE COPPER PIPE

1 Use a pipe-bending spring. Tie a length of string to the loop at the end of the spring. Insert the spring into the pipe and position it either side of the bend position.

2 Ensure that you hold the pipe within the length of the spring. Place a sponge block between your knee and the pipe as you bend the pipe – it will distort without the spring.

3 For deep bends retrieve the spring using the string, or use a screwdriver as shown if it cannot be removed easily.

Short lengths of hand-bendable, flexible, copper pipe can be bought which are useful for awkward connections. These must not be used for connecting shower pumps or in central heating systems. Special connectors are available for this.

1

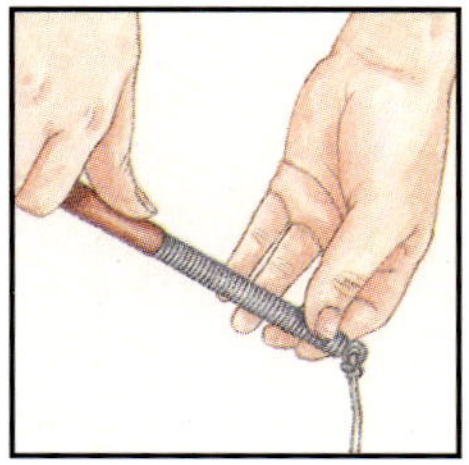

2

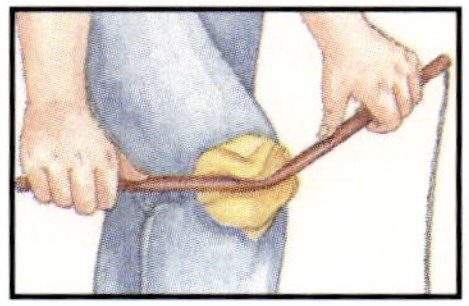

3

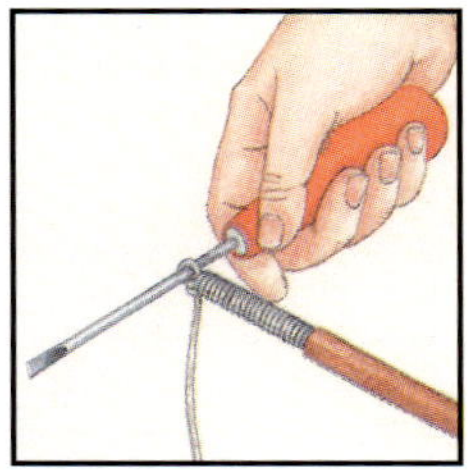

Below: A pipe-bending machine.

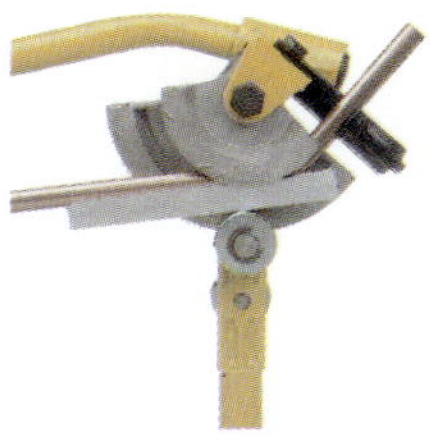

1

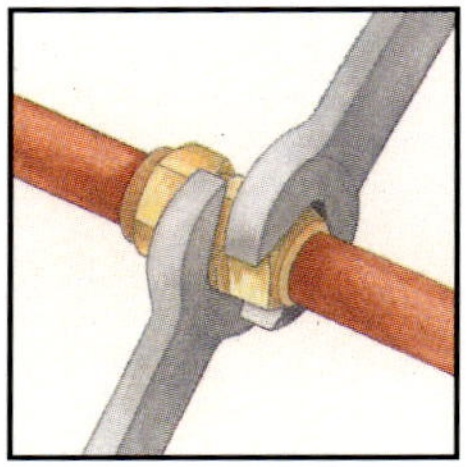

2

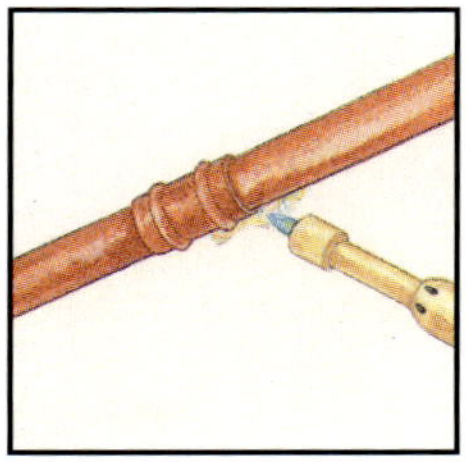

3

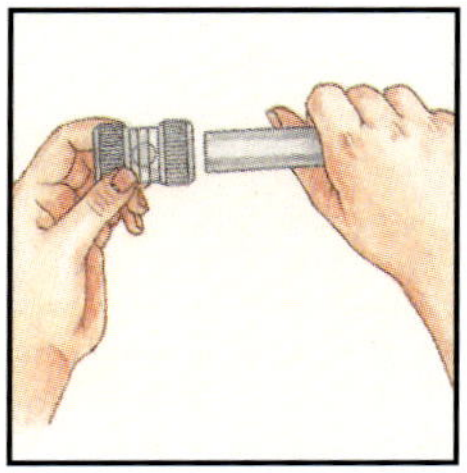

4

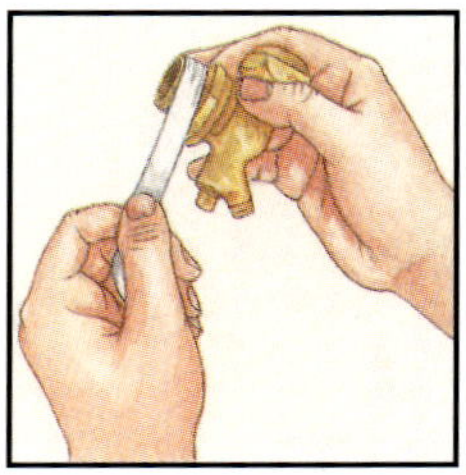

USING FITTINGS

A good selection of spanners (preferably adjustable ones) is essential for working on compression fittings.

Plumber's wrenches with serrated jaws are designed to turn iron pipes – they will damage the surface of nuts.

USING COMPRESSION FITTINGS

1 Place the components in sequence on the pipe with the 'olives' in position. Always use one spanner to turn the nut and a second spanner to hold the fitting.

USING CAPILLARY FITTINGS

2 Copper pipe ends must be scrupulously clean with flux applied to both the pipes and the inside of the fitting.

A gas blowtorch is the most convenient tool. Use a flame-resistant mat to protect flammable materials such as floorboards. Pipe-soldering tongs are safer to use in some situations though they take longer.

With the fitting in place, apply heat until solder appears at the rim of a solder-ring fitting – or until a neat ring of molten solder is built around the rim with an end-feed fitting.

USING PUSH-FIT FITTINGS

3 Push-fit fittings need no special tools, but it is essential to follow the instructions supplied with the fittings and to ensure that the copper inserts supplied are used with push-fit fittings on plastic piping.

USING THREADED FITTINGS

4 In plumbing there are many threaded connections – especially on hot water cylinders and central heating boilers. It is essential that screwed joints make a perfect seal. Traditionally hemp and plumber's mastic were inserted between the male and female threads. Today, white PTFE tape – available in rolls – is used.

Wind the PTFE tape around the threads – about seven times, in a clockwise direction – so that it is forced tight into the threads as the joint is made.

SERVICING VALVES

It is a requirement of the Water Bylaws that servicing valves be fitted to pipes leading to taps or ballvalves.

This is to make it easier to repair or replace either a tap or a ballvalve without the need to turn off the water and drain the pipe. Many repair jobs will involve turning off the water and draining the pipe. To avoid having to do this too often, it is a good idea, wherever possible, to fit a few in-line servicing valves.

Cut out a short length of pipe – without making the overall pipe length longer or shorter – and replace it with an in-line servicing valve. These usually have compression fittings on either end with a small, internal, shut-off 'ball' mechanism, that can be operated by a coin or screwdriver.

BLOCKED SINK OR BASIN

1 The first thing to try is the trusty sink plunger or the more powerful, hand-operated force pump. Nine times out of ten, this will force the blockage out of the pipe and allow the water to run freely.

2 If plunging does not work, use a length of wire through the plug hole to work the blockage free. A plumber will use a 'snake', a long length of flexible wire with a hook on the end. You can buy one of these yourself. Pull rather than push the blockage.

3 The next stage is to dismantle the trap. Wear rubber gloves to protect your hands and make sure you have a large bucket beneath the trap to catch the water.

4 Again, 'wiggling' the blockage with a length of wire will help. Remember to refit the trap before tidying up and dispose of the bucket contents outside!

5 Finally, when the blockage is partially clear, you can use a chemical – such as caustic soda.

Do not use chemicals on a completely blocked sink – the plastic trap may melt – and you could end up with a bucket of toxic chemicals!

Follow the instructions to the letter and wear rubber gloves. Use a dilute solution of washing soda at monthly intervals down bath, basin and sink plugholes to help keep them free from blockages.

1

2

3

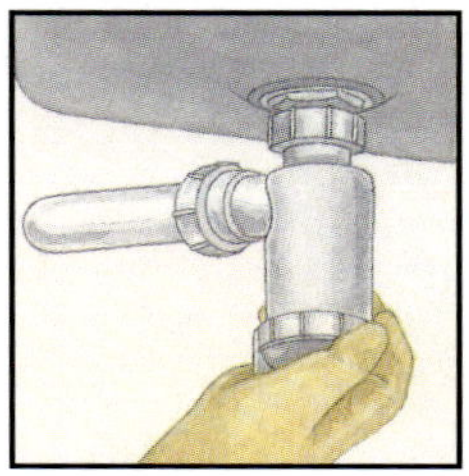

4

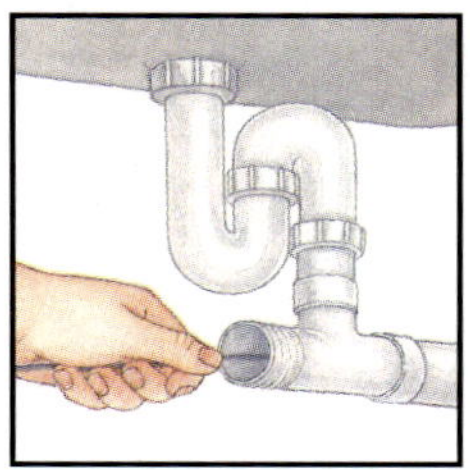

BLOCKED DRAINS

The first sign that indicates a blocked drain is usually an overflowing gully.

1 Trace the direction of the drains and the sequence of inspection chambers. Lift all the manhole covers until you find a dry inspection chamber – the blockage is between this dry one and the previous full one.

2 Remove the blockage with hired or bought drain rods. Drain rods are supplied with plunger discs for pushing the blockage out and with 'corkscrews' for dislodging it.

3

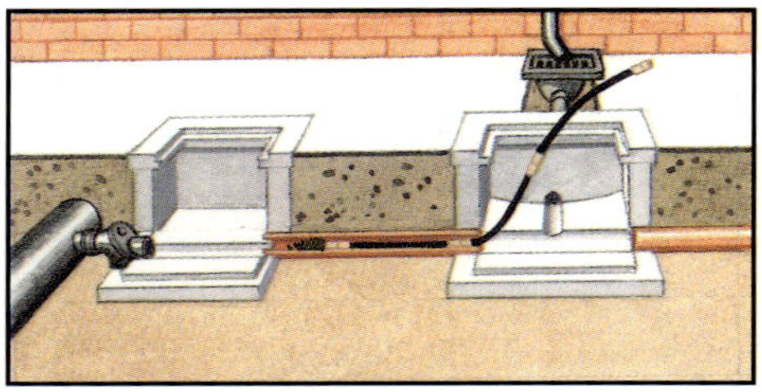

4

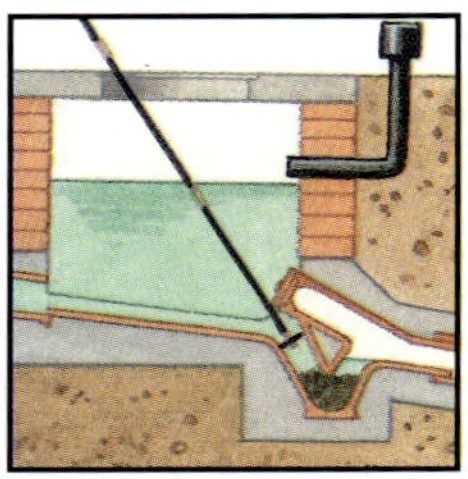

3 Push the drain rod into the outlet of the full inspection chamber, adding more extension rods as necessary.

Never twist the rods anticlockwise or they could unscrew underground.

4 If the blockage is in the final inspection chamber before the sewer, this is usually caused by the 'rodding arm' plug falling into the interceptor trap.

Use some stiff twisted wire or a 'snake' to pull the plug out and then rod with the plunger disc to clean out the trap.

Underground drains should be hosed down once a year and damaged concrete haunching repaired – to avoid broken haunching causing blockages.

DRIPPING TAPS

Taps often drip and cannot be turned off effectively when a tap-washer has failed.

1 Turn off the water supply – to the tap and open the tap to let the pipe drain.

2 Remove the tap handle – and the domed tap cover on old style taps. Unscrew the large nut formed around the barrel of the tap mechanism. This comes out in one piece with the washer at the bottom – usually held in place by a small nut or flange. Replace the washer with one that is of the same size and shape as the original.

3 Before replacing the tap mechanism, inspect the brass washer seat inside the tap. If it is badly scored, it will need to be re-ground with a tap reseating tool – which you can hire – or a new nylon seat inserted. If you do not do this, the new tap washer will not be effective.

4 Assembly is the reverse of dismantling – if the tap leaks from the top when the water is turned on, it could be that the O-ring seal needs to be replaced or, on older taps, that the packing has failed. Remove the packing by unscrewing the small nut under the dome cover, pick out the old, dried-out packing and replace it with wool that is smeared with petroleum jelly.

Re-packing should also cure a tap which is stiff to operate – no more than fingertip pressure should ever be required.

AIRLOCKS

An airlock is often the cause for water refusing to flow from a tap. The usual culprit is badly run pipework but sometimes the cause is either a cold water cistern or a pipe feeding the hot water cylinder that is too small.

TO CURE AN AIRLOCK

1 Attach one end of a hose pipe to a tap with mains pressure – the kitchen cold tap in an 'indirect' cold system or any cold tap in a 'direct' system – and the other end of the hose to the offending tap.

2 Turn both taps full on. Only if the primary cause of the problem is cured, will the airlock be removed.

LEAKING OVERFLOW

The overflow pipe from a cold water or WC cistern is a 'warning' and is meant to annoy you – so that you fix it.

It is usually a failed washer on an old-fashioned piston-operated ballvalve. It is possible to clean up and repair the washer on a piston-operated ballvalve but a much better solution is to replace it with a modern diaphragm ballvalve (brass or plastic). A diaphragm ballvalve is more compact and easier to adjust; also it is much quieter in operation.

To replace or repair a ballvalve, turn off the water supply to the cistern at the mains or at the cold water cistern. Unscrew the nut holding the pipe to the

2 (dripping taps)

4

1 (airlocks)

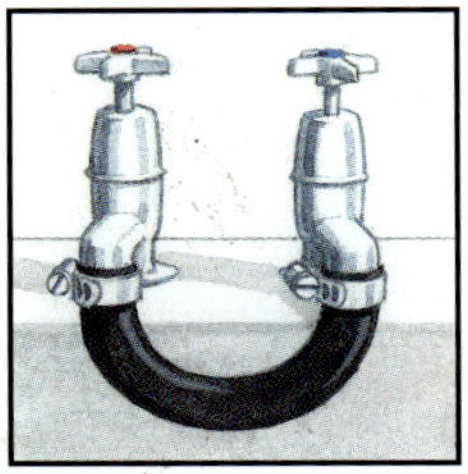

ballvalve. The tap connector on the end of the pipe can usually be connected directly to the new ballvalve – make sure the small fibre washer which makes the seal is undamaged and in place.

NOISES

CREAKING NOISES

Creaking noises are caused by hot water and central heating pipes expanding as they warm up and rub against notches cut in flooring joists.

The solution is to raise the floorboards and slip some foam pipe insulation around the pipes where they cross the joists – sometimes the notch may need to be enlarged.

NOISY FILLING OF THE CISTERN

This can be cured by replacing a piston-operated ballvalve with a diaphragm type (see page 21).

Make sure the ballvalve is the correct type – low-pressure for cistern-fed supplies and high-pressure for mains-fed supplies.

LOUD BANGING IN THE PIPES

This is known as water hammer and is caused by a shock wave passing down the pipe often started when a tap is turned off. It can be cured by closing the mains stopcock a little to reduce the flow of water. Sometimes a replacement diaphragm ballvalve will do the trick, and occasionally you will need to change one or more tap washers.

FROZEN OR BURST PIPES

Pipes will not usually freeze in houses which are occupied and heated.

If a house is left empty during the winter, ice can form in the pipes and joints which if left unattended will 'burst' – either splitting the pipe or 'blowing' a joint apart – with disastrous results as water pours all over the house.

DEFROSTING A FROZEN PIPE

1 A frozen water pipe is indicated when there is no water from a tap and it is known not to be an airlock.

This can be cured by opening the tap and using a hair-dryer to heat the pipe. Work back from the tap until the frozen blockage is reached. This will be where the pipe is exposed to the coldest temperatures – in an outhouse, in the loft or under any downstairs floorboards.

REPAIRING A BURST PIPE

2 Purchase a burst-pipe repair coupling – an elongated compression fitting – or a repair kit. Turn the water off – and drain the pipe system.

A burst pipe can be dealt with immediately using a burst-pipe repair clamp without turning the water off.

3 Mark off the burst part of the pipe to the effective length of the repair coupling.

4 Cut out the damaged pipe using a fine-cut hacksaw. File off any burrs and use wire wool to remove stain, grease or paint from around the ends of the pipe.

5 Fit the repair coupling elements in sequence ensuring that the 'olives' are correctly seated.

Minimise the danger of burst pipes by draining the water system before leaving a house empty in the winter. Do not drain the central heating system – add antifreeze instead.

WC FLUSH FAILURE

If a low-level WC fails to flush or is difficult to flush, the fault is usually the large clear plastic 'flapvalve' washer.

The function of this is to carry water over the inverted 'U' of the flushing mechanism to start the siphonic operation.

1 Turn off the water supply – to the cistern, then flush it to remove the water. Dismantle the flushing mechanism until you can get to the 'flapvalve' washer.

2 Replace the washer with a new one of the same size and type.

If you cannot get one of exactly the same size, buy a larger one and cut it down.

3 Complete flush failure may be due to a broken link which is easily replaced.

4 Difficult flushing on an old-fashioned, high-level cistern is usually due to dirt. A good clean is usually sufficient.

PROBLEMS WITH SCALE

In hard water areas, water will produce scale if heated above 70°C/160°F.

Scale can build up inside hot water pipes and cylinders, it can damage the element in hot water cylinders, and cause stains in baths, basins and sinks.

1 (frozen/burst pipes)

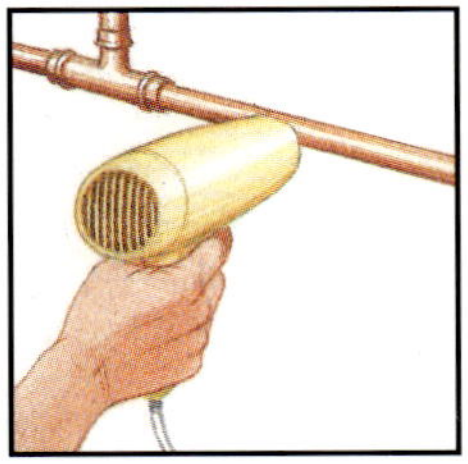

3

4

5

3 (problems with scale)

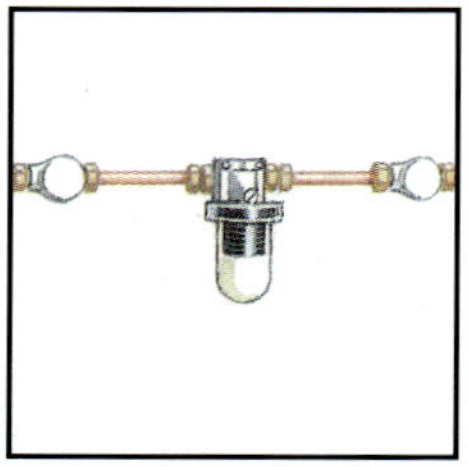

1 Minimise the formation of scale in electrically-heated hot water systems by setting an immersion heater thermostat to no more than 60°C/140°F.

2 Scale can be a particular problem in water heaters that produce instant hot water – gas multipoints, gas sink heaters and electric showers – since the temperature of the water at the heater is much higher than 70°C/160°F.

3 A solution is to fit a polyphosphate dosing unit in the cold pipe leading to the heater. The polyphosphate will prevent scale formation. Ensure stopcocks are fitted either side of the unit so that it can be removed for maintenance or repair.

STIFF STOPCOCKS

If left unused for a long period, stopcocks can become very difficult to turn and you do not want to find this out when you have an emergency.

TO FREE A STOPCOCK,

1 Apply heat with boiling water from a kettle and add a little penetrating oil to the spindle.

2 Once the stopcock is free, close it half a turn from fully open to prevent it sticking again.

LEAKING PIPE JOINTS

LEAKING COMPRESSION OR SCREWED FITTINGS

1 These can normally be cured by tightening the nut. With a compression joint, hold the fitting with one spanner and tighten the nut with a second spanner. Do not overtighten the nut – a deformed 'olive' will leak worse than before.

LEAKING CAPILLARY FITTINGS

1 Turn the water off – drain the pipe by opening taps and using draincocks if necessary.

2 Only when you are certain that there is no water in the offending pipe should you heat and unsolder the joint.

3 Clean up the pipe and fit a new capillary fitting. Any water inside the pipe will make the joint more difficult to make. A simpler solution may be to cut the pipe either side of the joint and fit a burst pipe repair compression coupling.

PUSH-FIT FITTINGS

1 Turn the water off – and drain the pipe, then replace the fitting.

2 Check the instructions with the new push-fit fitting for how to dismantle the old one.

INSTALLING A NEW BASIN

A new basin could be a replacement – where the pipework is already in place – or an addition in a bedroom or new cloakroom, where the pipes will have to be installed.

New 15mm copper or plastic supply pipes are connected via compression or capillary tee-fittings to existing pipes. They run to the basin position under the floorboards and along or up walls with clips at regular intervals. Ensure that horizontal pipe runs have a slight fall.

A new 32mm/1¼in plastic waste pipe must run to and be connected to the main soil stack or – in older systems – the waste hopper. This is not easy with old cast iron systems.

Drill a hole through the wall where the pipe passes through an outside wall. Then open this up from either side with a club hammer and cold chisel.

When buying a basin, remember to buy the taps, waste outlet and trap – make sure the basin has one hole for a mixer and two holes for pillar taps, depending on which installation is being used.

Planned properly, unsightly pipework can be avoided to give a professional and stylish look to your bathroom.

WHEN REPLACING A BASIN

Turn off the water and drain – before you disconnect and remove the old basin.

WHEN FITTING A NEW BASIN

Fit the basin and waste pipe, then turn off the water and drain to cut into the existing hot and cold water pipes to connect the new supply pipes.

2 (installing a new basin)

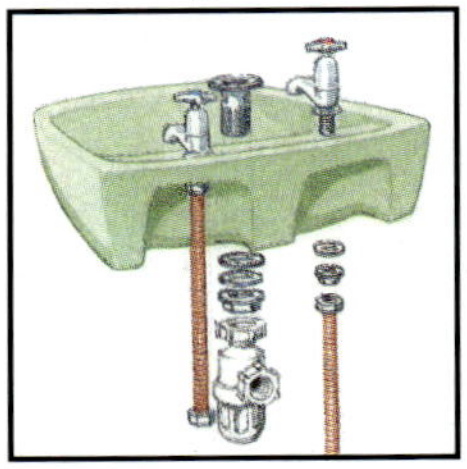

2 (installing a new bath)

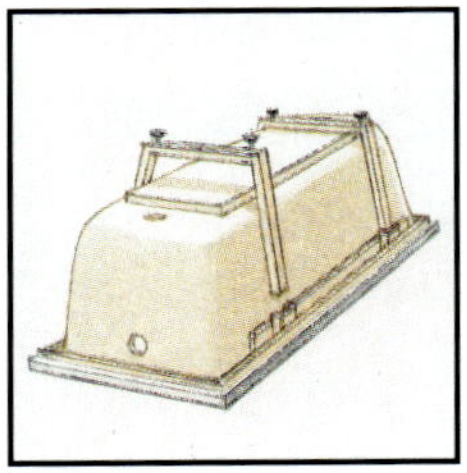

3

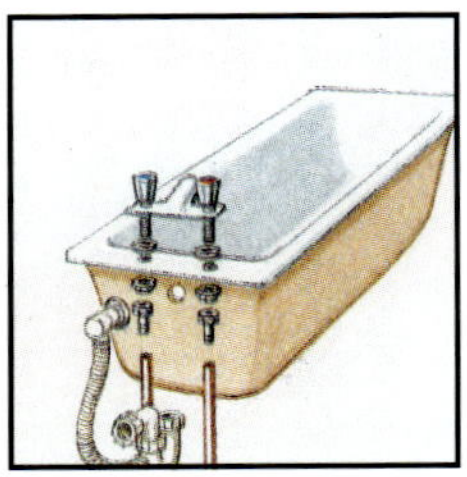

1 Ensure that the wall is strong enough to carry the weight of a wall-hung or pedestal basin.

On solid walls use heavy-duty wall plugs preferably with long-reach brass or zinc-coated screws.

On hollow or partition walls install a batten. To take the weight, this must be screwed directly to the upright studs in the wall. Cut away the plasterboard to install the batten and make good the plaster before fitting the basin.

2 Connect the taps before fitting the basin and make sure that the sealing washers provided are correctly fitted. Then connect the waste outlet, which also has a sealing washer.

3 Connect the supply pipes to the basin taps using tap connectors. If you have a modern basin mixer-tap, it may be supplied with 8mm, 12mm or 15mm pipes which will need pipe reduction pieces. Supply pipes must be connected using compression fittings – to allow removal of the taps in the future.

4 The waste pipe is connected to the plug assembly via a plastic trap – bottle-traps are the neatest.

INSTALLING A NEW BATH

Usually a new bath is a replacement so make sure that it will fit the space and that the size of supply and waste pipe can be routed and adapted to fit the new bath.

1 Turn the water off – drain the system. Use a bath/basin spanner to disconnect the supply pipes from the taps. A cast-iron bath is very heavy. Cover it with a blanket. Smash it with a sledge hammer and remove the pieces.

2 Fit the cradle support to the bath. If the bath is against a solid wall remove a strip of plaster so that the edge can be embedded and rigidly secured into the wall.

3 Run – or extend – the service pipes to new positions. Fit the taps, waste outlet – and overflow link – to the bath. Adjust the legs to level the bath and secure it in position.

4 Connect the waste and supply pipes. Make good the bath surround and seal around the edges with a flexible silicone sealant.

5 Run a $4mm^2$ earth wire from the main earthing point by the consumer unit. Use electrical earth bond connectors fastened to the supply pipes as close to the taps as possible.

A metal bath must be earthed.

FITTING A BATH/SHOWER MIXER

A bath/shower mixer is quite easy to fit as it simply replaces the existing bath taps.

The mixer usually has two taps – one hot and one cold – with a diverter lever or knob which allows mixed water to flow either through the spout into the bath or up a flexible hose to a shower-head mounted above the bath.

1 Turn the water off – and drain the bath hot and cold taps. Remove the bath side-panel. Use a bath/basin spanner to unscrew the nut securing the pipe on the nearest tap and then the nut on the furthest tap.

2 Use the spanner to unscrew and remove the taps. Clean off any dried sealing compound on the bath surface.

3 Check that the supply pipes reach the new bath/shower mixer – if short, use an adaptor – and fit the mixer.

4 Drill holes for the shower bracket and fasten to the wall. To comply with Water Bylaws, a restraining ring should be fitted to prevent the shower-head from dangling in the bath.

5 Turn on the water to check for leaks – tighten the nuts if necessary – and re-fit the bath panel.

PLUMBING IN A WASHING MACHINE/DISHWASHER

A permanently plumbed-in washing machine or dish-washer has to be the height of convenience.

PLUMBING IN

1 Do not turn the water off. Use a 'plumbing-in' kit – it has self-cutting valves which fit over the sink supply pipes. When the valve is screwed down it makes the connection.

Alternatively turn the water off – and drain the pipe. Cut the supply pipe to insert 15mm compression tee-fittings and run a 15mm pipe to the machine position. Fit a mini turn-off valve with ¾in BSP screwed fitting to the end of the pipe and connect the machine supply hose.

PLUMBING OUT

2 Close to the sink – connect the out hose direct to the sink waste pipe with a self-cutting connector. Alternatively fit a standpipe to the wall behind the machine with a trap at the bottom. Take the waste pipe from the trap out through the wall to a convenient gully.

1 (bath/shower mixer)

3

1 (plumbing in)

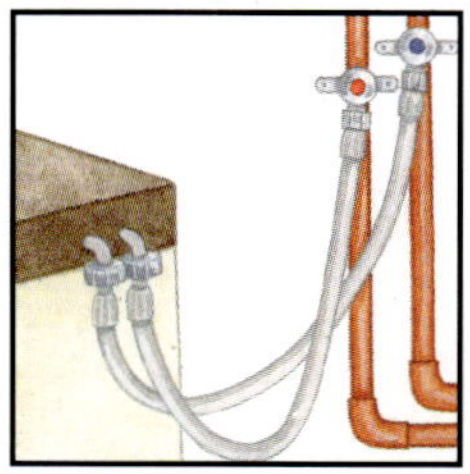

2 (plumbing out)

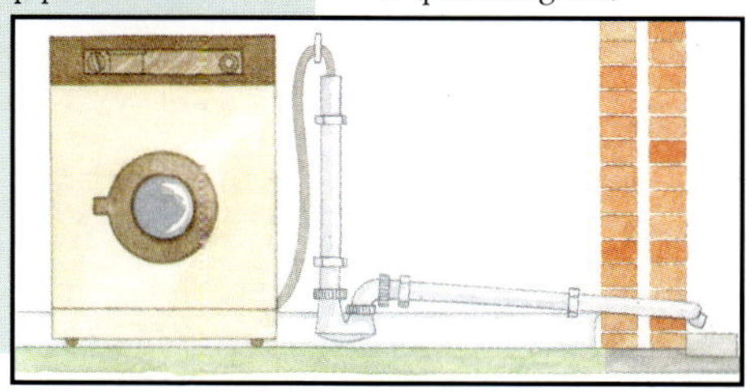

1 – 21mm hole for Part 2 or 3 diaphragm ballvalve – look for a strong part of the cistern.

2 – 25mm hole to take the plastic tank connector for the 22mm overflow pipe.

3 – two 30mm holes for tank connectors to the 22mm cold supply pipes to feed the bathroom taps, and to feed a hot water cylinder. Both these connections should be made at least 50mm/2in above the base of the cistern – the cold supply to the hot water cylinder should be slightly higher than any cold supply.

FITTING A NEW COLD WATER CISTERN

Modern plastic cisterns come in rigid – rectangular versions, which need a large loft hatch – and flexible – circular versions, which can be squeezed through a hatch. Make sure you buy a cistern with a capacity of at least 227 litres/50 gallons for a main cold water, or 18 litres/4 gallons for a central heating feed-and-expansion cistern. Buy also a 'Bylaw 30' kit which includes a lid and an insulating jacket.

1 Turn the water off at the mains and drain the cistern. Bale out the remains by hand. Disconnect all the old pipes – if it will not pass through the loft hatch, leave it in a corner.

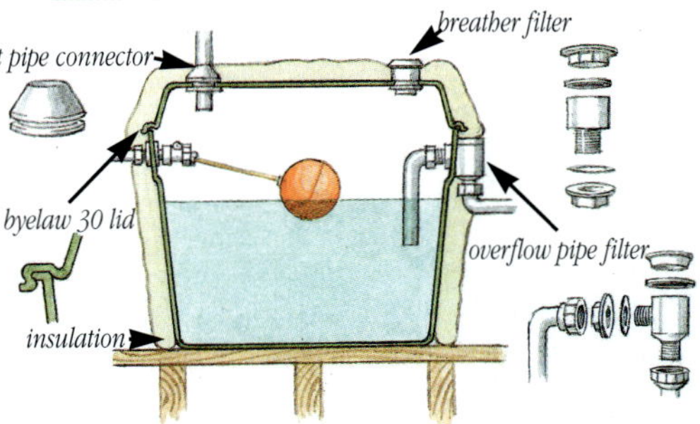

2 The cold water cistern will need a stout platform to support it, resting on at least three loft joists. Ensure all supply pipes are in proper order, and securely clipped in place.

3 Make holes in the tank for the supply pipes in line with the existing supplies so that you will not have to alter these pipes. Modify the rising main, but take the opportunity to fit a 15mm in-line servicing valve and a new tap connector. Make at least four holes in the cistern. See 1,2 and 3 (left).

Additional tank connectors will be needed for a power shower or a rim-supply bidet. Both of these must comply with regulations and have their own separate cold supply set in priority order, at water level safety heights to avoid scalding. Get professional advice if in doubt.

Drill any additional holes and then fit the ballvalve before turning the water on.

4 The 'Bylaw 30' kit has a downturn for the overflow pipe, a 'breather' in the lid, a grommet to take the safety open vent pipe (a hole for this should be drilled to match the position of the vent pipe) and an insulating jacket.

5 Run a small amount of water into the bottom of the cylinder to anchor it in place before closing the in-line servicing valve and making all the connections.

6 Fit the insulation jacket once all the connections are completed for the rising mains, cold water feed supply pipes, overflow pipes, jacket vent and breather connections.

ADDING OR MOVING A RADIATOR

Provided the boiler has the capacity, there is usually no problem with adding extra radiators to give more heat.

Replacing an existing radiator with one of greater output, for instance a double panel for a single panel, has the advantage that the same connections can be used because the radiator is the same length.

The main problem with adding, moving or replacing a radiator is having to drain down the system – particularly if a corrosion inhibitor has been added. The additive will be lost, and needs to be replaced if the system is fully drained.

1 Switch the boiler off and drain the system – draincocks can be found at the lowest points of the system. Attach a hose pipe to these, leading to outside drains. Start at the top and, working downwards, go around the system opening the air bleed valves on radiators (see page 31).

2 To run pipes to a new radiator you will have to cut into the existing flow and return pipes – the flow is the pipe which heats up first when the systems is turned on.

3 Use tee-fittings – reducing tees if joining 15mm pipe to 22mm pipe – so that the pipework goes from the flow to the radiator and then connects to the return pipe.

4 When a radiator is moved, cut through the existing pipes and fit stop-end fittings unless they can be used to extend new pipes to the new radiator position.

5 Fit pipe insulation to all pipes that are under ground-floor floorboards – or where expansion noise is likely (see page 22).

6 When refilling the system, progressively close the air bleed valves as the system fills up. If a new radiator has been added, it should be balanced (see page 31).

3

4

1

2

2 (replacing the pump)

FITTING A THERMOSTATIC RADIATOR VALVE

A thermostatic radiator valve reacts to the surrounding temperature, and reduces or increases the flow through a radiator.

It is a way of saving money on heating costs by limiting the central heating boiler demand in a room that has some other form of heating.

1 A special kit consisting of two special plugs is available which avoids the need to drain down the system.

One plug is fitted into the cold feed pipe at the point where it leaves the feed-and-expansion cistern in the loft.

The other is fitted over the end of the open vent pipe. The vacuum keeps the water in the system, provided that the radiator valves are removed one at a time – but you will still need cloths to catch any drips.

2 The valve is fitted in place of the existing valve, usually on the 'flow' side of the radiator. Simply disconnect the pipe and unscrew the valve from the radiator. Remove the plugs once the valves are fitted.

REPLACING THE PUMP

Central heating pumps need to be replaced if they fail. If the system was installed correctly – stop-valves are fitted either side of the pump – then this is an easy task.

1 Turn off the electricity supply to the system – while you disconnect the old pump and connect the new. The electrical connections to the pump are straightforward.

2 Turn off the stop-valves either side of the pump – which may need a special handle. The two large nuts either side of the pump can be unscrewed and the pump slid out sideways.

3 Provided the new pump is the same size, it can be slid in, the nuts tightened, and the stopcocks opened.

CORROSION PROTECTION

Many of the problems with central heating systems are the result of internal corrosion. The sludge in the system will cause noises and poor performance.

You can tell whether or not your system has corrosion protection by draining off a jam-jar full from a draincock and leaving a nail in the jar for a couple of days. If it rusts, you have no corrosion inhibitor.

The type of inhibitor needed depends on the type of boiler. The manufacturers of corrosion inhibitor products will be able to tell you which one you should use and also recommend the type of system cleanser you should use beforehand to flush out the sludge in the system.

Instructions are provided – both cleanser and inhibitor are added to the feed-and-expansion cistern in the loft – but you will need to be prepared to drain and refill the system several times.

BLEEDING AND BALANCING RADIATORS

If air gets into the central heating system – or corrosion produces hydrogen gas – the tops of radiators get cold.

1 Switch the boiler off. Use a radiator key to unscrew the air-bleed screw at the top of the radiator. Allow the air or hydrogen to escape. Hold a cloth under the key to catch any water which comes out when all the air is gone.

You will need to bleed the radiators whenever you drain and refill the system.

2 With the boiler on, balance radiators by adjusting the 'lockshield' valve – a free spinning handle – usually fitted on the return pipe. This can be turned with a spanner or by using the handle of the handwheel valve on the flow pipe which should be fully open for balancing.

If a radiator is correctly balanced, it has a temperature differential across it of 11°C difference between flow and return. If each radiator is correct, then the system is correctly balanced and will distribute heat evenly.

To measure accurately, you will need to buy or hire clip-on pipe thermometers – many plumbers rely on their fingers as temperature-sensing devices.

3 Start with the lockshield fully open and slowly close it until the correct temperature difference is achieved.

1

2

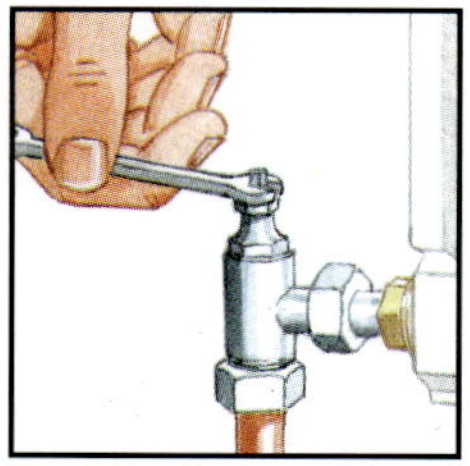

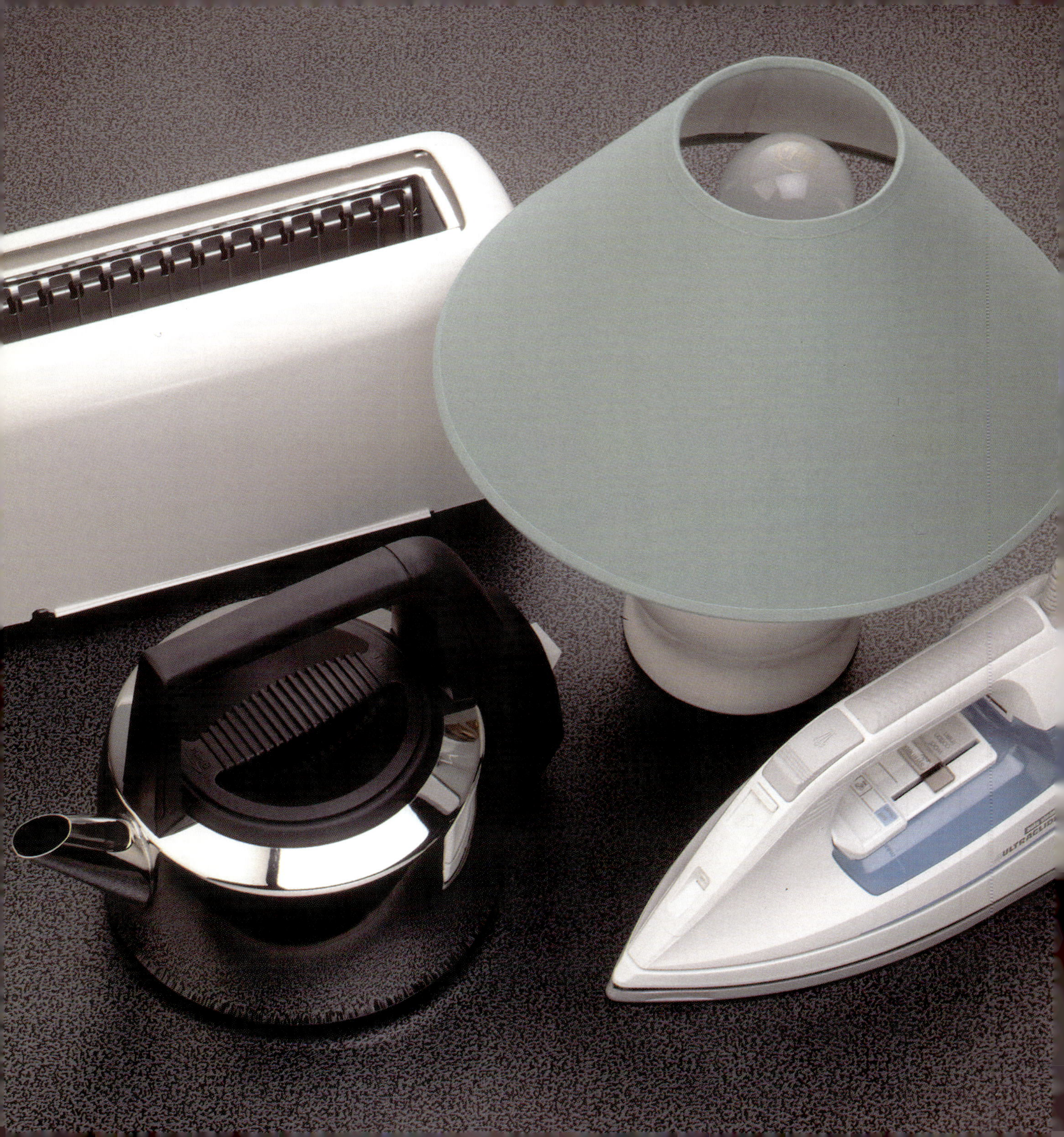

ELECTRICITY

SAFETY FIRST

Electricity is dangerous if it is not used safely or treated with due respect, but there are plenty of other do-it-yourself activities that can more easily lead to disaster if they are carried out without due care and attention.

As far as electricity is concerned, all you need to work with it safely is a clear understanding of the basic principles, together with the patience and skill to work methodically and safely. You need no special skills and few specialist tools, and all the materials you will require are widely available from retail outlets and DIY superstores.

Whatever wiring work you are tackling, always remember these basic safety rules:

1: MAKE SURE YOU KNOW WHAT YOU ARE DOING AND CAN COMPLETE THE JOB PROPERLY.

2: SWITCH OFF THE POWER SUPPLY AT THE MAIN SWITCH BEFORE STARTING WORK.

3: DOUBLE-CHECK ALL CONNECTIONS TO ENSURE THAT WIRES GO TO THE CORRECT TERMINALS AND ARE SECURELY ANCHORED.

4: ALWAYS UNPLUG ELECTRICAL APPLIANCES BEFORE TRYING TO INSPECT OR REPAIR THEM.

5: NEVER TOUCH ANY ELECTRICAL FITTING OR APPLIANCE WITH WET HANDS AND NEVER USE ELECTRICAL EQUIPMENT OUT OF DOORS IN WET CONDITIONS.

6: NEVER OMIT EARTH CONNECTIONS. THE ONLY APPLIANCES THAT DO NOT NEED AN EARTH ARE NON-METALLIC LIGHT FITTINGS AND DOUBLE-INSULATED APPLIANCES AND POWER TOOLS.

RULES AND REGULATIONS

In the United Kingdom, anyone can do their own wiring work. Professional electricians follow a code of practice called The Regulations for the Electrical Equipment of Buildings.

These regulations are published by the Institution of Electrical Engineers (IEE) and are known as the IEE Wiring Regulations, but they do not have the force of law except in Scotland, where they form part of the Scottish Building Regulations.

It is essential that do-it-yourself electricians follow the provisions of the

Regulations, to ensure that the system is safe to use. All the instructions given comply with the current (16th) edition of the Regulations.

EARTHING AND CROSS-BONDING

It is essential that every new wiring accessory or light fitting you install is connected to the house's earthing system.

This means connecting the earth conductor in the new cable both to the new accessory or fitting and to the existing circuit wiring at the chosen connection point. If you are installing an electric shower unit in a bathroom (see page 57), you must also ensure that its supply pipework – and any other exposed metalwork in the room – is cross-bonded to the earthing system. To do this you fit a special earth clamp on the pipework and run a $6mm^2$ single-core insulated earth cable from it to the earth terminal on the shower unit.

HOW ELECTRICITY WORKS

Electricity can do work only if it can flow round a complete circuit, rather like the water in your plumbing system.

Like water, it will flow through the cable carrying it only if there is a pressure difference between the two ends of the system. What drives electricity is the voltage difference between the supply (live or phase) cable and the return (neutral) cable; this is about 240 volts in the United Kingdom, 220 volts in Australia, New Zealand and the EEC, and 110 volts in the United States, Japan and South America.

How much electricity flows through a cable – the 'current' – is measured in ampères (usually shortened to amps), and depends on the 'resistance' to free flow of what lies between the live and neutral parts of the circuit. If resistance is low, the current flow will be high. Substances with low resistance are called 'conductors'. Metals such as copper are among the best conductors, which is why they are used for house wiring work.

Materials with high resistance to the passage of electricity are called 'resistors'. If the resistance is so high as to impede the flow of electricity completely, the material is called an 'insulator'. The best insulators are plastics, ceramics and rubber.

THE HOUSE SUPPLY

Your electricity supply originates at the local supply transformer and runs to your house through an underground or overhead power supply.

Shortly after entering the house, the supply terminates in a sealed box called the service head or cut-out (1).

1 - service head
2 - electricity meter
3 - fuse box
4 - earth conductor
5 - wire fuse

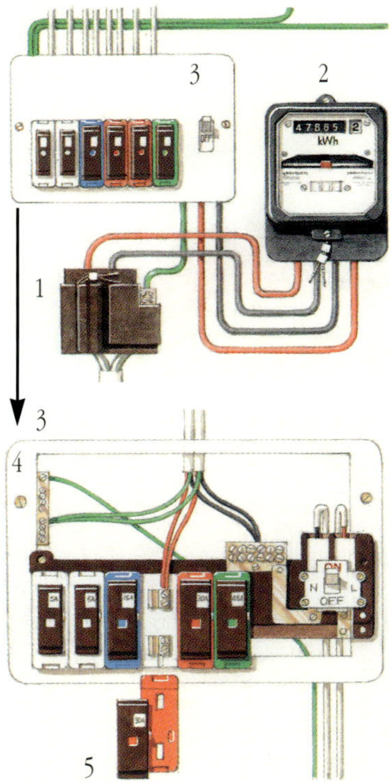

This contains a large fuse which is there to prevent the house wiring from demanding more current that the supply cable can safely carry without overheating, and which will 'blow' if its current rating is exceeded.

From the cut-out, two large single-core cables run to the electricity meter (2); if the house uses cheap night-rate (off-peak) electricity there will be a dual-rate meter and time clock instead of the conventional meter. Up to and including the meter, all the supply equipment is the property of the electricity supply company, and must not be tampered with in any way.

From the meter, two more single-core cables run to the main on/off switch and distribution centre of the dwelling – what everyone calls the fuse box (3). In a house or flat with an old-fashioned wiring system, the main switch may be in its own box, with cables running from it to individual fuse-boxes, each controlling an individual lighting or power circuit. In a modern home, everything is concentrated into a fuse-box that is called a consumer unit (3).

PROTECTIVE DEVICES

Every wiring installation is designed for maximum safety, to protect both its users and itself from the consequences of an electrical fault.

For example, if the insulation between the live and neutral conductors of the flex to an appliance breaks down, current will be able to pass from one to the other instead of flowing through the appliance. The result is a short circuit; this generates a lot of heat which could start a fire. Another fault that can occur is when something metallic, such as the casing of an appliance, comes into contact with a live conductor, perhaps due to a loose connection. This might give an electric shock to someone touching it as current flows through their body to earth instead of safely on round the system. Protective devices are installed to prevent faults like these having serious consequences.

The first is to provide a continuous electrical conductor all round the house wiring system which is then connected to earth. How earthing works can be difficult to grasp. Electricity normally completes its circuit by flowing back to the local supply transformer and then to earth, rather like used water running down a drain. If it gets out of the system where it should not – a 'leak' due to faulty insulation, for example – it needs an alternative path to earth, and this is the purpose of the earth conductor (4) in all home wiring cables and flexes.

The second protective device cuts off the flow of electricity if the demand for current becomes too great, a fault known as overloading. This happens if too many appliances are plugged into a circuit, and also if a fault, such as a short circuit or current leaking to earth, occurs. The oldest such device is the wire fuse (5), designed to melt and cut off the supply if the current flow becomes too high, but this has now been superseded by electro-mechanical devices called circuit-breakers. These switch themselves off under fault conditions, and cannot be switched on again until the fault has been cleared.

THE FUSE-BOX

The fuse-box – or consumer unit on a modern installation – distributes power to the various circuits within the home.

The live supply cable is taken to the system's main on/off switch. This supplies current to a metal bar within the box, and on this bar a protective device – a fuse or miniature circuit-breaker (MCB) – is mounted to protect each circuit. The live core of the circuit cable is connected to the other end of the protective device, while the neutral return core is connected to a separate neutral terminal block within the box. The cable's earth core goes to the earth terminal block, and this is itself connected to earth.

A modern consumer unit, as well as having circuit-breakers instead of fuses to protect each circuit, may also incorporate a separate protective device called a residual current device (RCD). This is often fitted in place of the main on/off switch, and can be switched off in the same way to isolate the whole system from the mains. When switched on, it monitors the balance between the flow of current in the live and neutral sides of the circuit, which should be equal if all is well with the system. If a current leak occurs, for example, because faulty insulation has allowed current to flow to earth through the system's earth conductor, the RCD will switch off the supply automatically. It therefore prevents a fire in the system caused by leaking current and, equally importantly, also protect the users. Anyone touching something live will receive a shock, but the RCD will detect the current flowing through the person's body to earth, and will cut off the supply within milliseconds – fast enough to prevent the shock from being fatal.

LIGHTING CIRCUITS

Most homes have two lighting circuits, so that if the protective device on one cuts off the supply, the house is not plunged into total darkness.

The circuit is wired up as a radial circuit, with the circuit cable running from the fuse box or consumer unit to each light position in turn, terminating at the most remote light on the circuit. It usually has a current rating of 5 or 6 amps, and is protected by an appropriately rated fuse or MCB.

The actual wiring connections along the circuit can be made in one of two ways, loop-in wiring (1) and junction-box wiring (2) . While loop-in wiring is more common on modern house wiring systems, junction-box wiring can be combined with it when this makes more economical use of cable. Junction-box wiring is also useful for adding extensions to the existing wiring.

CIRCUITS TO SOCKET OUTLETS

Portable or free-standing appliances with power ratings of up to 3kW are connected to the mains supply via a plug which fits into a socket outlet on the supply circuit.

Modern British wiring installations use a plug with three rectangular pins; this contains a small wire fuse in a cartridge which is designed to protect the appliance in the event of an electrical fault developing within it. The plug can deliver currents of up to 13 amps if fitted with an appropriately rated fuse, or can be fitted with a fuse of a lower rating to protect low-wattage appliances.

The circuit supplying the socket outlets can be wired up in one of two ways, a ring circuit (3) or a radial circuit (4).

The most widely used is the ring circuit because it is wired as one. Both ends of the live core of the circuit cable are connected to the circuit's protective device, allowing current to flow either way round the ring to an individual socket outlet, thus increasing the current-carrying capacity of the circuit. Such a circuit has a current rating of 30 or 32 amps, and is pro-

1: LOOP-IN WIRING

The circuit cable runs directly to each light and then on to the next, and a cable to the switch controlling the light is wired in at the light.

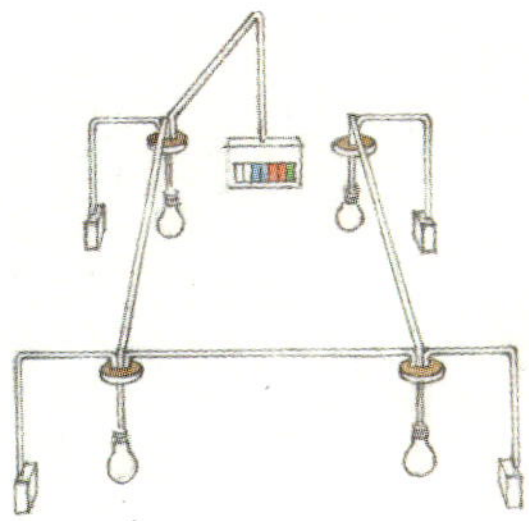

2: JUNCTION-BOX WIRING

The circuit cable runs to a series of junction boxes; from each box separate cables are run to the light and to its switch.

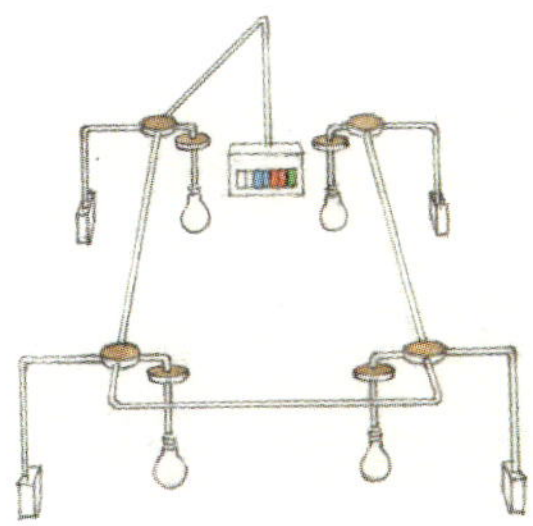

3: RING CIRCUIT

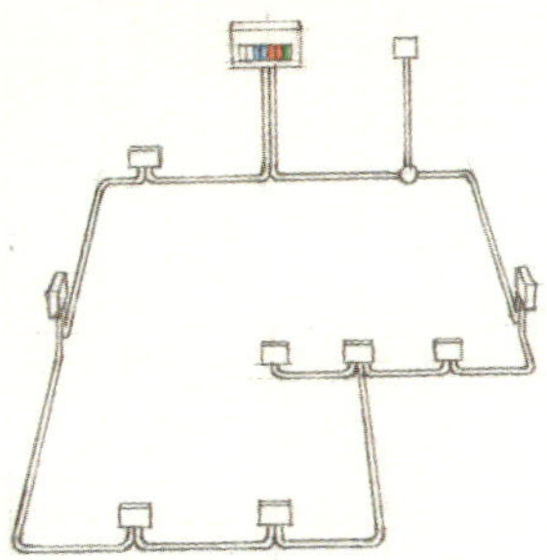

4: RADIAL CIRCUIT

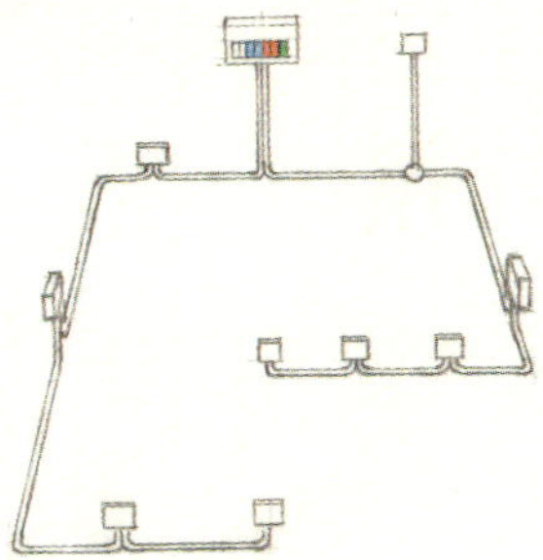

tected by an appropriately rated fuse or MCB. It can supply an unlimited number of socket outlets, but the total floor area of the rooms served by the circuit must not exceed $100m^2/1075ft^2$.

A radial circuit is a supply to sockets with the cable running from one outlet to the next and terminating at the remotest outlet. Such circuits are mainly used where running a ring circuit would involve excessive use of cable – for example, when providing a power supply to a new home extension remote from the fuse-box. The circuit can serve a maximum floor area of $20m^2/215ft^2$ if protected by a 20 amp circuit fuse or MCB, and up to $50m^2/540ft^2$ if protected by a 30 amp cartridge fuse (NOT a rewirable one) or, a 30 or 32 amp MCB. There is no limit to the number of socket outlets each circuit supplies.

Apart from supplying socket outlets, ring and radial circuits can also supply so-called fused connection units (FCUs). These allow the appliance flex to be wired directly into the FCU, instead of taking its power supply via a plug and socket, and are used mainly for appliances such as freezers, waste disposal units, cooker hoods and the like which do not need to be plugged in and unplugged regularly.

Older installations used plugs with round pins which were not fused, and had matching socket outlets which came in three sizes to match the current demand of the appliance. The smallest, rated at 2 amps, was for lamps and appliances such as radios. The second, rated at 5 amps, was for larger appliances without heating elements. The third, rated at 15 amps, was for electric fires and the like. Each socket outlet was originally wired individually to its fuse-box, where an appropriately rated circuit fuse provided the only protection in the event of an electrical fault. However, such systems have often been extended as demand for additional outlets increased, and may no longer be safe.

If you have such a system, get it checked over by a professional electrician before carrying out any work on it yourself.

CIRCUITS TO OTHER APPLIANCES

Large appliances such as cookers, showers and immersion heaters consume more current than a ring or radial circuit can supply, and so have their own individual circuits. These run from a fuse or MCB in the fuse-box or consumer unit, and have current ratings to match their needs. They range from 15 or 20 amps for an immersion heater up to 45 amps for a powerful cooker or shower. Each circuit cable runs to a double-pole (DP) switch that interrupts both the live and neutral sides of the circuit, allowing the appliance to be isolated from the mains for maintenance.

OUTDOOR POWER SUPPLIES

If you want to use an electrical appliance or power tool outdoors, you can plug an extension lead into a socket outlet inside the house.

However, for safety's sake you should always use a plug-in adaptor containing a high-sensitivity RCD, even if your house has an RCD at the fuse-box, to guard against the risk of shock in what is always a dangerous environment for electricity. New homes have to have a socket outlet containing such an RCD and designated for powering outdoor appliances.

If you want to take a permanent power supply to an outbuilding – a detached garage, a garden shed or a greenhouse, for example – then you must provide a separate circuit to it, run from its own fuse or MCB in the fuse-box or consumer unit.

Below: Electric lighing installed correctly can look attractive and warm even in the most modern of environments.

TOOLS FOR WIRING

You need few specialist tools to do electrical wiring, although you will make extensive use of your general tool-kit for things like drilling holes in walls and lifting floorboards.

CABLE AND FLEX

You use 'cable' for all fixed wiring work, such as power supplies to new wall lights or extra socket outlets. 'Flex' connects electrical appliances and pendant lampholders to the mains supply.

1 – cable and flex cutters.

2 – continuity tester – for checking that there is a continuous current path in components.

3 – pliers – for gripping and bending conductors, and for twisting cable cores together.

4 – screwdrivers – a thin-bladed terminal screwdriver with an insulated blade, and drivers with tips for slotted and cross-head screws.

5 – torch – similar to a small miner's lamp, leaving both hands free.

6 – wire-strippers to remove the insulation without damaging the conductors inside.

1: CABLE

Cable has a tough grey or white PVC sheath containing the conductors, known as cores. Except in two-way switching arrangements (see page 53), you will be using cable containing two current-carrying cores plus an earth core. The current-carrying cores have colour-coded PVC insulation – red for the live core and black for the neutral. The earth core is bare, but is covered in a slip-on length of green/yellow PVC sleeving whenever it is exposed for connection to a wiring accessory terminal. Special three-core-and-earth cable used for two-way switching has colour-coded red, blue and yellow cores for identification, plus a bare earth core.

2: COAXIAL CABLE

This special cable is needed if you want to provide extra TV or telephone outlets – coaxial cable for TV outlets and multi-core cable telephone outlets.

3: FLEX

Flex or flexible cord also has cores contained within an outer protective sheath – generally white PVC, but it also comes in black and orange. Unkinkable flex, often used on appliances such as irons, has a vulcanised rubber sheath covered in fabric braiding.

Most flex has three cores, each of which is insulated in PVC and colour-coded so that brown is for live, blue is for neutral and green/yellow is for earth.

4: TWO-CORE FLEX

This has no earth core, and is used for wiring up non-metallic lamps and light fittings, and also for hand-held appliances and power tools that are double-insulated and so need no earth connection.

COMMON CABLE AND FLEX SIZES:

CABLE

1mm^2	for extensions to lighting circuits
2.5mm^2	for extensions to power circuits
6mm^2	for circuits to electric showers

FLEX

0.5mm^2	for wiring light fittings
0.75mm^2	for light fittings and small appliances rated up to 1.3kW
1mm^2	for appliances up to 2.3kW
1.25mm^2	appliances up to 2.9kW
1.5mm^2	for appliances up to 3.6kW

All of the above are sold by the metre length.

1

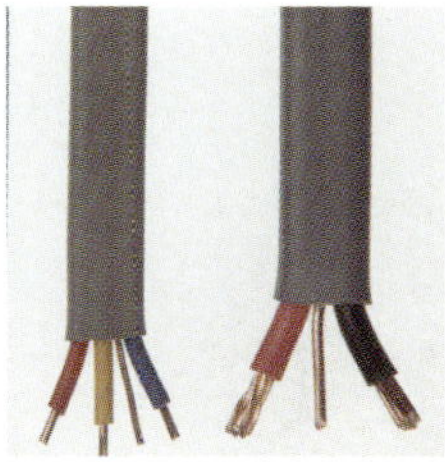

2

3

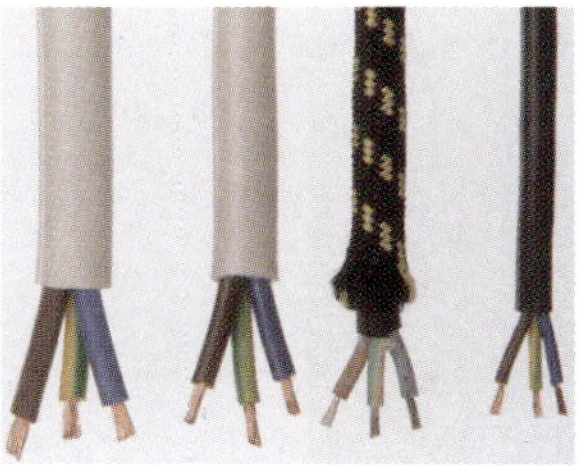

4

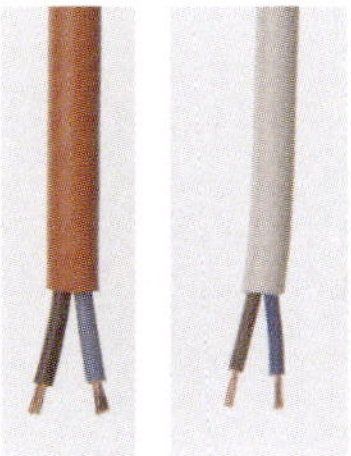

CONNECTING CABLE AND FLEX

All wiring connections are made at screw-down terminals within wiring accessories, light fittings and plugs.

1 To make a sound connection, the cable or flex sheathing must first be cut back to expose the cores inside; these must then be bared ready for connection to the terminal.

2 When cutting back the outer sheath, remember that the flex or cable cores must not be visible outside the plug or mounting box to which they are connected.

3 Core insulation should run right up to the terminal when the bare conductor has been connected and not be trimmed too short.

4 Bare earth cores within wiring accessories must be covered with a slip-on PVC earth sleeving right up to the terminal.

5 Cable can be connected to flex at light fittings, using strip connectors housed in a mounting-box; this can either be surface-mounted or recessed into the wall or ceiling.

WIRING ACCESSORIES

1: SOCKET OUTLETS

Available in single, double or triple, with or without on/off switches and neon indicators.

2: FUSED CONNECTION UNITS (FCUs)

FCUs are used as an alternative to a single socket outlet for appliances which do not get moved around – things like extractor fans. The appliance flex passes into the FCU through a hole in the faceplate, which contains a small fuse carrier holding a cartridge fuse like those fitted in fused plugs.

3: DOUBLE-POLE (DP) SWITCHES

These are used to control individual appliances permanently linked to the mains, such as cookers and electric showers. They are available in wall- and ceiling-mounted versions, the latter cord-operated, in current ratings from 16 to 45 amps.

LIGHT SWITCHES

Also called plateswitches, these are used to turn lights on/off. The basic type has a single switch on its faceplate, but versions with up to six switches are available. You can also buy narrow plates called architrave switches, which fit on door frames.

4: ONE-WAY SWITCHES

These have just two terminals, and operate the light from only that switch.

5: TWO-WAY SWITCHES

These have three terminals and are linked to a similar switch to provide two-way switching.

6: CORD SWITCHES

These are ceiling-mounted, cord-operated switches for use in bathrooms or wherever cord operation is more convenient than a wall-mounted switch.

7: DIMMER SWITCHES

These light switches allow you to vary the brightness of the light as well as to turn it on/off, usually by rotating a knob on the switch faceplate.

8: CEILING ROSES

These are used to connect pendant lampholders to the lighting circuit. The flex to the lampholder can either be wired permanently into the rose, which is screwed to the ceiling surface, or connected to it via a special plug that fits into a socket in the rose; known as a luminaire support coupler (LSC). The big advantage of LSCs is that they allow the light to be taken down easily for cleaning.

9: JUNCTION BOXES AND CONDUIT BOXES

These are used to make wiring connections on lighting and power circuits, normally hidden above ceilings or beneath floorboards.

WIRING ACCESSORIES

10 – PVC sleeving (green/yellow).

11 – PVC insulating tape (red).

12 – rubber grommets to fit the holes in flush metal mounting-boxes to stop the cable sheath from chafing.

13 – strip connectors used for making connections to some ceiling and wall lights.

14 – mini-trunking to carry cable safely either in or over surfaces.

15 – cable clips for fastening cable securely to a surface.

LAMPS AND TUBES

1: GENERAL SERVICE LAMPS

These are available in a range of squared-off and round shapes including candle and pygmy lamps, either with clear or pearl glass in plain and a range of colours, and various wattages.

2: REFLECTOR LAMPS

Used mainly in spotlights, have an internal silver coating – either round the base and sides so the light is thrown forwards (an ISL lamp), or inside the crown (a CS lamp) so the light is thrown back into the fitting and then forward by the reflector inside it. Parabolic aluminised reflector (PAR) lamps have armoured glass envelopes and are for outdoor use. All come in a range of colours and wattages.

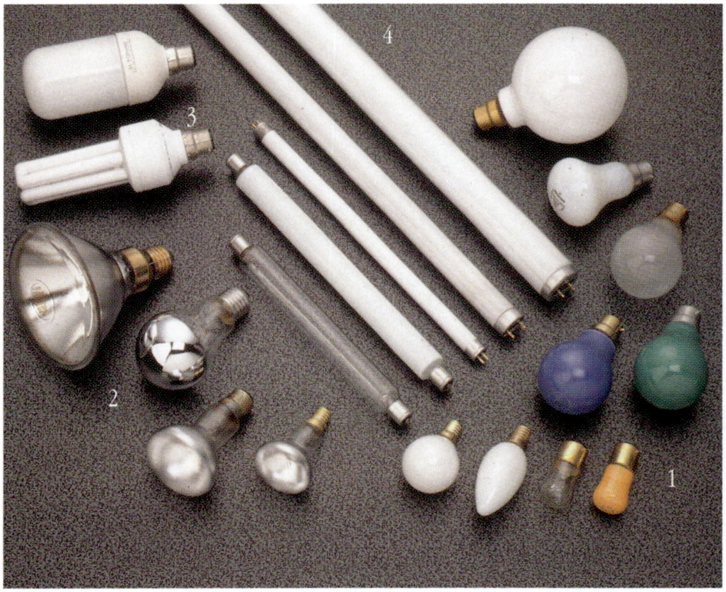

3: COMPACT FLUORESCENT LAMPS

These contain a miniature fluorescent tube and its control gear inside a lamp small enough to fit a standard lampholder. There are several types, some having a cylindrical or spherical glass envelope and others having a cluster of four small glass 'fingers' projecting from the lamp base. They use about a fifth as much electricity as a GLS lamp, and have a lamp life of up to 8,000 hours. They are expensive to buy, but over a period of years cost less than half as much to run as GLS lamps.

4: FLUORESCENT AND FILAMENT LAMPS

In tubular form these are available in a range of sizes and wattages. Standard fluorescent tubes are 38mm in diameter, slimline ones 28mm across and miniature tubes 15mm. Tungsten filament strip-lights are smaller (between 220mm and 285mm long) and are mainly used for concealed lighting.

RUNNING CABLE

1 Ideally cable should be concealed – under floorboards, above ceilings or in channels (called chases) cut in the walls of the room. However, this means wrecking your decorations and probably having to lift fitted carpets or furniture, so it is generally best to surface-mount the cable temporarily and then to conceal it the next time that the room is stripped for redecoration.

2 You can simply clip white-sheathed cable along the top edges of skirting boards or along the edges of door architraves.

3 A neater solution is to use slim plastic ducting known as mini-trunking. This consists of a U-shaped channel that is stuck or pinned to the wall, and a clip-on cover that conceals the cables once it is snapped into place. Used with surface-mounted accessories, this results in a neat job with the new cables concealed yet readily accessible, and it is far less disruptive than traditional concealed wiring.

4 When the time comes for the wiring to be concealed, cut chases up and down walls with a sharp brick bolster and a club hammer, clip the cables in place before plastering over them.

5 Lift floorboards and thread the cable through holes drilled in the joists if it crosses them, or run it between the joists if it runs parallel to them.

MOUNTING WIRING ACCESSORIES

Light switches and socket outlets can be fitted to flush or surface-mounted boxes. It is simpler to fit a surface-mounted box but a flush box looks much neater. The following instructions are for the mounting only and do not involve live cables.

IN MASONRY WALLS

1 The best way of making the recess for the box is to drill a series of closely-spaced holes into the wall to the required depth.

2 Chop out the resulting honeycomb with a brick bolster and club hammer.

Push out one of the pre-stamped knockouts (cable entries) and fit a rubber grommet into the hole to protect the cable from chafing.

3 Screw the box into the recess and make good round it with plaster or filler.

ON TIMBER STUD PARTITION WALLS

4 Simply mark and cut out a square or rectangle of plasterboard using a trimming knife. Use a screwdriver to break out one knockout in the box before fitting it.

5 Clip in a special hollow wall box with side lugs that grip the edges and hold the box in place.

1 (mounting accessories)

2

3

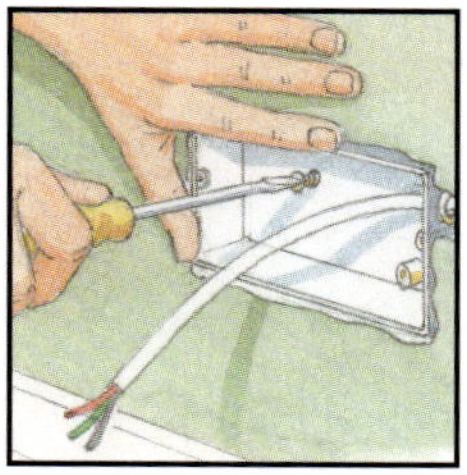

5

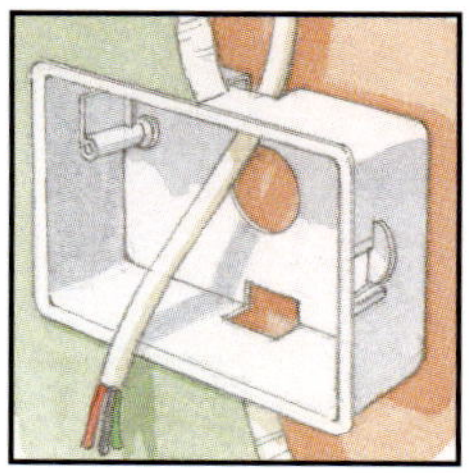

2

3

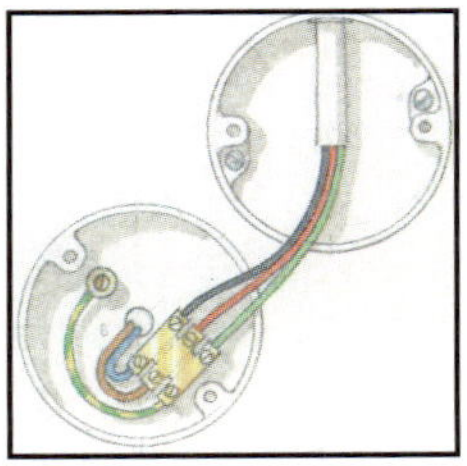

5

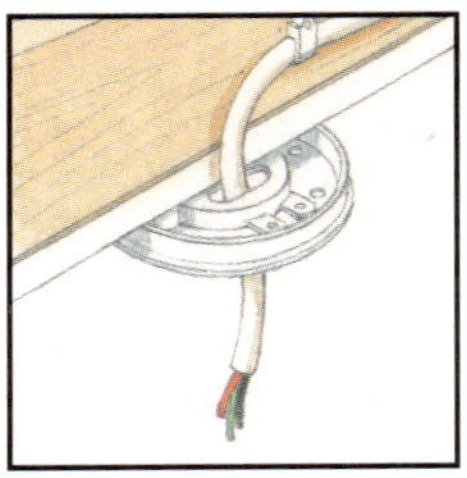

6

CONNECTING NEW CABLE TO AN ACCESSORY

1 Turn off the power at the mains. Feed in the cable and strip the sheathing and core insulation to size as required.

2 Then connect the live and neutral cores to the labelled terminals (L and N) on the accessory.

If there is an earth terminal on the accessory, slip a PVC sleeve over the bare earth core before connecting it.

If the accessory is metal, link its earth terminal with the terminal in the box – use a short length of earth core from a cable off-cut and cover it with PVC sleeving.

Light switches are not earthed unless they are metallic.

3 If the light accessory has an earth, take the earth core to the terminal in the accessory mounting box.

4 Fold the cables neatly back into the mounting box and fit the faceplate to its lugs.

ON CEILINGS

5 Screw ceiling roses and light switches to the undersides of the joists if possible, running the circuit cable down the side of the joist and into the accessory.

6 If screwing the ceiling rose into a joist is not possible because of the positioning, you have to gain access to the void above the ceiling and fix a support batten between the joists. The accessory is then screwed to this through the ceiling surface.

Push the excess cable back into the ceiling void and fit the cover after making the connections.

WIRING JOBS

The following pages contain some of the jobs most frequently carried out by 'do-it-yourselfers'. None are particularly difficult and all are within the general abilities of the practical householder. However, as with all home improvements, it is common sense to ensure that personal safety during installation, and user safety after installation, is complete.

Always comply with specific appliance regulations and manufacturers' installation instructions. If in doubt, consult a knowledgeable specialist.

ADDING EXTRA TV/TELEPHONE POINTS

Most homes have television sets and FM radios in more than one room. Unless you live in an area of good reception and can rely on set-top or built-in aerials, you will need a rooftop or loft aerial.

ADDING TV POINTS

1 The aerial supplies a TV/FM signal via a coaxial cable to the socket outlet. To ensure that each outlet does not suffer from loss of signal strength, you need to install a special electrically-powered distribution amplifier, and then to run coaxial cable from this to the various rooms in the house

2 A single coaxial cable can be used to carry both TV and FM signals if it terminates at a special double TV/FM outlet fitted with a device called a diplexer. These outlets are mounted on a standard single mounting-box.

ADDING TELEPHONE POINTS

It is useful to have telephone socket outlets in more than one place in the house.

Householders are now allowed to fit extension socket outlets themselves so long as there is a master plug-in socket outlet installed by a telecoms operator

3 Kits are available that contain everything needed for the job – extension outlets, connectors, clips, multi-core cable, detailed instructions and a special tool for connecting the flimsy cable cores to the outlet terminals.

You can install as many extra outlets as you like, but the phones will not ring if you plug in more than four at once. The outlets can be wired using a junction box (A) if this makes more economical use of cable, or in series (B).

1

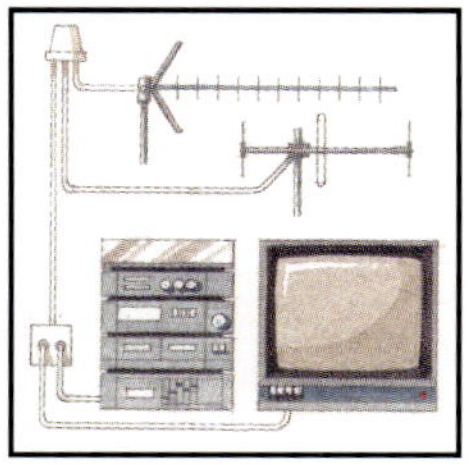

2

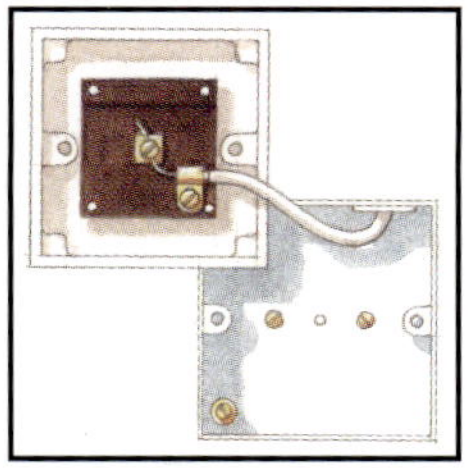

3

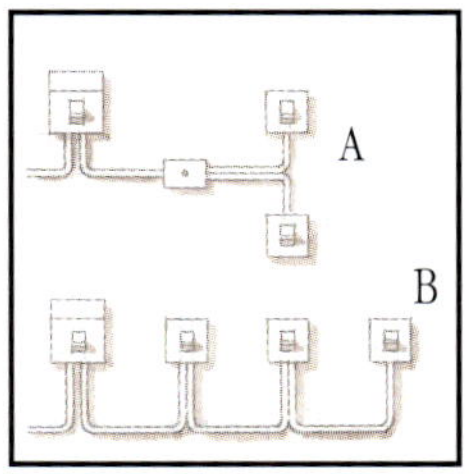

3

FITTING A DIMMER SWITCH

Replacing an existing light switch with a dimmer switch is one of the simplest electrical jobs you can tackle.

There are two points to check before you go to the store to buy the new switch.

1: YOU NEED TO FIND OUT WHETHER THE EXISTING SWITCH IS A ONE-WAY OR TWO-WAY TYPE.

Turn off the power to the lighting circuit.

Loosen the switch faceplate screws so you can ease the old switch away from the wall and see whether it has two terminals (a one-way switch) or three terminals (a two-way switch).

2: CHECK THE WATTAGE OF THE LIGHT(S) THE DIMMER WILL CONTROL TO ENSURE IT FALLS BETWEEN THE MINIMUM AND MAXIMUM OPERATING WATTAGE OF THE DIMMER.

1 Turn off the power at the mains.

2 Unscrew the switch faceplate and ease it away from its mounting box. Make a note of which cable core goes to which terminal before disconnecting them.

3 Reconnect the cores to the new switch. The terminals on dimmers are often arranged and labelled differently to those on plateswitches, so follow the maker's instructions carefully.

4 If the dimmer has a metallic faceplate, it will also have an earth terminal. You must link this to the earth terminal in the mounting box, so scrounge a few inches of lighting-circuit cable from someone and pull out the bare earth core. Slip a piece of green/yellow PVC sleeving over the two earth terminals and connect them.

5 Fold the cable(s) neatly back into the mounting box, secure the dimmer faceplate to it and restore the power.

INSTALLING A NEW CEILING LIGHT

To replace an existing ceiling rose, check the wiring arrangement at the rose and on the new fitting.

If the rose has only one cable and the light has a fixed terminal block (many fluorescent light fittings do), remove the rose, disconnect the cable and connect it directly to the terminal block before securing the light to the ceiling.

If the new light has flex tails emerging from its baseplate or if there is more than one cable at the rose (indicating that loop-in wiring has been used), you will have to remove the rose and replace it with a recessed round conduit box which contains the connections between the light flex and the circuit cables. The light is either screwed to the lugs on the conduit box or the ceiling to hide the box and connections.

1 Turn the power off at the mains.

2 Unscrew the rose cover. Make a note of which cable cores go to which rose terminal, then disconnect them. If only one cable is present and the new light has a terminal block, connect the cores to the block terminals L, N and E.

3 Screw the fitting to the ceiling – screw into the joist to which the original rose was secured.

TO FIT A RECESSED CONDUIT BOX

4 You need access to the ceiling void from above, either through a loft or lift a floorboard in the room above.

5 Remove the rose and draw the cables into the void. Drill a hole between the joists to mark the new light position.

Mark around the conduit box position then use a padsaw through the drilled hole to cut round the outline of the box.

6 Fit a piece of wood between the joists, and nail a short batten to each end. Wedge the wood between the joists over the hole and offer up the conduit box to check that its lip will be flush with the ceiling surface. Adjust the level of the support, then nail through the battens into the joist sides to secure the support in place. Screw the box to it.

7 Feed the circuit cables into the box, and connect them to strip connectors as shown. Attach the flex cores from the new light to the strip connectors and push any excess cable back into the ceiling void.

8 Screw the light to the lugs on the conduit box if its base-plate has 51mm fixing holes, or to the wooden support.

2

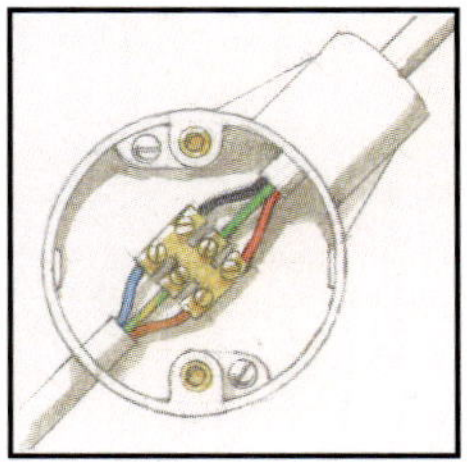

7

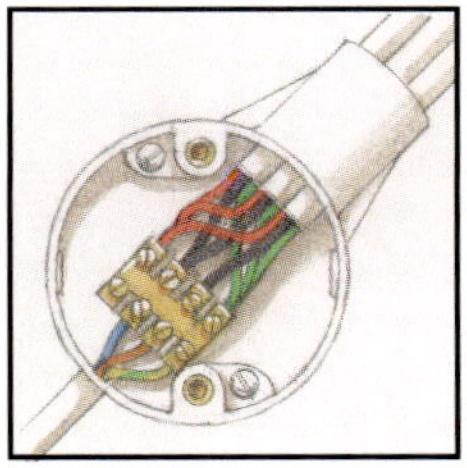

2

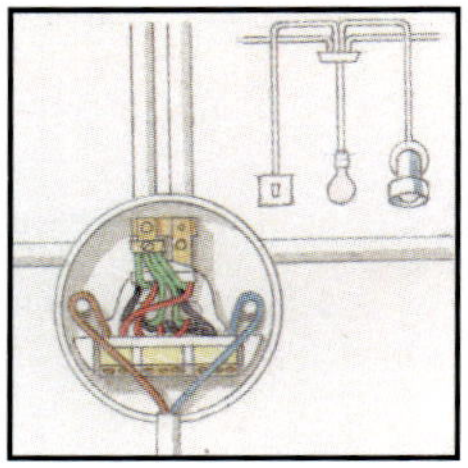

5

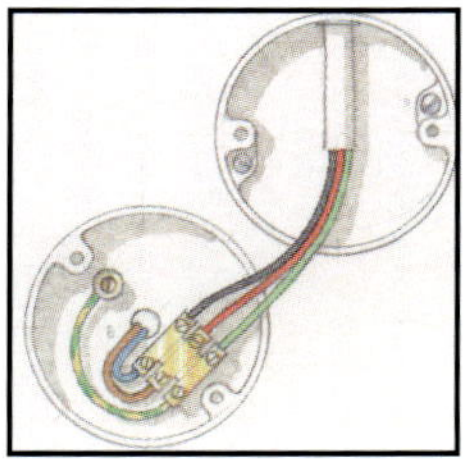

INSTALLING WALL LIGHTS

There are several ways in which you can provide a power supply to new wall lights. The method you choose will depend on:

1: HOW EASY IT IS TO GAIN ACCESS TO THE EXISTING WIRING.
2: THE SORT OF SWITCH CONTROL YOU WANT.
3: HOW MUCH YOU ARE PREPARED TO DISRUPT YOUR EXISTING DECORATIONS.

The two ways suggested here are the simplest. Unless you are redecorating the room at the same time as fitting the light(s), it is easiest to run the cable to them in surface-mounted mini-trunking, and to bury it in a chase cut in the wall surface when you next redecorate.

OPTION 1

Take a power supply for the new light from an existing ceiling rose in the same room. The new light will be controlled by the rose's switch.

1 Turn the power off at the mains.

2 Connect the branch cable to the rose as shown, run it across the ceiling to a point immediately above the new light position and pass it down through a hole in the ceiling.

3 At the chosen light position, chop out a recess for a round conduit box and secure it in place. If the wall is a plasterboard wall, fit a slim architrave partition wall box in a hole cut in the plasterboard.

4 Cut a chase in a solid wall, clip the cable into it and feed it into the conduit box. With plasterboard walls, feed the cable down inside the wall and into the architrave box. Alternatively, use surface-mounted mini-trunking.

5 Connect the cable cores to the flex tails on the wall light using strip connectors as shown. Then fold the cable into the box and secure the light, either to the box lugs or to the wall surface, so that its baseplate conceals the box.

OPTION 2

Take a power supply from a conveniently-sited socket outlet. The new light is controlled by its own switch.

1 Turn the power off at the mains. Run a spur cable from a suitable socket outlet (see page 55) to a point immediately above or below the new light position.

2 Fit a mounting box for the light as in Option 1 step 3, and run in the cable as in step 4.

3 Just before the cable reaches the mounting box, fit a mounting box for a switched fused connection unit, which will control the light.

4 Connect the spur cable to its 'FEED' terminals. Then connect a short length of $1mm^2$ lighting cable to the 'LOAD' terminals and run it on to the light's mounting-box. Connect it to the light and secure the light to the wall as in Option 1 step 5.

5 Fit a 5 amp fuse in the fuseholder of the connection unit, and fit this to its mounting box.

PROVIDING TWO-WAY SWITCHING

Most lights are controlled from just one switch position, using a one-way switch with two terminals on its faceplate. If you want control from two positions, you have to replace the existing switch with a two-way switch (this has three terminals), and run special three-core-and-earth cable from it to the new switch position, where another two-way switch is fitted.

1 Turn off the power at the mains. Unscrew the faceplate of the original switch and disconnect the switch cable.

2 Reconnect the existing switch cable cores to the new two-way switch.

If the top terminal at one end of the terminal block on its own is marked C, use the two terminals next to each other at the other end of the block marked L1 and L2.

If the lone terminal is marked L1, use L2 and L3.

3 Run three-core-and-earth cable from the existing switch to the new switch position, running it up the wall and across the ceiling void or down the wall and beneath the floorboards, depending on which route is more convenient.

4 Connect the cores of the three-core-and-earth cable to the two switches as shown.

At each switch the red core goes to the lone top terminal. The blue and yellow cores go to the bottom two terminals. Earth cores go to the mounting-box earth terminal.

5 If the switches have metal faceplates, link the faceplate earth terminal to the one in the box with a short length of sleeved earth core.

5 (wall light - option 2)

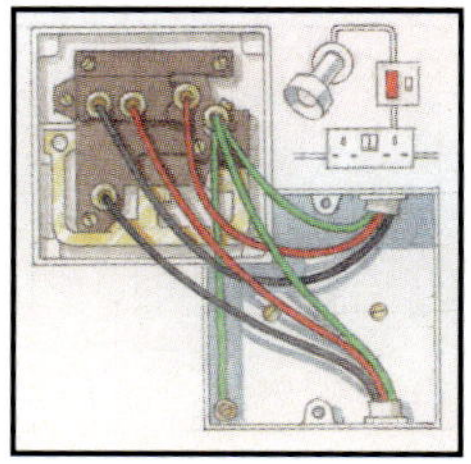

5 (two-way switching)

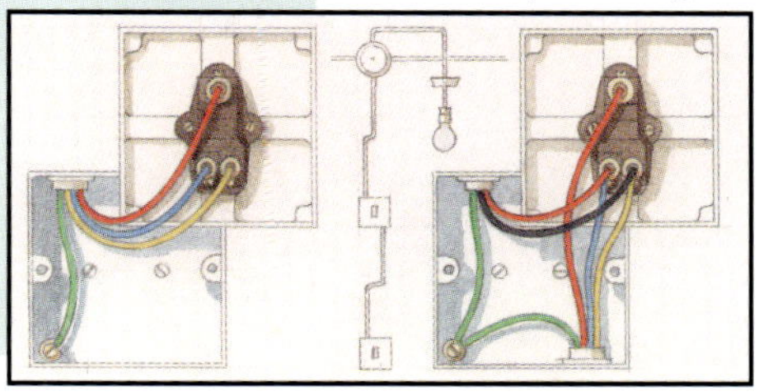

3

5

CONVERTING SINGLE SOCKET OUTLETS

If you need more socket outlets and most of the ones you have are single outlets, you can gain extra capacity by converting them to double or triple outlets without having to do any extra wiring work. Select from the options below, for sockets that are either flush- or surface-mounted.

1 always start by turning off the power.

2 unscrew the existing socket faceplate and disconnect the cable cores.

OPTION 1

NEW FOR OLD SURFACE-MOUNTED OUTLET

3 Remove the old mounted box. Remove the knockout in the new larger box, so that the cable(s) can be fed in.

4 Screw the new box to the wall and connect the cable cores: red to L, black to N and earth to E.

OPTION 2

FLUSH-MOUNTED FOR SURFACE-MOUNTED OUTLET

This only works if there is sufficient cable within the original box to reach the new faceplate terminals.

5 Fit a twin converter frame over the existing flush box, screwing the frame to the lugs in the original box.

6 Connect the cable cores to the new outlet – red to L, black to N and earth to E and screw it to the frame.

OPTION 3

A NEW FLUSH-MOUNTED OUTLET

Care must be taken over the box position to ensure the existing cable cores reach the terminals on the new outlet.

7 Remove the original box. Mark the outline of the new mounting box on the wall.

8 On solid walls, chop out the recess. Feed in the cable(s). Screw the new box in place. On plasterboard walls, cut out the plasterboard and fit a partition wall box (see page 52).

9 Make the connections to the new socket outlet – red to L, black to N and earth to E.

ADDING EXTRA SOCKET OUTLETS

Extra sockets can be added by running spur cables from the existing ring circuits.

The only restriction the Wiring Regulations impose is that the total floor area of the rooms served by the circuit, including any socket outlets on spurs, must not exceed $100m^2/1075ft^2$. You can add extra outlets in one of two ways. In both cases $2.5mm^2$ cable must be used for the spur.

OPTION 1

Connect the spur cable into the circuit at an existing socket outlet. This outlet must be on the main ring circuit, must not already be supplying a spur (when it will have three cables connected to it) and must not itself be a spur (just one cable).

1 Turn the power off at the mains. Open the chosen socket. If there are two cables present, it is on the ring circuit and can be used to connect in the spur cable.

If it has one or three cables, it must not be used and another outlet will have to be found.

2 At the new socket position, fit a mounting-box and run cable back by the most convenient route and method to the existing outlet position.

To prevent lifting floorboards, cable can run around a room either clipped to the top of the skirting board or concealed in mini-trunking. It can also pass through walls to feed a new outlet mounted back-to-back with the existing one.

3 Connect the cable to the terminals of the new socket faceplate and fit it to the mounting box.

4 At the existing socket, connect the new cable cores into the terminals, matching like to like.

All the live (red) cores go to the L terminal, black to N, and green/yellow to earth.

5 Fold the cables carefully back into the mounting box and replace the faceplate.

2

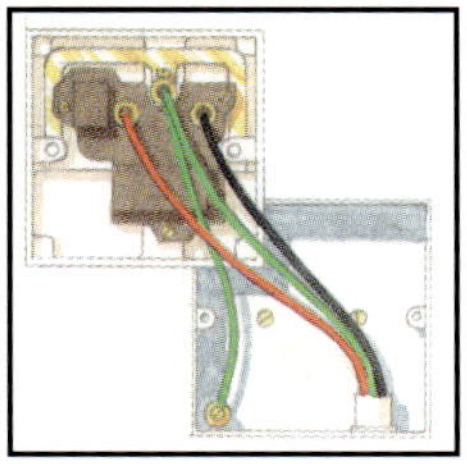

4

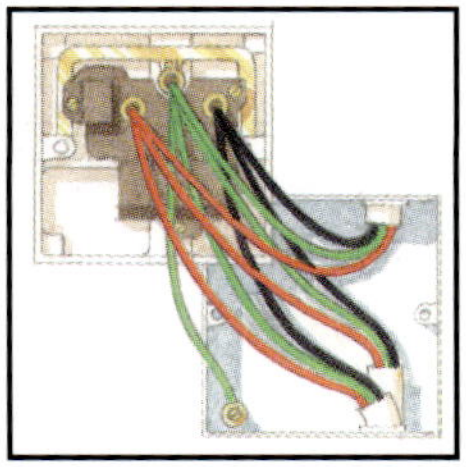

Left: Mini trunking used to conceal cable.

1 (option 2)

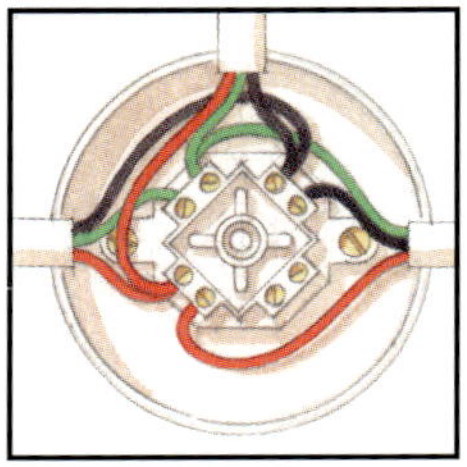

2 (fixed appliances)

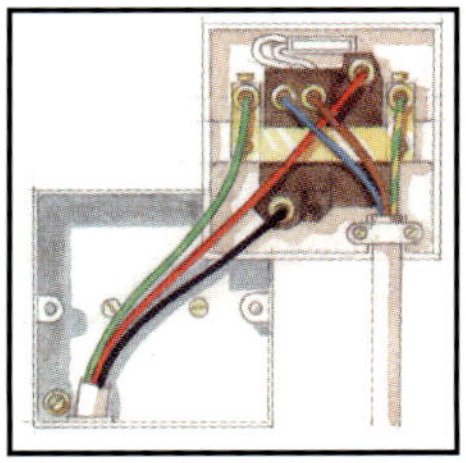

OPTION 2

Connect the spur cable into the circuit using a three-terminal junction box. Use this method if there is no socket outlet available, or if running cable from an existing outlet is inconvenient.

1 Turn the power off at the mains. Lift a floorboard or two in the room where you want to fit the new outlet, and locate the ring circuit cable. Check it has enough slack to make the connection.

2 At the new outlet position, fit a mounting box and run cable between the joists to your chosen connection point. If the joists run contrary, then drill holes in the centre of the joists and pass the cable through.

3 Connect the spur cable to the new outlet faceplate, then fit this to the mounting box.

4 At the connection point, screw the base of a 30 amp junction box to the side of a nearby joist.

5 Cut the main circuit cable, strip back the sheathing and remove some of the core insulation. Connect the cores, like to like, within the junction box.

6 Prepare the spur cable for connection, and wire it into the junction box, again linking like to like.

Sleeve all the earth cores, then fit the box cover.

WIRING 'FIXED' APPLIANCES

Fixed appliances such as cooker hoods or waste disposal units can be plugged into nearby socket outlets but it is better to give this type of appliance a permanent connection to the socket circuit, using a switched fused connection unit (FCU). This allows you to switch the appliance off for maintenance or repair but as the flex is wired directly to terminals, it cannot be accidentally disconnected.

The unit contains a cartridge fuse to protect the appliance and the FCU power supply is from a spur cable, connected to the ring circuit in the same way as the spur for an extra socket outlet (see page 55).

1 Install the appliance, then decide on a position for the FCU. Fit a mounting box for it, then plan the cable route back from it to the ring circuit. Run the cable by the most convenient method and route.

2 At the FCU, connect the spur cable to the 'FEED', and the appliance flex to the 'LOAD' terminals. Secure the flex sheath in the cord grip provided.

3 Fit the FCU to its mounting box. Check that the fuse is the correct rating for the appliance; fit a 3 amp fuse if its wattage is less than 720W, a 13 amp fuse if more.

4 Turn off the power at the mains. At the connection point, link the spur cable to the ring circuit at a socket outlet or using a junction box.

INSTALLING AND WIRING AN ELECTRIC SHOWER

This is a major DIY job combining plumbing installation with electrical installation. The electrical wiring is straightforward so long as you have available a spare fuseway in your consumer unit. If not, it is important to get a professional electrician to fit and connect an additional enclosure that contains one or two spare fuseways.

PLUMBING IN

If you install the shower in a cubicle, suitable drainage must be installed to the main soil stack. Alternatively an electric shower can be safely installed over the bath, provided that the casing is not in the direct line of the spray. All this needs is two or three holes to take wall plugs for the screws to support the shower unit.

1 Run a length of 15mm pipe from the rising main, via a stopcock, to the shower position. Often the easiest place to make the connection is in the loft space, running the (insulated) pipe down through the ceiling to the shower position.

2 Turn the water off and drain through the kitchen taps. Make two cuts 18mm/¾in apart to fit a compression tee-fitting. Clean the cut pipe ends and insert the fitting with the new length of pipe running to the shower.

An electric shower

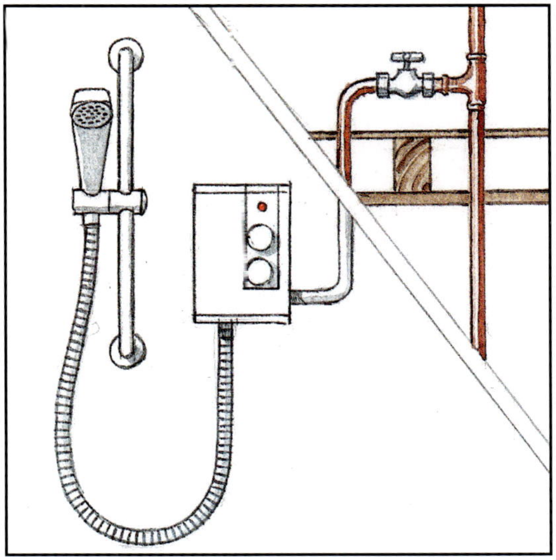

1

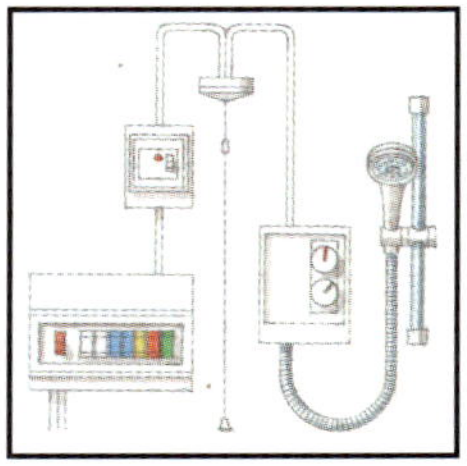

1

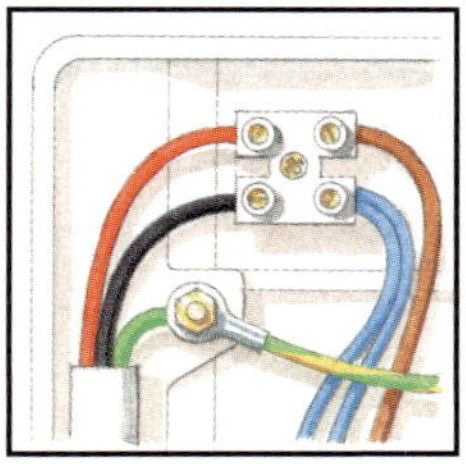

2

3

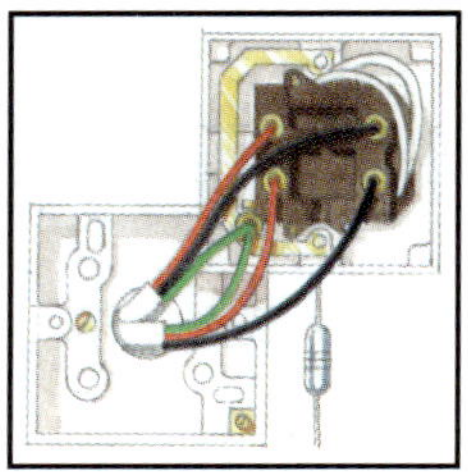

ELECTRICAL INSTALLATION

Showers up to 7.2kW need a 30A circuit run in $4mm^2$ cable – $6mm^2$ if the consumer unit has rewirable fuses or if the cable run is longer than 20m. Showers of more than 7.2kW need a 40A: $10mm^2$ cable.

1 Install the shower heater unit and plumb it in (see above) Connect $6mm^2$ cable to the shower terminal block and run it up the wall to a ceiling-mounted, cord-operated, 45 amp, double-pole on/off switch. The cable may be either surface-mounted, in a chase cut in the masonry or concealed within a partition wall.

2 Fit a special earth clamp to the shower supply pipework, and link its terminal to the earth terminal on the shower unit using $4mm^2$ single-core earth cable to cross-bond the pipework to earth.

3 Screw the mounting box for the ceiling switch to a joist, then pass the cable down the side of the joist through a knockout in the box. Connect it to the 'LOAD' and earth terminals of the switch, then connect a second cable to the 'FEED' terminals; this will run back to the consumer unit by the shortest convenient route.

IF YOU HAVE A FUSEWAY AVAILABLE IN YOUR CONSUMER UNIT

4 Turn off the power at the main isolating switch. Move the existing fuseholders along to make a space for a new 45 amp fuseholder or MCB to be fitted next to the main switch – fuseholders must be arranged so that the highest-rated is nearest to the switch (get an electrician to do this if you are unclear how to proceed).

5 Connect the cable's live core to the terminal on the fuseholder or MCB, its neutral core to the main neutral terminal block and its earth core to the main earth terminal block. Restore the power and test the shower.

6 To protect the shower circuit and its users, have an electrician specify and install a residual current device (RCD). This can be installed in the same enclosure as a new fuseway, if he is fitting one, or in its own enclosure.

TRACING FAULTS

It is essential to trace and correct the cause of an electrical fault. The secret to electrical repairs is to be thorough and methodical in your approach as you systematically eliminate elements of the problem to trace the fault.

The following are examples of frequent faults that will assist your understanding of the principle of fault finding.

A LIGHT DOES NOT WORK

A component such as a lamp bulb may have failed, a connection come loose or a fuse may have blown.

1 Turn off the light switch.
Replace the lamp bulb.

2 Turn off the power.
Check the circuit fuse or the MCB.

With fuses – remove and inspect the fuseholder; rewire or replace the fuse.

With MCBs – switch MCB back on.

3 Turn off the power.
Open ceiling roses and lamp-holders to check for loose or damaged connections. Remake the connections if necessary.

4 Disconnect the power.
Check flexes for continuity, and replace any damaged flex.

AN APPLIANCE DOES NOT WORK

5 Plug another appliance into the same socket outlet. If it works, the fault is in the original appliance – go to 6. If it does not work, the outlet is at fault – go to 8.

6 Remove and open the plug.
Check for and remake any loose connections you find. Check the plug fuse with a continuity tester, and replace it if necessary. Replace the top and plug in.

7 Unplug the appliance, open its casing/body and locate the terminal block. Check for any loose connections and remake as required.

Check the flex cores for continuity and replace if faulty.

8 Turn off the power.
Open the outlet, check the cable terminals for loose connections and remake if necessary.

2

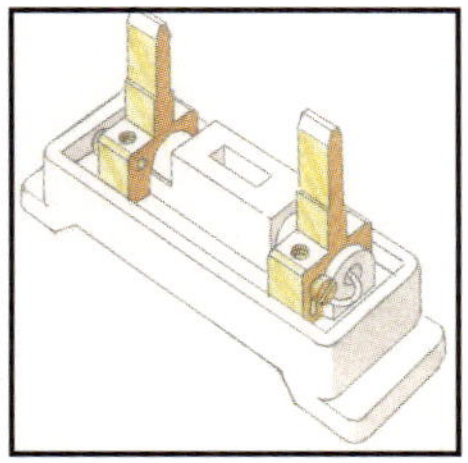

2

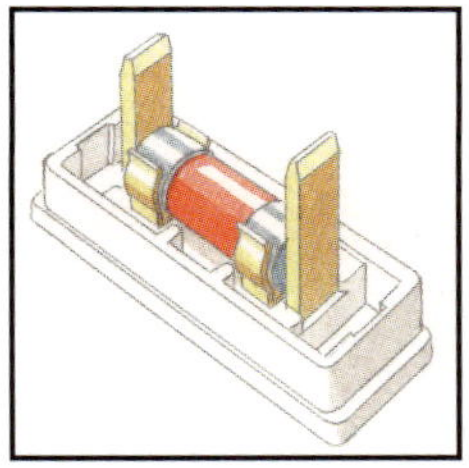

6

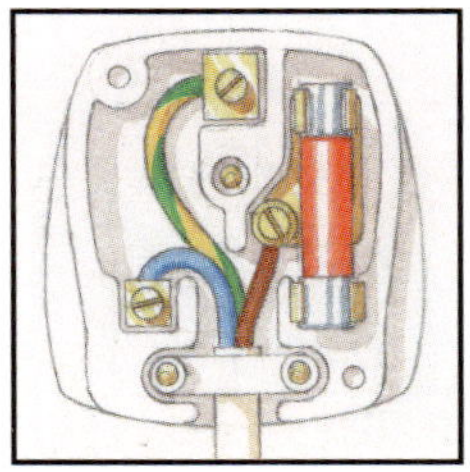

1 (a circuit is dead)

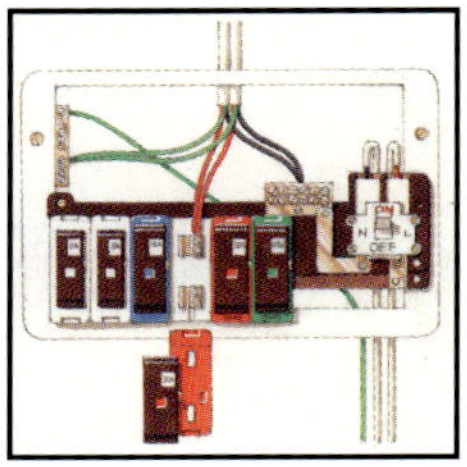

A CIRCUIT IS DEAD

1 Turn off or disconnect the power.
Check the consumer unit. If the fuse has blown, replace it. Reset the MCB (if it will not reset, the fault is still present).

2 Switch lights on or plug appliances in, one by one. If one blows the fuse, isolate and check it as described above. Check appliance ratings and calculate whether the circuit is overloaded.

3 Turn off the power.
Open accessories and check for loose connections, damaged insulation or signs of overheating. Remake connections, and repair insulation with PVC tape. Replace overheated accessories.

4 If you have drilled through or driven a nail into a cable, turn off the power. Replace the fuse or reset the MCB. Expose the damaged cable. In a void you may be able to cut and rejoin the cable using a junction box. Otherwise cut out and replace the damaged cable.

5 If the circuit is still dead, call in an electrician to test the circuit and trace the fault.

THE WHOLE HOUSE HAS NO POWER

1 Is it a power cut?
Check the neighbourhood for signs.

YES:

Call your area 24-hour emergency number.

NO:

Turn off the power – check and replace the fuses.

2 If you have an RCD.
Check whether it has tripped off. Reset the RCD. If you cannot, the fault is still present.

3 Are you the only house without power?

NO:

Call your area 24-hour emergency number.

YES:

There is either a fault on your main supply cable or your main service fuse has blown. Call the emergency number and ask for an engineer to trace the fault.

EMERGENCY REPAIRS

BE PREPARED FOR ELECTRICAL EMERGENCIES.

Temporary repairs to things like cracked plug tops, damaged wiring accessories and frayed flex sheathing can be made using PVC insulating tape. A repair is not permanent – replace the damaged component at the earliest possible opportunity.

1 Keep a supply of 3 amp and 13 amp plug fuses, plus a spare plug or two. If your fuses are rewirable – keep a card of fuse wire or spare fuseholders already wired for 5 amp, 15 amp and 30 amp.

2 If your fuses are cartridge fuses – keep a spare fuse of each size close to the fuse-box.

3 It is a good idea to keep a small container holding: all of the above, an electrical screwdriver, an ordinary screwdriver, wire strippers, a small utility knife, a pair of pliers and a torch close to the fuse-box.

REPLACING CIRCUIT FUSES

AN EMERGENCY KIT MAKES THIS SIMPLE.

If you think a circuit fuse has blown – find your emergency container near the fuse-box.

Turn off the power – then remove the suspect fuseholder.

1 If it is a rewirable fuse – loosen the terminal screws and remove the remains of old wire.

2 Select wire of the correct rating and cut a new length. Feed it down the protective sleeve, then wind each end around its terminal. Tighten the screws and snip off any excess.

3 If it is a cartridge fuse – test it with a continuity tester and, if it has failed, fit an identical replacement. Replace the fuseholder and restore the power.

In the absence of a proper fuse – NEVER use any other metallic object (nail, paper clip, aluminium foil) to restore power. The circuit will not have any fuse protection, and your dangerous action could actually kill someone.

REPLACING APPLIANCE FLEX

AN APPLIANCE WITH A DAMAGED FLEX IS DANGEROUS.

If an appliance flex is damaged or too short for use – replace it. Unplug the appliance from the mains, then open the plug and the appliance casing.

1 Disconnect the old flex – from the plug and the appliance's terminal block – and release it from any protective grommets in the appliance. Take the flex with you when you buy the replacement, to ensure that you get the correct size and type. Remember that double-insulated appliances need two-core flex.

2 To fit the new flex – strip the sheathing to expose the cores. Strip away their insulation. Feed the flex through any protective grommets.

Connect the cores – brown to live terminals; blue to neutral; yellow/green to earth on the terminal block of the appliance and plug.

Fit the flex in the cord-grip, then close the plug and the appliance casing.

REPLACING DAMAGED ACCESSORIES

DAMAGED ACCESSORIES ARE DANGEROUS.

If a light switch, socket outlet or other wiring accessory is cracked, temporarily repair the damage with PVC insulating tape and buy a replacement at the earliest opportunity.

1 Turn off the power at the mains – unscrew the damaged faceplate.

2 Ease it away from its mounting box – note which cable cores go to which terminals and disconnect them. Discard the old accessory.

3 Connect the cores to the terminals on the replacement and screw the faceplate to the mounting box. Reuse the old mounting screws if the new ones will not thread.

REPLACING AN IMMERSION HEATER

If an immersion heater fails, first check whether the heating element or the thermostat is at fault.

1 Turn off the power to the heater at its isolating switch, remove the heater cover and use a continuity tester on the thermostat terminals, then on the heater terminals.

A:

Wiring to a single element heater and thermostat.

B:

Wiring to a dual element heater and thermostat.

2 If the thermostat has failed – disconnect it and slide it out of the heater; fit a matching replacement and reconnect the wiring as on the original thermostat.

If the heating element has failed – turn off the water supply to the hot cylinder and run the hot taps until the flow stops.

3 Attach a length of garden hose to the draincock at the bottom of the cylinder. Draw off two or three bucketsful of water – enough to lower the water level inside the cylinder to below the boss.

4 Disconnect the flex from the heater terminals after making a note of the wiring connections.

Unscrew the old heater – use a hired immersion heater spanner. Heaters tend to get clogged with limescale; if the heater will not budge – use a blowtorch to heat it before trying again with the special spanner. Lift it out and clean round the boss.

5 Slide in the new heater, complete with sealing washer, and screw it in hand-tight. Give it a further half a turn with the spanner.

6 Reconnect the flex and fit the heater cover, then restore the water supply and the power.

1A

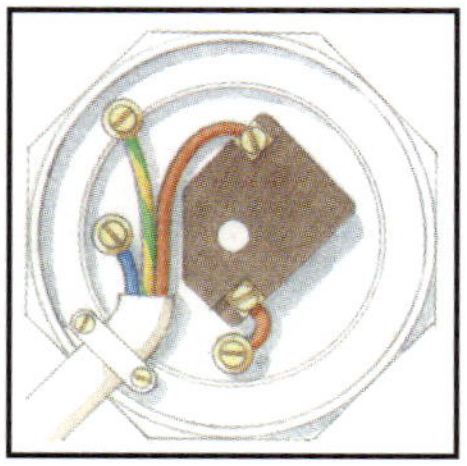

1B

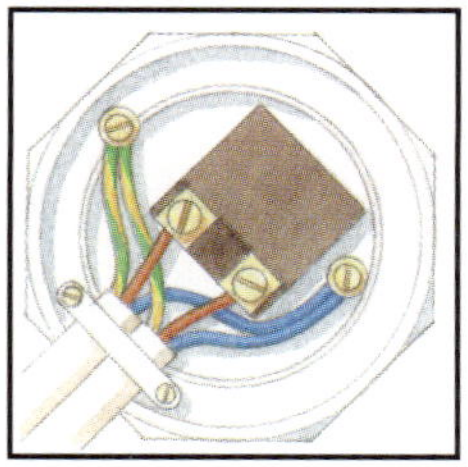

2

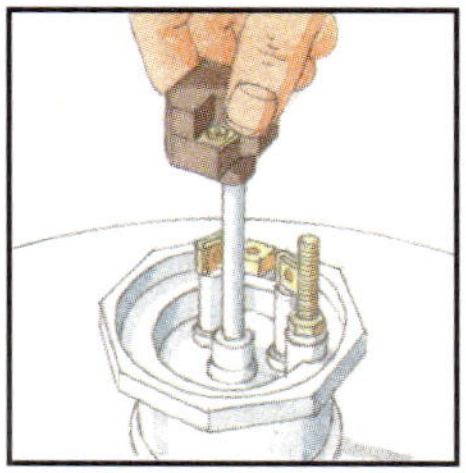

PATHS AND PATIOS

PLANNING

Draw up a plan

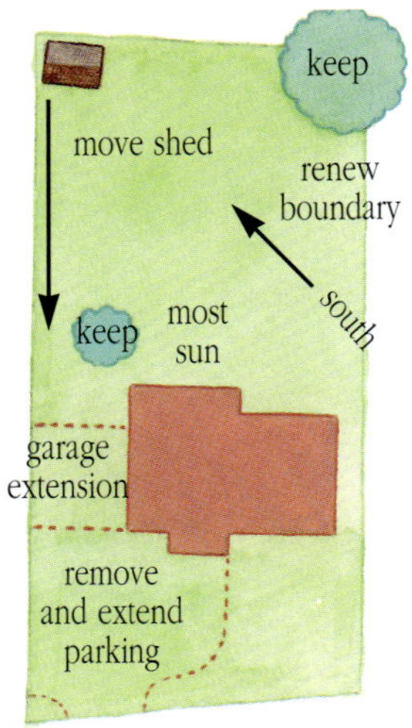

Design

Building a patio or garden path might seem like a back-breaking chore, but it is not difficult. With basic do-it-yourself skills it can be achieved without great cost.

LOCATION AND PLANNING OF A PATIO

The ideal location for a patio is at the back of the house, where it will provide a convenient spot for relaxing and eating outdoors, but with easy access indoors.

Ideally, a patio should catch the sun for at least half the day, so if the garden area adjacent to the house is shaded by buildings or large trees, or swept by the prevailing winds, its use will be limited.

It is easier to rub out pencil lines than change your mind once a patio or path has been laid, so planning it on graph paper using a simple scale is essential.

Use measurements that are like for like – measure and plan using either metric or imperial – never mix the two. For a garden of 10–30m/30–100ft long, a scale of 1:100 (10mm:1m/⅛in:1ft) will be adequate. For a smaller garden or backyard, details will be clearer on a scale of 1:50 (20mm:1m/¼in:1ft).

DRAW UP A PLAN

Choose a reference point (a wall of the house), and take measurements of length and angle to each corner of the garden. Mark in the position of doors, windows and airbricks, and all the garden features and plants.

OBSERVE THE GARDEN THROUGHOUT THE DAY

Make a note of where shadows lie in the morning and afternoon, and sketch these in. Note the prevailing winds and mark in exposed areas.

DESIGN

Several attempts may be needed until you are happy, so sketch out the design on tracing paper stuck firmly in place over the graph paper with tape. Work out the design precisely so that you can calculate the size of foundations, number of slabs needed, and see how any pattern will fall around the edges.

SIZE AND SCALE

A small patio can be made to look larger by careful design. Trying to plan a patio that leaves room for an area of garden in a small town walled garden is an impossible task. A wall-to-wall patio with plenty of 'pockets' for plants is the best solution.

Proportions of scale for gardens tend to be larger than for interiors because garden furniture has more bulk. To ensure that your patio will be large enough, measure your furniture, and allow at least 1m/3ft of space all around for easy access.

In family gardens provide a play area for children too. Do not forget to add in extra space for a sand pit and a courseway for wheeled toys away from the main sitting area.

In a small garden, the bare minimum for a patio is $2.3m^2$. For medium-sized and larger gardens, plan for a patio that is at least $3.6m^2$.

WHERE TO SITE A PATH

From a practical point of view, the ideal route for a path is the shortest and in a straight line, making it faster to lay, more economical and quicker to use. Over a short distance, a straight line is probably the only practical choice.

However, diagonals, zigzags and serpentine curves are more attractive, so choose whichever you think will be in keeping with the style of the garden, but remember that the route must be practical so that people do not take shortcuts where you would rather they did not.

Avoid steep sections on the land altogether, or turn them into steps. Slopes of more than about 1:10 are usually better converted into shorter, flatter lengths with individual steps between them.

LONG AND NARROW GARDENS

Snaking curves can look fussy in a small area, but a series of short, straight paths that move from side to side of the garden will break it up neatly into a series of 'rooms' that are much more interesting, and provide larger, more useful, areas of space.

SQUARE GARDENS

A straight path going in any one direction will reduce accessibility to other large areas of the garden. A curving path makes a complete circuit of the garden leading the eye away from boundaries and visually breaks up wide flat spaces. It will also bring every corner within easy reach.

DOGLEG GARDENS

When one part of a garden is at an awkward angle, it is often treated separately. A circuitous path, or a path of stepping-stones in the lawn, will draw the dogleg back into the main garden without fragmenting the view.

1

2

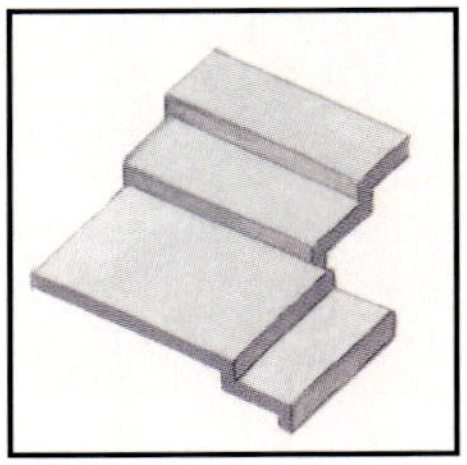

3

4

SIZE AND SCALE

The minimum practical width for a path is around 450mm/18in, but for two people to be able to walk side by side, or to accommodate a wheelbarrow, the width should be 900mm/36in.

Where flowerbeds border the path on both sides, constructing a path that is around 1500mm/60in wide will allow for the invasion of mature plants over some of the surface.

PLANS FOR STEPS

Although steps have a very practical purpose, they should also be regarded as an integral part of the path and designed along with it.

1: GRADUAL SLOPES

A series of steps with wide treads and low risers, or a series of 'landings' gradually sweeping around in a fantail design can make an impressive feature.

2: STEEP SLOPES

On steep slopes either build the steps out from the bank, or dig into it and set the flight within the bank. A solid flight of steps will look like a staircase, so break up the slope with several small sets of steps, interposed with a wide flat landing.

3: CHANGING THE DIRECTION OF THE STEPS

Changing direction or turning them back on themselves at each landing will also make the overall effect of the steps less imposing.

4: STAGGERED STEPS

If a long continuous flight of steps is essential, the simplest variation is to stagger individual steps in an irregular way so that they seem much wider. Allow plants to grow in around them to soften the overall shape.

STEP SIZE

In general, long treads are needed for steps on a gentle slope and short treads are advisable to keep pace with a steep slope.

Steps need to be safe and comfortable to use, should be evenly spaced and not less than 610mm/24in wide. In family gardens, where children are likely to rush about, a width of 1400mm/56in is more desirable.

Steps are easiest to climb comfortably when a long tread is combined with low riser, or a shorter tread is used with a high riser. But a tread should never be less than 300mm/12in deep, or a riser higher than 180mm/7in nor shallower than 100mm/4in.

The table gives the most comfortable tread and riser combinations:

TREAD	RISER
400mm/16in	130mm/5⅛in
380mm/15in	145mm/5¾in
360mm/14in	150mm/6in
330mm/13in	165mm/6½in
300mm/12in	180mm/7in

Below: Concrete paving slabs with a gravel edge look effective as a pathway and the gravel softens the effect of the bare concrete.

CHOOSING MATERIALS

The choice of the materials you use will be dictated by how much you want to spend, and the effect you wish to achieve.

Take into consideration how well it will blend with the exterior of the house and garden as well as the amount of work involved in laying the material, and how confident you are of your DIY skills

ASPHALT

This is hard wearing, but laying can be expensive. Cold-lay versions you can put down yourself, but hot asphalt needs a reputable, specialist contractor.

Suitable for paths that lead from a driveway, but the appearance of asphalt is flat, which can be improved by dressing the surface with stone chippings (see page 87).

CRAZY PAVING

Ideal for an informal patio further away from the house where the overall effect can be softened by plants. Broken concrete slabs can be used, but generally pieces of natural riven stone look better. Select stones which are 40–50mm/1¾–2in thick. Although simple to lay, crazy paving requires a 'good eye'.

Below: riven flagstones.

Below: granite setts.

Below: clay pavers.

Below: concrete slabs.

FLAGSTONES

Used for paving, stone flags give a handsome feel to a garden and regular pieces work well when laid simply in a large, flat area. They look best in rural gardens, but unless this material is readily available locally transport costs may be high.

GRANITE SETTS

These are similar to bricks, and are available in either brick or half-brick sizes, and cubes. Colours range from steel greys to rich browns, and the finished effect has a rough, earthy quality.

Simulated granite setts are cheaper and easier to lay because of their regular shape. They can be laid in lines, circles or fantails with ease, and used for edging. However, the small proportions mean that this is a time-consuming job.

GRAVEL

Gravel creates a relaxed, informal path that can accommodate curves and uneven ground with ease and is available in a variety of colours.

When selecting gravel, remember that the cheapest available will probably be made from the type of stone that is quarried or dredged locally, and the colour should blend beautifully with its surroundings.

Gravel needs raking every so often to keep it looking tidy, and should be topped up each summer to keep it crisp. It tends to 'walk' onto lawns unless restrained by an edging strip.

PAVERS (CLAY)

Brick-size clay pavers are made in a range of clays with a wide colour variation from traditional reds, through to red-blue mixes and brown. They are finished in numerous ways to create different surface textures, and used for radial and circular designs.

They are light and easy to handle. They are a perfect complement to mature gardens, but can cost twice as much as alternative paving materials, and are time-consuming to lay.

PAVERS (CONCRETE)

These are usually rectangular but decorative, interlocking shapes are also available. Colours include grey, red, charcoal, brown, buff and red-grey. Similar in appearance to natural clay pavers, they have a more precise character and are a cheaper alternative.

Concrete pavers are light and easy to handle and will adapt easily to almost any shape. They are well suited to town and formal country gardens, but are time-consuming to lay.

PAVING SLABS

These are inexpensive, and quick to lay on a straight site (each one covers the same area as 10 or 18 small pavers). They are heavy to handle and difficult to form into curves so careful planning is needed on awkwardly shaped sites.

CONCRETE PAVING SLABS

These are available in a variety of shapes and a small range of colours including grey, buff and red. The cheapest are uncoloured slabs with a smooth surface finish.

ARTIFICIAL 'STONE'

These have a textured or riven finish and irregular edges to give the appearance of natural stone that has been weathered by time and water.

POURED CONCRETE

This is composed of varying quantities of sand, cement and gravel aggregates. A variety of finishes can be achieved by varying the size of the gravel used and by applying texturing techniques when the material is nearly dry.

Concrete is one of the cheapest ways of covering large areas, but it is an uninteresting surface that does not improve with age.

USING MATERIALS

Concrete and clay pavers are the most versatile particularly for radial and circular patterns on patios, but materials can be mixed to create some interesting effects.

BASKETWEAVE

Adapts well to either formal or informal gardens and makes a large patio seem more compact.

HERRINGBONE

Suits both town and country gardens and will 'stretch' a small patio. It looks impressive arranged at a 45° angle to the external wall of the house.

STRETCHER BOND

Looks like a brick wall that has been laid on its side and is perfect for use with textured multi-coloured pavers in mature cottage gardens.

STOCK BOND

Looks particularly good in strong blue-greys and buff, and has a sharp modern urban appeal.

STAGGER JOINTS

Stagger joints brick bond style to break up the uniformity of plain smooth slabs.

basketweave

herringbone

stretcher bond

stock bond

ESTIMATING QUANTITIES

Draw an irregular shaped patio on square paper, count the whole squares and average out the portions of part-squares to find the approximate area.

UNIT SIZES:	METRIC SLABS	METRIC PAVERS
	610 x 610mm	215 x 105mm
	610 x 460mm	200 x 100mm
	460 x 460mm	
	460 x 690mm	
	450 x 450mm	

FOR A WORKING QUANTITY –

divide the length and breadth of your plan by the selected size of slab or paver.

Estimate quantities using the information below.

SIZE:	METRES	YARDS	FEET	INCHES
LENGTH	1m	= 1.0936yds	= 3.2808ft	= 39in
LENGTH X BREADTH	$1m^2$	= $1.1960yds^2$	= $10.7639ft^2$	= 39in x 39in
LENGTH X BREADTH X DEPTH	$1m^3$	= $1.3080yds^3$	= $35.3147ft^3$	= 39in x 39in x 39in
WEIGHT:	12cwt	= 112lbs	= 50.80kg	

SHAPE:	FORMULA	$AREA^2$	$VOLUME^3$
RECTANGLE	L X B	= LENGTH X BREADTH	X DEPTH
TRIANGLE	L X B ÷ 2	= $\frac{\text{LENGTH X BREADTH}}{2}$	X DEPTH
CIRCLE	πr^2	= $\frac{22}{7}$ X RADIUS X RADIUS	X DEPTH

When ordering quantities from your merchant, always give them your measured dimensions so that they can check the quantities and ensure that you only buy what you need. A simple calculating error can be expensive.

DO NOT MIX MEASUREMENTS – USE EITHER METRIC OR IMPERIAL.

PREPARING THE GROUND

A patio that looks enormous on paper can be quite small in reality, and the way in which a tree will block the view from your new patio will only become obvious once the full size plan is laid out *in situ*. In the same way you will only know whether a path is fully successful and steps are practical for use once they are plotted and have been tried out.

1 Plot out the perimeter of the patio or the edges of the path by driving pegs into the ground and stretching string-lines between them. For curves, scribe arcs on the ground with a rope tied to a peg and mark the lines with stakes or a row of bricks. Hold string in place by hammering nails into the tops of the pegs and bend them over to form a hook. Mark out irregular curves using a garden hose laid along the edges of your shape.

2 Remove all grass, topsoil and organic matter from within the pegged area, and then roughly mark out with a spade an area that is 150–200mm/6–8in larger than the pegged area to allow for edge restraints.

3 Calculate the combined thickness of the paving and base materials, and dig out the ground roughly to a depth that will be 150mm/6in below the top of the finished surface.

If the site is adjacent to the house, the finished surface height must be two courses of brickwork below the damp-proof course.

4 Compact the excavated ground with a garden roller or tamp it down firmly using the end of a stout timber post.

REMOVING OLD PATHS

An old cracked concrete path or paving slabs may come up easily but for more resilient surfaces the hire of a power hammer may come in useful. Always protect your eyes with safety spectacles or goggles and wear thick protective gloves.

BEFORE YOU START

Check the position of gas, electric and water services and mark their approximate position on the surface with chalk. Hire a skip to load and clear away all the old rubble.

Work across 300mm/12in strips of path at a time. Use a sledge hammer to break up a line across the path (on asphalt a pickaxe will be adequate). Lift large pieces into the skip, and tackle stubborn remains with a hammer and bolster.

Work carefully around gulleys and manhole covers. Break up the surface around the edge first with a hammer and chisel. Take care not to let any rubble fall down the drain.

COPING WITH A MANHOLE COVER

Under no circumstances must a manhole be buried under paving materials. There are many ways it can be disguised or raised to blend in with the new surface.

RAISING A MANHOLE COVER

1 Remove the manhole cover. Place a polythene sheet over the drains to catch any falling debris.

2 Use a club-hammer and cold chisel to carefully chip away the mortar around the frame and on top of the brickwork around the chamber.

3 Build up the height of the chamber walls with a course of bricks, or brick slips if the thickness required is less than 75mm/3in.

4 Reset the frame on a bed of 3:1 sand-and-cement mortar. Tap the frame gently into position with a club-hammer cushioned by a piece of softwood, and use a spirit level across all surfaces to check that the frame is level.

5 Neaten the mortar around the perimeter of the frame by sloping it downwards to form a run-off for rainwater.

DISGUISING A MANHOLE COVER

Special recessed replacement covers are available from builder's merchants which will act as a tray in which the new paving material can be laid. These are made from pressed steel and measure around 610mm x 460mm. Once laid flush with the surrounding surface, all that is visible is the outer framework.

TAKE CARE NOT TO STRIKE THE FRAME OF A MANHOLE COVER – IT WILL SHATTER EASILY!

HOW TO RESTRAIN EDGES

Unless a surface is laid against a wall, the edges of paving laid dry on sand must be supported in some way. This can be achieved with a decorative row of small unit pavers or an edging strip, or more simply with concrete haunching or timber treated with a chemical preservative.

A decorative edging or timber restraints are usually installed before hardcore and sand are laid. This means that your calculations for setting out the design must be very accurate.

With decorative patterns like herringbone, the paving material can be used to form its own edging, using either a soldier course – pavers used end on around the edge of the surface or, a string course – one or two rows of pavers placed sideways to the edge of the surface.

Paving slabs, flagstones and materials that are bedded in concrete do not require an edging strip, though one can be added for decorative effect.

1 Dig out a trench deep and wide enough to accommodate the edging material plus 100mm/4in for the foundations. Fix temporary restraints along the inner edge, and then lay foundations 75mm/3in thick using a 1:3:4 mix of cement:sand:gravel and leave for at least 24 hours.

2 For a straight edge – bed the edging over a 25mm/1in thick mortar bed of a 3:1 sharp sand-and-cement mix. Pack more mortar behind the edging, and slope it up the outer edge to make a small haunch. Fill the joints between blocks.

3 For a curved edge – bed the edging onto a 25mm/1in thick mortar bed of a stiff 2:1 sand-and-cement mix. Make the joints as regular as possible, and no wider than 25mm/1in. Leave for 24 hours, then fill the joints with mortar up to the bottom of the chamfered edge and smooth off.

4 Edge restraints can be removed after 24 hours, but wait three days before laying the paving.

FOR HAUNCHING

Leave the surface for 24 hours to settle, then carefully remove the edge restraints. Fill the gap with a foundation mix of 1:3:4 cement:sand:gravel. Slope the mix up the outside of the edging to within 30–40mm/1½in from the top edge of the patio, to form a generous triangular haunch about 150–200mm/6–8in wide. Once the concrete has set, landscape by replacing the topsoil and turf.

MAKING A START

1 (the correct fall)

2

1 (laying the patio)

3

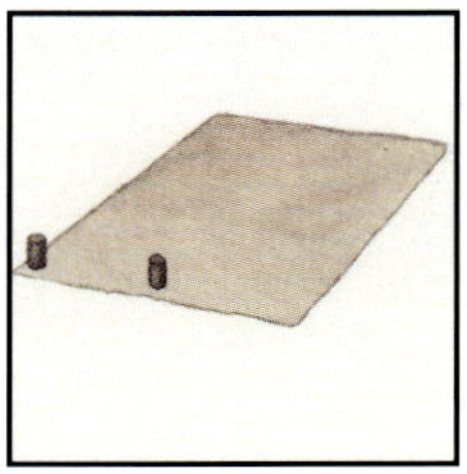

HOW TO ACHIEVE THE CORRECT FALL

A fall of about 1:60 (16mm:1000mm/58in:40in) is adequate to allow rain water to run off the surface without affecting the stability of garden furniture.

To set a fall, you will need a shim – a thin piece of wood of the correct thickness. For a crossfall of 1:60 on a surface where the marker pegs are set at 1500mm/60in intervals, you will need a shim 25mm/1in thick.

Once all the marker pegs are in place, you can adjust the height to create the correct fall. Start at the top of the surface and work down each row of pegs towards the lower edge.

1 Lay a spirit level on a length of timber across the first two level marker pegs.

2 Place the shim under the wood on top of the second peg. With the shim in position, tap down the second peg until the bubble in the spirit level is exactly central. With the shim removed, the fall between the top of both pegs will be 1:60.

3 Now lay the timber and spirit level across the next pair of pegs, placing the shim on top of the third peg in the row. Work along all the pegs in each row in this way. If a surface is set against two house walls, then the correct fall should be set across as well as along the length.

LAYING THE PATIO

Although the patio area has been roughly marked out, it is essential to install precise string-lines and accurately levelled pegs over the entire area before any groundworks can commence.

1 First create a corner with intersecting string-lines – a corner at the top of the patio nearest the house is a good place to start. Fix pegs outside the work area so that they will not be disturbed if you need to excavate into corners.

MARKING OUT THE SITE

2 Cut a number of timber pegs about 450mm/18in long, and mark on them the depths of the various layers of the patio. Work from the top down.

3 Drive a marked peg into the ground in the top corner nearest to the house.

4 At 1500mm/60in intervals drive a row of levelled pegs in across the top edge of the patio.

5 Drive a second row of levelled pegs into the ground 1500mm/60in farther down the patio, and continue in rows 1500mm/60in apart so that the last row is along the bottom edge of the patio.

You can adjust the pegs to set the fall of the patio as you work, or do this afterwards.

6 Once the correct fall has been set, fix taut string across the top of the pegs and measure down from the string-lines to work out whether there are any high or low spots to be dealt with.

Use a builder's square to ensure that all the corners are at perfect right-angles.

IRREGULAR CURVES

7 Mark out a base line parallel to the intended shape with pegs and string. Use the scale plan to calculate the distance from the baseline to the outer edge of the patio at 1000mm/40in intervals, and mark these measurements on the ground with your pegs marked with various layers.

Use a builder's square to make sure that string-lines are at right-angles to the baseline.

Right: A water feature is enhanced by radiation cobbles in this rustic garden.

CIRCULAR PATIOS

8 Peg string-lines on the ground in a square – each side should equal the diameter of the circle. Stretch string-lines across the corners and knock a peg into the centre of the circle.

9 Scribe the circumference on the ground by using a peg on a string of the required radius. Use one end of the square as the baseline for pegging out the site.

5

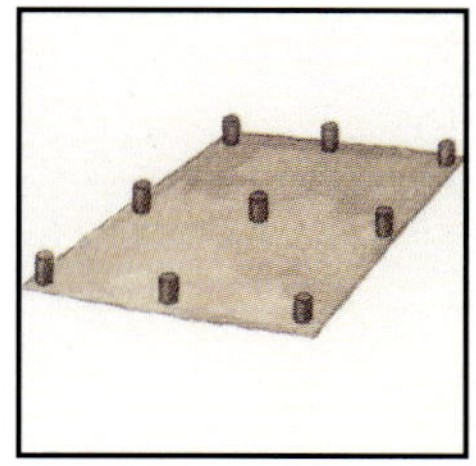

6

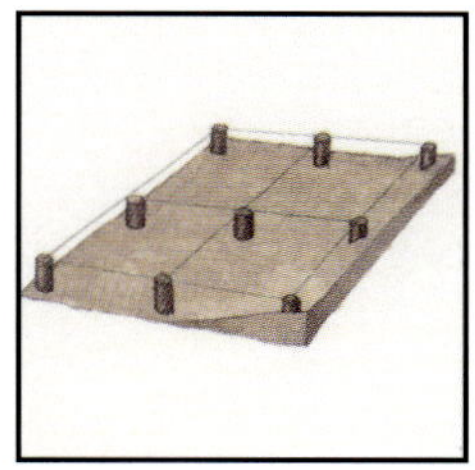

7

9

2 (constructing steps)

3

4

5

LAYING NEW STEPS

Build steps from the base upwards – the bottom step takes most of the weight and the foundations must be solid.

For this reason, it is wise to construct steps in the early stages of garden design and layout. It is then a simple task to link patios and secondary features by paths.

MARKING OUT THE STEPS

1 Set a post at the foot of the bank and run a string-line from the top of the bank to the post. Check that it is square, and measure the height (the post) and depth (the string-line) of the slope.

2 Divide the height of the slope by the number of steps required – this will give the height needed for each step (riser plus the thickness of the tread).

3 Divide the depth of the slope by the number of steps – giving the depth needed for each tread.

4 Start at the top of the slope and cut out a slope slightly above the level of the intended steps.

5 Roughly cut out where the finished steps are to be, then dig out the extra soil needed for sub-base materials.

CONSTRUCTING STEPS

1 Dig a footing 125mm/5in deep and wide enough for the first riser.

2 Fill and compact the trench with 25mm/1in of hardcore. Fill and level the footing with a 100mm/4in deep mix of 1:2½:3½ cement: sand: 20mm aggregate, or 1:5 cement:all-in-one aggregate. Cover the footing with polythene sheeting and leave for three days to cure.

3 Construct the riser using normal bricklaying methods, and leave it to harden for two hours before backfilling with well compacted hardcore.

4 Lay the tread on a full mortar bed of 4:1 sharp sand-and-cement so that the front edge overhangs the riser by 25–50mm/1–2in.

5 The next riser is laid on a bed of mortar on the back edge of this tread, and steps 3 and 4 repeated.

Use a spirit level – tap down the front edge of each tread. The slight slope will allow rainwater to run off and prevent ice forming in winter months.

Instructions are for steps constructed from concrete paving slabs for the treads and pavers for the risers, but the method is similar whatever material you use.

LAYING A NEW PATH

Ensure a constant width – unless the path rambles among greenery – and make sure you achieve the correct fall (see page 76).

A path should have a slight crossfall of about 1:80, especially where it runs alongside a house wall.

MARKING OUT THE SITE

The easiest way to construct a path from paving units is to make sure that an exact number will fit across its width.

1 Lay out a row of slabs or pavers dry, positioned to allow for any joints.

2 Mark the full length of the path to this width (allowing for any edging) with pegs and string. On curves use a garden hose to mark the outline.

3 Excavate the full area. Drive pegs down each edge and along the path centre at 1000–2000mm/40–80in intervals.

4 Adjust the pegs to set the correct fall of the path, and level any high or low spots.

HOW TO LAY A CONCRETE PATH

The surface layer of a concrete path must be at least 50mm/2in thick, but increase the thickness to 75mm/3in where the path will carry a heavy wheelbarrow.

To construct a concrete path use either a paving mix of 1:1½:2½ cement:sharp sand:20mm/¾in aggregate or 1:3½ of cement and all-in-one aggregate.

Prevent the path cracking by incorporating expansion joints in the concrete.

1 Clear the site to a firm base. Fix temporary supporting side edge restraints to the path position. On very wide paths an additional centre stake support will be needed every 1500mm/60in dividing the path into bays.

2 Fit a hardboard filler strip between, and at right-angles, to the two edge restraints. Support the strip on the outer edge with pegs.

Filler strips are permanent so make sure they are level with the surface of the concrete.

3 Shovel concrete into the bay, and for about 300mm/12in into the next bay. Use the back of a rake to level the concrete so that it is about 13mm/½in higher than the top of the framework.

Air pockets will weaken concrete so make sure it is pressed well into corners and against edges.

3 (laying a new path)

4

1 (a concrete path)

2

2 (laying the sub-base)

4 Move the filler strip support pegs to the next bay. Repeat step 3 above.

5 Compact the concrete by tamping it down with the edge of a heavy plank laid across the edge restraints. Then remove excess concrete by working the plank in a sawing action across the surface.

6 Before the concrete hardens, smooth with a float, the back of a shovel or broom according to the finish required and leave it to cure under polythene for three days.

If the path is curved, position the filler strip so that it meets both side edge restraints at right angles.

MATERIAL	GROUND CONDITION	SUB-BASE
PATIO:		
PAVING SLABS	soft	100mm/4in hardcore plus
	firm	35mm/1⅜in sand compacted to 30mm/1⅛in
CRAZY PAVING	soft	100mm/4in hardcore plus
	firm	35mm/1⅜in sand compacted to 30mm/1⅛in
PAVERS	soft	150mm/6in hardcore plus
	firm	65mm/2½in sand compacted to 50mm/2in
PATH:		
ASPHALT		75–100mm/3–4in hardcore plus
		50mm/2in top layer of ballast
COBBLESTONES		100mm/4in compacted hardcore plus
		25mm/1in binding layer of sand
CONCRETE		50mm/2in compacted hardcore plus
		25mm/1in binding layer of sand
GRAVEL		100–150mm/4–6in compacted hardcore plus
		25mm/1in binding layer of sand

LAYING THE SUB-BASE

A patio or path that is laid on soft ground (ie clay or peat), or subjected to heavy loads such as a large lawn-mower or cast-iron furniture, will need a well compacted hardcore base.

1 Choose timber boards which are an equal width to the required depth of the sub-base and position them along the outer edge(s) of the surface. Break up a large surface into manageable bays with timber boards 1000mm/40in apart that are parallel to the outer board(s).

2 Lay another board across the rails and shovel hardcore into each bay up to this level. Fill and level 1000mm/40in of each bay at a time, moving the top board as you work.

3 When the hardcore has been laid, draw out the inner boards and check the level with string-lines. Fill any dips and scrape flat any high spots.

4 Compact the hardcore to the sub-base level using a garden roller, or plate vibrator.

5 With edge restraints in position, rake on a layer of sharp sand and damp it down with a watering-can fitted with a fine rose (the sand should form a ball if squeezed).

LAYING SAND

Sharp sand will even out slight variations in a levelled area of soil or a hardcore sub-base, to provide the final smooth surface over which paving materials are laid.

1 Erect temporary edge restraints (25mm/1in thick planks) nailed to pegs around the perimeter of the surface (except where it butts a wall), so that the top of the board is the finished height (30mm/$1\frac{3}{16}$in plus the thickness of slabs, flagstones or crazy paving, and 50mm/2in plus the thickness of concrete and clay pavers).

2 Use a builder's angle to ensure that the restraints are at right angles, or measure across diagonals – dimensions from corner to corner should be equal.

3 Break the area into manageable bays with boards parallel to edge restraints (3000mm/120in bays for two people working together or 1500mm/60in bays if working alone).

4 Shovel sand into one bay at a time, roughly level it with a rake, then draw a screed rail across the surface to level it. Complete each bay in turn and then thoroughly compact the sand.

CONSTRUCTING A SCREED RAIL

An easy method to level sand is to draw the edge of a timber board across the surface. To construct a screed rail, you will need to cut notches in each end so that it sits neatly on the perimeter boards.

For paving slabs, flagstones and crazy paving, the notches should be the same depth as the paving material (usually 38mm/$1\frac{1}{2}$in).

For concrete and clay pavers, the sand should be slightly higher to allow for compaction. Cut notches 35mm/$1\frac{3}{8}$in deep for 50mm/2in thick pavers, and 50mm/2in deep for 65mm/$2\frac{1}{2}$in thick pavers.

3

4

Below: Hexagonal pavers can be attractive and versatile for paths and patios alike.

LAYING METHODS

HOW TO LAY CRAZY PAVING

Sort the pieces into piles of different colours and sizes, so that you can select from the various piles as you work.

Place large stones with a straight edge in a separate pile and save these for edges. The stones will not all be of the same thickness, so additional mortar will be needed under thin pieces to maintain a level surface.

Below: A mixture of symmetrical pavers and crazy paving adds interest to this small patio and garden setting.

1 Lay a full bed of mortar about 32–50mm/1½–2in thick over an area of $1m^2/1yd^2$, using a dry 4:1 sand-and-cement mix.

2 Lay as many medium-to-large pieces over the area as you can. With a wooden mallet or piece of stout wood, tamp each stone into place until it is stable.

3 Use a spirit level to check and adjust the level of the laid stones, then fill any small gaps with small pieces and tamp these to the surrounding level.

4 Continue working in bays of $1m^2/1yd^2$ until the whole area is laid, and then leave for two days before pointing.

It is not necessary to maintain uniform joints between stones but, for appearance, joints should be no wider than 25mm/1in.

FINISHING TOUCH

Use an almost dry mortar of 2:1 sharp sand-and-cement mix and press it well into the joints with a trowel. Draw a well defined groove in the mortar around each slab using the tip of a brick trowel, then use an old paintbrush to smooth the joints. Wipe the stones clean with a damp sponge.

HOW TO LAY FLAGSTONES AND SLABS

For a patio alongside the house, an obvious starting point is against a house wall.

If it is sited elsewhere in the garden, work from a string line along the top edge of the patio. Lay on a full bed of semi-dry 4:1 mix of sharp sand-and-cement.

1 Start in one corner. Use a brick trowel to spread mortar 32–50mm/1¼–2in thick over an area large enough for the first slab. Roughen or ridge the surface of the mortar with the trowel.

2 Lower the slab into position so that the outer edges are aligned with string-line(s).

3 Place a short piece of 100mm x 50mm/4in x 2in timber on the slab as a cushion and tamp it down firmly with a club hammer until it is level with the finished height shown on the marker peg.

After tamping down slabs, the compacted mortar should be about 25mm/1in thick.

4 Lay mortar for the next slab and position it so that there is a 5mm/¼in gap between the two. Tamp it down and check it with a spirit level. To maintain accurate joints, place temporary spacers (small pieces of wood) in each joint.

When laying mortar, lay a strip where the slab joints will be. Draw the mortar up the side of the last flags laid, tapering it to the top edge. When the next flag is laid, the joint will be almost ready pointed.

5 Work across the top edge of the patio, and then down one side. You can then begin to fill diagonally across the area. Continually check levels in all directions as the slabs are laid.

If a slab is too high, lift it and re-lay it with less mortar. If a slab is too low, lift it and add more mortar.

6 When a small area (around $2m^2/2yds^2$) has been laid, check that the fall from the house is consistent. Lay a spirit level on a length of timber on the surface and place the shim under the lower end. The spirit level should give a level reading.

7 Leave the surface for 24 hours for the mortar to harden, and do not walk on it during that time. Wait for 48 hours before removing the wooden spacers and filling the joints.

2

3

5

6

FINISHING TOUCH

To grout paving slabs and flagstones, you will need a stiff, dry 2:1 mix of sharp sand-and-cement. Mask off either side of the joint with thin sheet material, and trowel mortar in to 5–10mm/¼–½in below the surface level of the slab. Force it well into the gap, and use a short length of small-bore pipe (bent at an angle to provide a hand grip) to smooth the joint neatly. Wipe off any excess mortar immediately with a damp sponge.

A quicker method is to fill the joints with a dry mortar mix of 4:1 sharp sand-and-cement, and set it by wetting with a watering-can fitted with a fine rose.

You must remove all traces of the cement from the surrounding surface or it will leave unsightly stains on the new patio as soon as it rains.

Below: Radiate the joints of paving slabs and fill the gaps with gravel to create a curving patio.

For a path, you can use the five-spot method of laying – a fist-sized blob of mortar under each corner of the slab and one more in the centre.

CUTTING PAVING SLABS

1 Mark the cutting line on both faces and edges, then lay the slab on a bed of sand so that it is well supported.

2 Use a club-hammer and bolster to make a 3mm/⅛in groove along the marked line on all edges. You will need to strike the bolster a few times in each spot to achieve this.

3 Gradually work round the slab, deepening the groove.

4 Place the slab face down in sand, and tap firmly in two or three places along the cut line with a club-hammer.

The slab should split cleanly in two.

HOW TO LAY A PAVER PATIO

Use string-lines at all times to keep control of the pattern and prevent a small error growing out of all proportion.

Pavers laid at edges should stand about 10mm/½in proud of the edge strip – they will bed down when compacted.

1 Start in one corner and work gradually along the two adjacent sides and towards the middle of the patio, keeping a diagonal front to the work. Do not allow one side of the work to proceed faster than the other, and check the progress of the pattern regularly with string-lines.

2 Place the pavers on the sand – do not press them in or slide them across the surface. Leave a 2–5mm/⅛–¼in gap between clay pavers. Concrete pavers have spacer nibs so butt them together.

3 Work in sections of $2m^2/2yds^2$, moving forwards on a kneeling-board across the laid blocks. Lay whole pavers first, then cut and fit half-pavers.

Check that the fall has been maintained as you proceed (see page 76).

4 On clay pavers only, make two or three passes over the patio with a plate vibrator to within 1000mm/40in of the edges. This will compact the sand and drive some of it up into the joints.

A vibrator will displace sand easily so get a helper to brush it towards the vibrator as you work.

5 Brush dry-joint filling sand over the entire area so that it fills the joints, but leaves a covering of sand on the surface, and make another two passes over the patio with the vibrator to compact the surface.

6 Remove the temporary edging restraints and brush any remaining sand into the joints. Do not walk on the patio until the edges have been permanently supported.

To prevent scuffing the pavers, make sure that the vibrator is supplied with a rubber sole-plate.

1

4

1

3

HOW TO LAY A PAVER PATH

1 Start from the bottom of the path and work along it on a kneeling-board, laying the pavers.

2 Butt concrete pavers closely together, but leave a 2–5mm/⅛–¼in gap between each one.

3 Complete 1 linear metre/yard, then cover sections of the laid pavers with a piece of wood and hit it with a club-hammer to bed the pavers in.

4 When the path is complete, work back over the surface, compacting the pavers with a club-hammer cushioned by a piece of timber that is long enough to cover several bricks at one time.

5 Leave the path to settle for 24 hours before haunching the edges.

FINISHING TOUCH

After compaction, use a soft broom to sweep what sand is left on the surface neatly into the joints.

CUTTING PAVERS

1 Mark the cutting line on all sides of the paver then, using a bolster and club-hammer, score the marked line by tapping gently.

2 Lay the paver face down on sand and rest the bolster in the scored groove.

3 Tilt the handle towards the waste end of the paver and strike the bolster sharply once with the club-hammer. The brick should break in two. Designs such as herringbone often need a large quantity of cut bricks. Hiring a block splitter will be faster and less wasteful.

ALWAYS protect your eyes with safety goggles and hands with thick gloves, when cutting slabs and pavers whether by hand or machine.

HOW TO LAY ASPHALT

Cold asphalt is best used for resurfacing old paths, but it can be used to construct a new path providing the sub-base has been thoroughly compacted with a plate vibrator. Without this, it is very difficult to get good results.

1 With edge restraints and compacted sub-base laid, tip bitumen emulsion over about $3m^2/3yds^2$ at a time and spread to an even thickness with a stiff broom.

2 When it has turned from brown to black (about 20 minutes), tip asphalt onto the surface. Use the back of a rake to break down lumps and level it to a thickness of about 20mm/1in.

3 Wet a garden roller and roll it over the surface. Add extra asphalt to depressions and to build up the drainage slope, then roll the surface again.

4 Scatter stone chippings over the surface and roll in several directions to compact the asphalt to 13mm/½in thick.

Asphalt is easy to level and roll on a warm, dry day. Keep the roller wet so that it does not pick up lumps of asphalt, which will mark the surface.

HOW TO LAY COBBLESTONES

1 Sort the cobblestones into different colours and sizes, so that you can select from various piles as you work to create a well balanced design.

2 Lay cobbles on a 50mm/2in thick dry mortar bed of 4:1 sharp sand-and-cement.

3 Position the cobblestones so that they fit tightly together and project well above the surface of the mortar.

4 Using a long stout piece of timber as a cushion, compact the cobblestones with a club-hammer and, finally, lightly sprinkle the surface with water.

HOW TO LAY A GRAVEL PATH

1 With edging strip and sub-base laid, shovel in 10–20mm/½–¾in diameter pea gravel to a depth of 50mm/2in.

2 Use a rake to level the gravel and then compact the surface with a garden roller.

HOW TO LAY STEPPING STONES

1 Lay individual stones or slabs in position across the lawn, and cut around the edge of each one with a trowel.

2 Remove the turf and soil deep enough to allow for a 25mm/1in bed of sharp sand plus the thickness of the stone, and so the stone will sit about 15mm/½in below the level of the turf.

3 Dampen the sand and bed the stone in place so that it does not rock when stood on.

TILING

TILES AND TOOLS

1

3

4

Clay tiles, while they are primarily used in kitchens and bathrooms, can be used throughout the home and on a wide variety of surfaces.

Today more materials are available in tile form than ever before – carpet, cushion vinyl, polystyrene, rubber, cork and glass, to name but six. Tiles are considerably easier to lay than sheet materials and suit the inexperienced home decorator far better. They have practical benefits too. You can lay carpet tiles in a kitchen, knowing that, if one or two are spoilt, they can be quickly and cheaply replaced.

The key to achieving a good result in every case of tiling you attempt is careful preparation and planning.

CHOOSING WALL TILES

The vast majority of wall tiles are ceramic, with a smooth glazed surface.

1: FIELD TILES

Standards are the most common type. These have square edges, which need to be separated by spacers when laid. Field tiles may have one, two, or all four edges glazed. This is to allow tiles to be used at the tops of partly tiled walls and on external corners where more than the face of the tile will be seen. Tiles with no edge glazing are suitable for plain walls, but border tiles will be needed to cover any exposed edges.

Field tiles are available in a range of sizes. The most common are 108mm/4¼in and 150mm/6in square. The standard thickness is 4mm/5⁄32in, but wall tiles are available up to 10mm/3⁄8in thick.

Some field tiles have small wings or 'lugs' on their edges to create an even gap between them, so there is no need for spacers.

2: UNIVERSAL TILES

These have angled rather than square edges, which are again designed to space them automatically. Again, the most common sizes are 108mm/4¼in and 150mm/6in square.

3: BORDER TILES

Border tiles are for use with field tiles which have unglazed edges. Border tiles with one rounded edge are traditionally known as RE tiles and are used along the top or side of a tiled panel. Tiles with two rounded edges are known as REX tiles and are used to form corners.

4: HEAT-RESISTANT TILES

These are designed for use around cookers and fireplaces. They are thicker than standard ceramic tiles to reduce the risk of cracking. All ceramic tiles have some degree of heat-resistance (none should crack in temperatures up to 100°C/212°F).

5: EMBOSSED TILES

Embossed tiles have a design moulded into their surface. They may be the same size as the plain field tiles around them but can also be found in numerous sizes as well as strips for edging.

6: DADO TILES

These are specially shaped to resemble wooden dado rails. In hallways, bathrooms and kitchens their use is purely decorative, to cap a part-tiled wall.

7: MOSAIC TILES

These are small ceramic chips held together by a backing material. This backing material automatically creates even spacing between the tiles.

The backing sheets are made from string, paper or nylon. In some cases, the chips are held together by a paper facing that is soaked off once the tiles are in place (see page 97).

CERAMIC TRIMS

These are designed to fill gaps around the edges of baths and kitchen worktops. Bath trims are quadrant in shape and can be fixed in place using a silicone sealant that will flex with the bath when it is in use. Worktop trims are L-shaped and are fixed in place before the rest of the tiles.

ALTERNATIVES TO CERAMIC

CORK TILES

These are invariably 300mm x 300mm/12in x 12in square. They can give a room a warm appearance and will help to insulate a cold room. Covering walls with cork is a quick way to hide slightly uneven or stained surfaces but is no cure for damp.

MIRROR TILES

Covering a wall with mirror glass tiles is effective in making a small room appear more spacious.

BRICK SLIPS

These are thin strips of masonry which can be attached to interior walls to imitate the appearance of plain brickwork. They are often used to cover chimney breasts, breakfast bars and pillars.

5

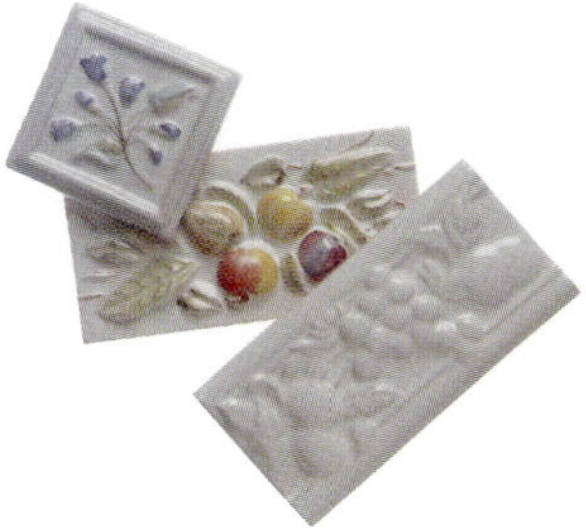

6

7

TILING TOOLS

There are a number of inexpensive hand-tools available which are used for cutting and shaping tiles.

1: ADHESIVE SPREADER

2: CHINAGRAPH PENCIL

Used to mark the glazed surface of a tile.

3: FLOOR SCRIBER

This can be made from an offcut of wood and 2 nails knocked through at either end.

4: GAUGE STICK

A gauge stick will help you decide how best to arrange your tiles so that there are no ugly slivers at either end of a row. To make one, simply place a stick of wood on the floor and lay out a line of tiles along it, complete with spacers. Mark the corners of each tile on the stick in pencil.

5: HOLE SAW

This is useful to cut a tile to fit around a large-diameter pipe.

6: PLUMB BOB

7: PROFILE GAUGE

This is useful for shaping around awkward objects.

8: SPIRIT LEVELS

Both pocket-sized for checking individual tiles and full-sized to check rows and columns.

9: TILE CUTTER

Cheaper hand-held versions may not offer a measuring facility and will require you to provide rather more of the leverage when snapping a tile.

10: TILE DRILL

A drill bit with a spear-shaped tip able to make holes in glass and ceramic tiles without shattering them – essential when fixing things to tiled surfaces.

11: TILE FILE

An inexpensive tool ideal for smoothing off rough fragments and forming curves along the edges of tiles that have been cut roughly to shape.

12: TILE NIBBLERS

These are pincers with hardened teeth used to nibble small sections of tile away to fit around an awkward obstacle like a doorframe or pipe.

13: TILE SAW

This is a hacksaw fitted with a tungsten carbide-coated blade. The ideal tool for cutting awkward curves and other intricate shapes, it produces a much finer finish than a pair of nibblers.

14: TILE SNAPPER

This tool looks like a pair of pliers, but with one tip flattened and the other set at right angles to it. Snappers are only suitable for breaking tiles up to 4mm/$\frac{5}{32}$in thick.

15: TILE SPACERS

The size of gap you leave between tiles for grouting is a matter of personal taste, but symmetry is critical and spacers make this a lot easier to achieve. Plastic spacers are inexpensive, but you may prefer to use spent matchsticks, or even strips of card. Many modern tiles have edges shaped to create this gap automatically.

16: TILE SPIKE OR SCORER

A tool used for scoring the surface of a tile before snapping it. Use in combination with a snapper as an alternative to an all-in-one tile cutter.

TILING ADHESIVES

There are a number of different adhesives available for fixing tiles to various surfaces around the home. For this reason, it is very important to read the manufacturer's instructions carefully when choosing an adhesive.

If you are tiling around a shower area, for example, it is essential to choose a waterproof adhesive. If you are tiling around a stove, a heat-resistant adhesive will be needed.

MAKING A START

1

5

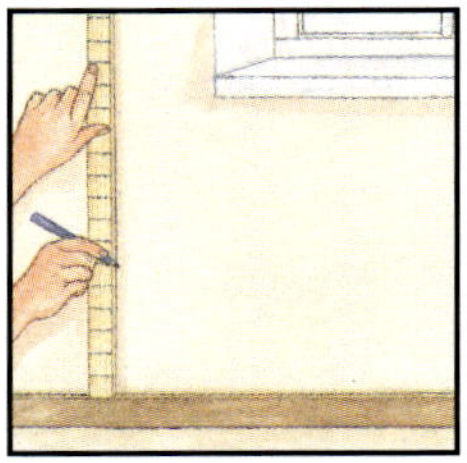

WHERE TO START TILING

There are two points to consider when deciding where to start. You need to get your first row of tiles as near to horizontal as you can; and you need to avoid fitting tiny slivers of tile at the ends of rows and columns. Do not assume that your skirting board will be level because it is in contact with the floor. The floor itself will almost certainly have a slope.

1 To guarantee that you are starting from a level plane it is best to use a wooden batten nailed lightly to the wall just above the skirting. The size of your tiles will determine roughly how far above you fix it – with 150mm/6in tiles, the gap between the top of the batten and the top of the skirting should be 100mm–120mm/4in–5in. Lay your first row of tiles along the top of this batten.

2 Your horizontal guide batten should be fixed at the bottom of the wall rather than the top. If you started tiling at the top of a wall and worked downwards, you would waste a lot of time re-positioning tiles that had slipped out of line.

3 You should use your gauge stick to avoid tiny slivers of tile around the edges of the room.

Spend some time sizing up the room in this way before starting work and you will save a lot of time and effort. You will need to consider every surface and obstacle, every window and doorway.

4 If you have never tiled before, you may choose to start in an unobtrusive corner of the room to build up confidence in the use of spacers and adhesive. This is fine, but you must still plan the rest of the job before that first tile goes up.

5 To do this, actually mark the wall with a pencil to show where each row of tiles will be fixed. This will show you if you are going to have an awkward gap to fill and allow you to adjust your starting point without wasting materials.

TILING A PLAIN WALL

Once you have marked out your wall and your starting point takes account of all the obstacles you are going to encounter, you are ready to fit your horizontal batten. A piece of timber 50mm x 25mm/2in x 1in is ideal for this, but size is not critical.

1 Nail one end of the batten to the wall at the chosen height, taking care not to drive the head right in – you are going to want to remove this batten later without disturbing the tiles above it.

Use your spirit level to establish a horizontal and nail the other end of the batten in place. If your batten is going to stretch along the whole wall, you will find a second pair of hands useful here. If you cannot run a single batten along the entire wall because of obstructions, use two or three short ones, but make sure that they are all correctly aligned.

2 Nail a second batten at right angles to the first in the corner in which you have chosen to start work. This ensures that the vertical is correct from the beginning. Like your horizontal batten, this one should be fixed to the wall approximately two-thirds of a tile's width in from the edge of your tiling surface.

3 Use a notched spreader to cover an area of wall $600mm^2$–$1m^2$/$2ft^2$–$3ft^2$ above your horizontal batten with adhesive. Do not apply any more than this or the adhesive may start to set before you have laid all the tiles. Aim to apply just sufficient adhesive so that no part of the wall behind is visible. The spreader will create ridges in the adhesive to improve the grip on the back of the tile. Applying adhesive to the wall rather than the back of each tile individually saves time, ensures a more even thickness is used and makes each tub of glue go a lot further.

4 Lay six tiles along the top of the batten, inserting spacers between them if necessary. As you press each tile against the wall, give it a twist to the left and right to spread the adhesive evenly under the tile. Then carefully slide it into its final position. Twisting the tile also prevents any movement when you release it.

5 Double-check that each tile is level as you go. You will find a bullet/torpedo spirit level the most convenient tool for doing this.

6 Wipe any traces of adhesive off the face of the tiles with a damp cloth before it dries. It will still be possible to remove spots of glue after they have set with the aid of a trimming knife, but you will risk scratching the surface of the tiles

1

3

4

6

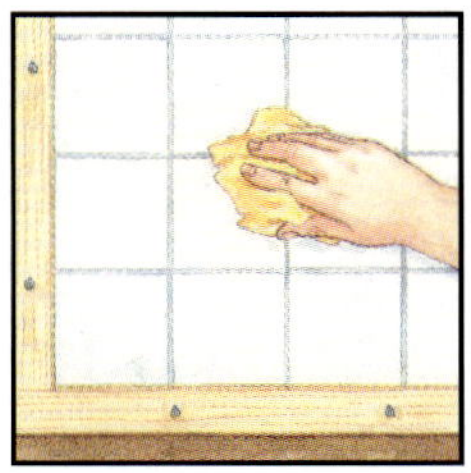

1

3

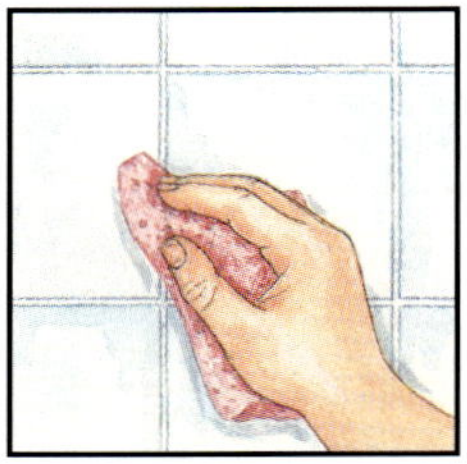

GROUTING

Grouting stops dirt and mould building up in the gaps between the tiles. To be effective, it must be pressed firmly into place.

Some grouts are sold in powder form and have to be mixed with water. Others are sold ready-mixed. If you are tiling around a shower that will regularly get soaked, use a special epoxy-based waterproof grout.

Below: Coloured, water-proof grouting around a bathroom basin can be used for decorative effects as well as being practical.

Grouting should not be applied for at least eight hours after tiling, to allow the adhesive to set. In practical terms, this means an overnight break in the work.

Special tools are available for applying grout, but the back edge of an adhesive spreader will do the job. A professional will use a special squeegee, but you may find this device difficult to use for forcing the grout into the gaps.

Concentrate on getting a liberal amount of grout into the gaps initially – the excess can be removed quite easily with a damp cloth or sponge.

1 You can buy a special tool to smooth over the surface of the grout, but this can be done just as effectively with a piece of dowelling or the blunt end of a pencil.

2 Draw your smoothing tool towards you – never push it away or it may dig in and dislodge some of the grout.

3 When the grout has dried, you will inevitably find traces on the surface of the tiles themselves. These can be removed with a clean dry cloth, which can be used to polish the surface of the wall.

TILING INTERNAL CORNERS

You will invariably have to cut both tiles to form the angle at an internal corner. Try to ensure that you cut about the same amount off each tile to achieve a balanced appearance. Overlap the tiles in the corner so as to hide the cut edges. Leave a standard grout gap between the tiles to allow for any movement between the walls.

TILING EXTERNAL CORNERS

Overlap the tiles so that you see the full face of the one on the more prominent wall. If you have to cut this tile, fix it in place with the cut edge hidden by grouting and the uncut edge on the corner where the glazing can be seen.

TILING AROUND A WINDOW

A window is often one of the focal points in a room, so it is important that the tiles here fit well. You may decide that you would like the row of tiles just below the window to consist of whole tiles. In this case, you will need to adjust your starting point accordingly. A gauge stick will help you to achieve this goal.

1 If you opt for whole tiles here, these should overlap the edge of the window recess by the thickness of one tile. This will allow you to butt the strips of tile laid inside the recess up against them to form a right angle.

2 All the tiles fitted in the recess, both horizontally and vertically, must be carefully aligned with those on the adjoining walls.

(tiling around a window)

APPLYING MOSAIC TILES

Take great care to maintain a consistent grouting gap when you are butting one sheet of mosaic tiles up to another. Tiles that have a face paper covering need to be grouted prior to hanging:

1 Lay the sheets face down on your workbench and apply a coat of grout with a spreader.

2 Let this dry for five minutes while you are spreading adhesive over the wall.

3 Hang the sheets of tiles on the wall with the paper covering facing towards you.

4 Leave to dry overnight, then soak the paper off with a little warm water. If you get the entire surface moist, the paper should peel off in one go.

5 Apply fresh grout to any bare patches between the tiles.

1 (bathroom fittings)

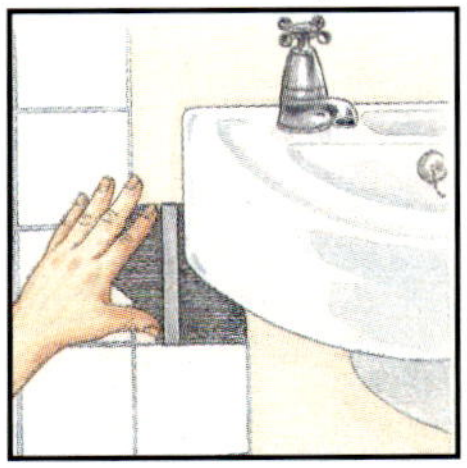

2

3

1 (drilling holes)

CUTTING TILES TO FIT AROUND BATHROOM FITTINGS

If you are tiling a bathroom, you will have to cut and shape tiles to fit.

1 A profile gauge – a measuring device consisting of a row of sliding pins held between two handles – will help here. Press the gauge against the obstacle and mould the pins to its outline.

2 Transfer this outline on to the front of the tile to be cut using a chinagraph pencil. Make sure you keep the sides of the gauge square to the sides of the tile as you do this.

3 Cut the waste portion of the tile using a tile saw (for tiles up to 4mm/5⁄32in thick) or a pair of heavy-duty nibblers.

4 Nibble off any rough spots and then smooth the edge of the tile with a file.

5 It may be more convenient to apply the adhesive to the back of the tile rather than the wall.

6 Any gap between the edge of the tile and the obstacle should be filled with a flexible silicone sealant that will allow for movement between the two in the future. A bath filled with warm water, for example, will flex outwards quite considerably in use and quickly crack a conventional filler.

DRILLING HOLES IN TILES

You may wish to hang mirrors, cupboards and the like from your newly tiled walls. You will need to use a special drill bit to make the holes for any fixings.

A tile/glass drill bit has a tip that has been shaped to reduce the risk of cracking. It can be used here with either an electric drill or a hand drill (use a hand drill only when making holes in glass).

1 Stick a piece of masking tape over the spot where the hole is going to be made. This prevents the drill bit slipping on the smooth, surface.

2 If you are using an electric drill, set it at a low speed to minimise vibration. Drill through into the wall behind.

3 When you are attaching the fixing, take care not to overtighten the screw as this could crack the tile.

CUTTING TILES TO FIT AROUND PIPES

1 Draw a vertical line down the front of the tile using a chinagraph pencil. The line should pass through the centre of where the pipe will be when the tile is fixed to the wall. Mark the point on this line where the pipe will pass through the tile.

2 Split the tile in two along the line and lay the two halves side-by-side on your worksurface. Take a coin, about 1mm–2mm/$\frac{1}{32}$in larger in diameter than the pipe and trace its outline on the two tile halves to mark where the pipe will go.

3 Use a tile-scorer to etch this outline into the surface of the tile. Then remove the waste with a pair of nibblers.

4 File the rough edges of the two semi-circles using sand-paper wrapped around a pencil.

5 Spread the back of both parts of the tile with adhesive and ease them into position.

Cutting large diameter holes to accommodate waste pipes can be tackled another way if you are able to disconnect the section of pipe that passes through the outside wall. The all-important tool here is a tungsten carbide, toothed hole saw which fits on to the end of an electric drill.

REMOVING DAMAGED TILES

1 Tape the damaged tile area around the outside edge. Place a strip of tape near the centre of the tile to prevent the drill bit from slipping.

2 Make a hole in the middle of the damaged tile using an electric drill fitted with a masonry bit.

3 Enlarge this hole with an old chisel; drive the blade in at an angle, striking the back of the handle with a hammer. As fragments of tile split, pull them away with your hands. Take care not to work the chisel blade under any neighbouring tiles or you will loosen them.

4 When you have removed the whole tile, you will be left with a patch of wall covered in hard ridges of old adhesive. This can be chipped away with the chisel blade, but you can get the job done a lot more quickly using a hot air gun.

5 Heat the blade of a metal scraper and then use this to strip off the old adhesive. Do not apply heat directly to the adhesive as this may crack the adjoining tiles.

6 Lightly smear adhesive over the back of the new tile with a notched spreader and press it against the wall. You may need to use strips of card to wedge it into place until the adhesive has partially set. Leave the repair to dry overnight before grouting.

2 (fitting around pipes)

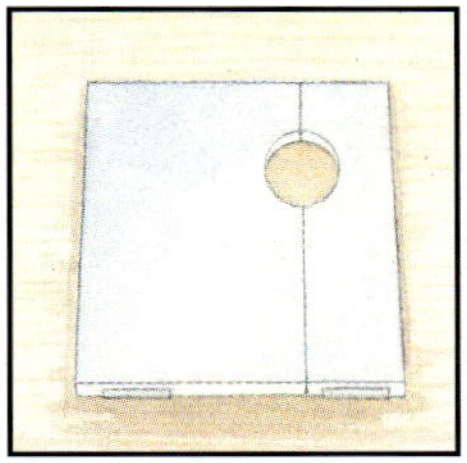

3 (damaged tiles)

5

6

FLOOR TILES

cork floor tiles

vinyl floor tiles

CHOOSING FLOOR TILES

Floor tiles need to be harder wearing than wall tiles, and they must not become slippery to walk on when wet. For these reasons wall tiles must not be used on floors.

CERAMIC TILES

These are the most durable and are available in a wide range of colours and patterns.

SLATE AND STONE TILES

Both are expensive but offer a beautiful natural finish. Neither material is particularly easy to cut using DIY tools and you may prefer to hire a professional to carry out the installation.

CORK FLOOR TILES

These contain a higher percentage of wood than cork wall tiles and are far more durable as a result – check packaging labels to ensure that you have the right sort.

VINYL TILES

These are available in a range of thicknesses – generally speaking, thicker tiles will last longer.

CARPET TILES

They combine the warmth and comfort of wall-to-wall carpeting with the convenience of a covering that can be replaced in small sections should it be damaged by burns or liquid stains.

RUBBER TILES

These were originally made for use in offices but look good in a modern home. They usually have a dimpled finish to improve grip.

Left: Vinyl and cork tiles are simple to lay and provide a warm and comfortable surface on which to walk but neither will last as long as a hard floor-covering.

PREPARING SOLID FLOORS FOR TILING

Solid concrete floors must be dry and level. A newly laid concrete floor should be left for at least a month to dry out.

1 Prime the surface first, using a diluted PVA adhesive applied with an old paintbrush.

2 Fill minor dents and cracks using a fine sand-and-cement screed. Fill larger depressions using a mix of one part cement to three parts sharp sand. Add just enough water to bind the two together, plus a little PVA.

3 A gently sloping floor or one that is deeply cracked or pitted will need to be re-surfaced using a self-levelling compound. If the floor is very uneven, you may have to apply a full screed.

4 A self-levelling compound must be applied to a clean, grease-free surface to achieve a good contact. Brush dirt out of recesses or cracks and wash the floor with warm, soapy water. Mix the compound in a bucket following the manufacturer's instructions; make sure there are no lumps.

5 Pour the compound over the floor, starting in the corner furthest from the door. Use a steel float to spread it evenly over the surface. Any lumps or marks can be smoothed off with the float and a little water when the floor has dried out.

You do not need to remove old floor tiles if they are firmly attached – simply lay the new tiles over the top. If the tiles are very uneven apply a self-levelling compound over them first.

SAND-AND-CEMENT SCREEDS

If your floor is very uneven or slopes by more than 12mm/½in from one side of the room to the other, you will have to cover it with a sand-and-cement screed before laying the tiles on top. This is not too difficult, since the tiles can be laid directly over the screed while it is still wet.

However, you will be raising the level of the floor so check that the bottoms of any affected doors can be trimmed.

With a screed, tiles are laid in sections or 'bays', between 12mm/½in thick wooden battens fixed across the room width.

To establish your starting point, find the centre of the room (see page 104) and dry-lay tiles out from this point to the walls. Adjust the rows to avoid any narrow gaps at the room edges.

Next, find the highest part of the floor. At this point, the screed is going to be

2

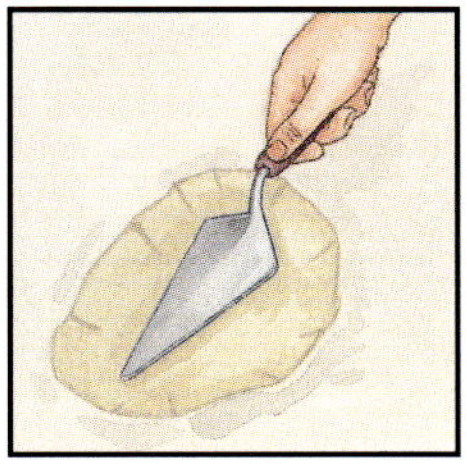

3

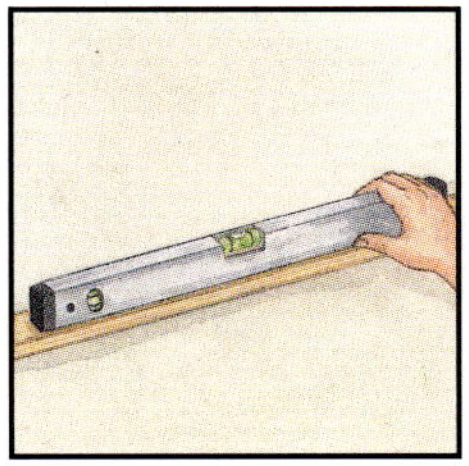

5

1

4

5

6

12mm/½in thick and the rest of the floor will have to be built up to match it.

To avoid stepping on freshly laid tiles, start work below the wall furthest from the door. Mark the position of the last full tile you have dry-laid up to this wall and draw a line on the floor along its front edge, extend this line in both directions to reach the side walls and fix your first guide batten along it.

1 Find the high spot using a long batten and a spirit level. Mark the spot with an offcut of wood 12mm/½in thick.

2 Mix the mortar in the ratio three parts sharp sand to one part cement. Mix it dry and then add just enough water to produce a stiff paste.

3 Spread a thin strip of mortar along your starting line and press your first batten down over it. Stretch a spirit level between the offcut you placed at the high point of the room and this batten.

4 Adjust the height of the batten until the two are level. Then level the batten along its own length. If the spirit level will not stretch between the high point and the batten, tape a straight edge to it to extend its range. Fix a second batten parallel to the first about 1m/3ft nearer the door. Again use the spirit level to even it up in relation to the first batten and along its own length.

5 Fill the space between the two battens with the screed, spreading it out with a steel float. A spare batten will come in handy to level the screed off with the tops of the battens.

6 Mix up a thin solution of cement and water (in a ratio 1:1) and pour a little over the top, spreading it out with your float. Immediately lay the tiles on to this slurry. Tap each one down and insert spacers as you go, using your spirit level to check that you are laying them horizontally.

7 When you have filled the first bay with tiles, detach the first batten from the side of the front row and re-position it 1m/3ft behind the second to form a second bay.

8 Repeat the process until you have laid all the whole tiles and reached the door. You can cut and lay the edge tiles at a later date if you prefer. Scrape the top 3mm–4mm/⅛in off the screed before it sets and fix them in place using adhesive.

PREPARING WOODEN FLOORS FOR TILING

Wooden floorboards that are in good condition can support the heaviest ceramic tiles but need to be covered with chipboard or plywood first to create an even sub-surface.

1 Go over the floor on hands and knees, hammering down any protruding nail heads and fixing loose boards back in place with special nails called cut floor brads.

2 Before you cover the boards, make sure that you will be able to gain access to any pipes or wires beneath them from adjoining rooms.

Once the tiles have been laid, you will not be able to get at them directly without spoiling your new surface. If you are unsure on this point, ask a professional to take a look before proceeding any further.

3 Use 12mm/½in thick chipboard or plywood to cover the floorboards – anything less will be too flexible. Nail the sheets down at 10mm/⅜in intervals right across the room, taking care to sink each nail head below the surface with a nail punch. This is especially important when laying soft floorcoverings, as even the slightest bump will show – and eventually wear through.

Use nails that are long enough to penetrate the floorboards without going through them into any pipes or wires below.

1

3

LAYING FLOOR TILES

1

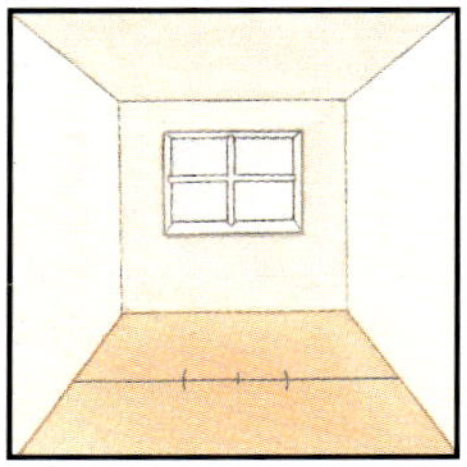

2

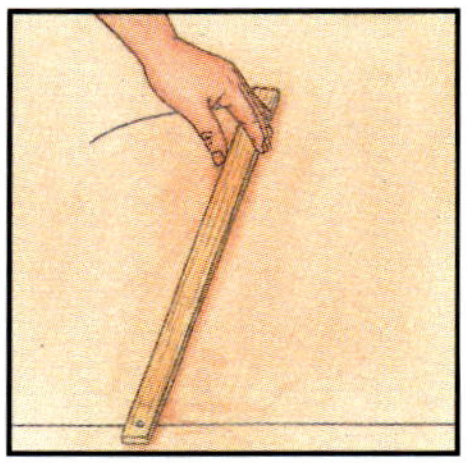

4

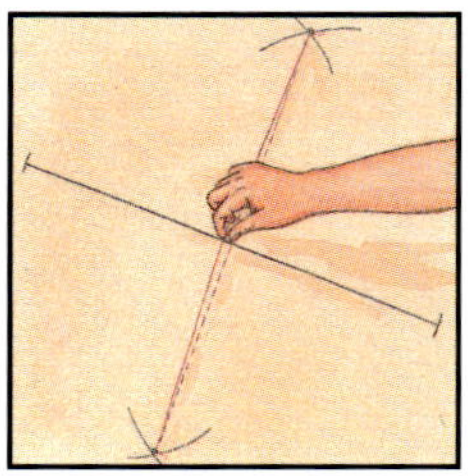

5

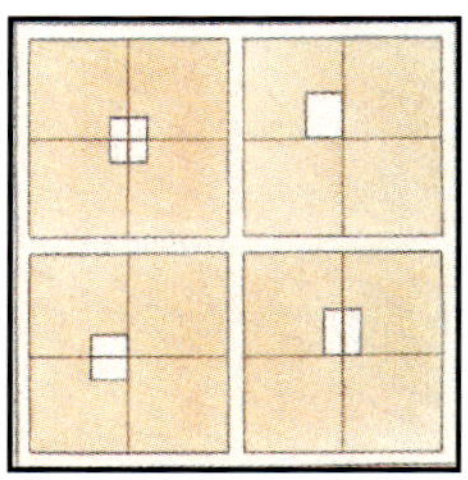

All floor tiles are laid in basically the same way. The only exception is tiles where you are laying them on a wet sand-and-cement screed (see page 102).

WHERE TO START

Generally the best place to start tiling is in the centre of the room.

1 To find the centre of the room, measure along the bottom of two facing walls and mark the floor at their mid-points. Hold a chalk line between the two marks and snap it on the floor. Make a mark half-way along this line.

2 You now need to make a second line at right angles to this one to help you locate your first four tiles using a floor scriber (see page 92).

3 Place one nail on the centre point of your first line and scratch either side, across the line. Place your scriber on each of these side-marks in turn and make two arcs.

4 Snap a chalk line between the two intersections to create your second guideline.

5 Dry-lay four rows of tiles from this central axis out to the four walls. Adjust the starting point as necessary to avoid laying narrow strips around the skirting boards.

6 Dry-lay as many tiles as possible before reaching for the adhesive. Any awkward projections should be tackled 'dry' first to avoid cutting ugly narrow tile strips.

When dry-laying solid floor tiles, allow for the recommended grout gaps.

LAYING SOFT FLOOR TILES

With this type of tile instead of a batten you can follow a pencil line on the floor.

Soft floor tiles can be trimmed to fit around obstacles using a trimming knife or even a pair of scissors.

LAYING HARD FLOOR TILES

1 Nail a batten along one of your starting lines, marking on it the position of the first tile before spreading a suitable adhesive over the floor.

2 Spread no more than $1m^2$/$3ft^2$ of adhesive over the floor at a time. It is very important to bed tiles down before the adhesive starts to set. Use a notched trowel to spread the adhesive – this will improve the 'grip' on the back of the tiles.

3 Lay three or four tiles along the batten, inserting spacers between them as you go.

4 Give each floor tile a twist as you lay it to remove any air pockets. Use a spirit level to

check that all the tiles are bedded down evenly.

5 Start to lay tiles at right angles to the batten. Keep each row as straight as possible.

6 Keep a damp cloth handy to wipe off any adhesive that gets on to the faces of the tiles.

7 When you have tiled the centre of the room, spread more adhesive along one side and continue as before.

Most tiles need to be left for 24 hours before they can be walked on, so you may decide to tile only half of the room at a time if you are decorating a busy kitchen or bathroom.

CUTTING EDGE TILES

You will need to use a heavy-duty tile cutter to snap floor tiles to fit around the edges of the room.

Gaps around the edges of the room will rarely be square so rather than use a tape measure it is far better to adopt a measuring technique that transfers the shape of the wall directly on to the tile you are going to cut.

When fitting tiles in a corner, you can mark the tile first along one edge and then along the other.

Do not fix the last row of whole tiles in place until you have cut the edge-tiles that will be laid next to them.

1 Dry-lay a whole tile next to the last one you have fixed down in the row, inserting spacers.

2 Lay another loose tile on top of the first, but slide this one across to touch the wall.

3 Mark the position of this top tile's back edge with a wax crayon on the loose tile below. Draw along its entire length so that when you lift it off you have a clear line on the tile below.

4 Remove the tile below and place the top tile on the floor next to the last fixed tile. Take the tile you have marked to your tile cutter.

5 If you were now to cut along the line marked on its face, portion 'A' would exactly fit the gap left between the last tile (as yet not fixed in place) and the wall but you need to allow for grouting. Mark a cutting line allowing for the thickness of the grout, using a straight edge, and cut along this.

GROUTING FLOOR TILES

Floor tiles can be grouted using a standard cement or a product specifically designed for the job. The technique is identical to that for grouting wall tiles (see page 96).

1 (laying hard tiles)

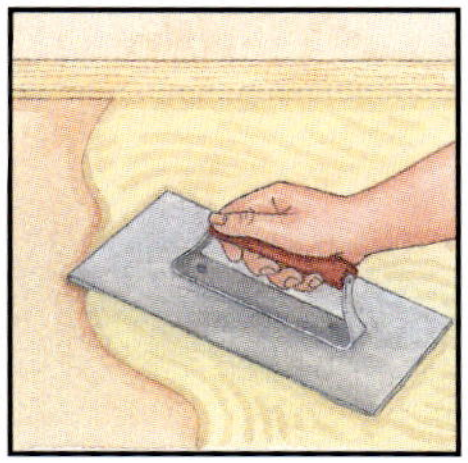

4

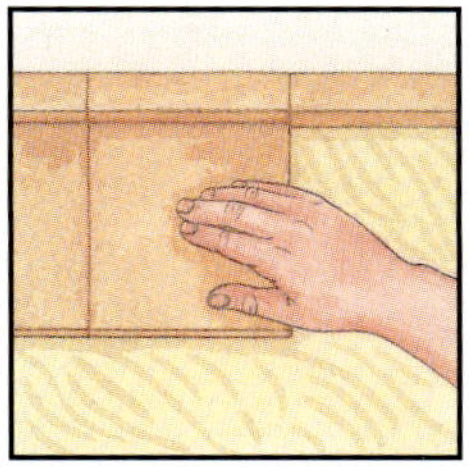

3 (cutting edge tiles)

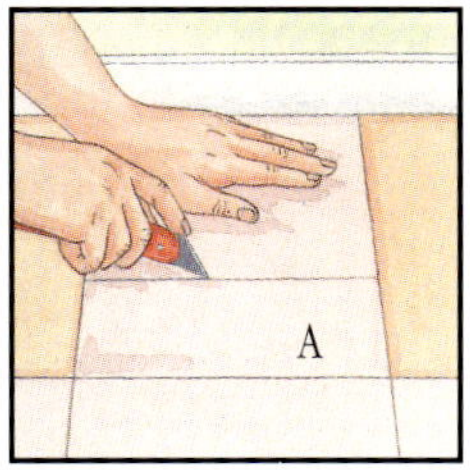

4

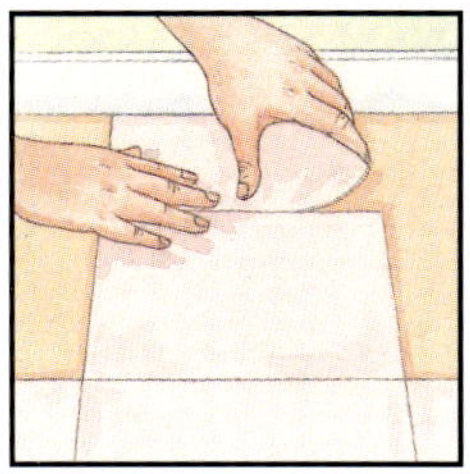

STAINING AND VARNISHING

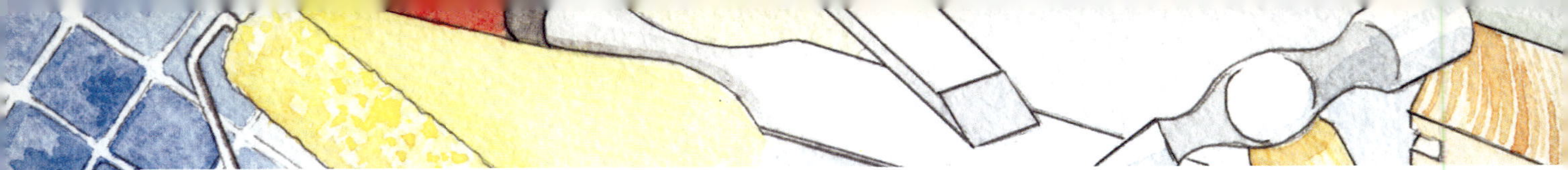

TOOLS

The purpose of stains, varnishes, and other wood finishes is to enhance and preserve the natural beauty of wood.

We are not interested here in paint which covers up the wood nor in preservatives used structurally in house-building, fences and sheds. We are interested in the warm, earthy colours which go to make up natural timber, in the formation of the characteristic grain and in what wood finishers call the 'patina' – that deep sheen a piece of wood acquires over a period of years when it has been finished properly and has been well cared for.

You will need four types of tools for preparing surfaces and applying stains and varnishes.

GENERAL TOOLS

If you are getting involved in wood finishes and applying stains and varnishes, it is likely that you will also be doing some furniture restoration, which may involve considerable amounts of woodworking, often on a very small scale.

1: ADHESIVES

Both polyvinyl acetate wood adhesive and natural (animal or 'Scotch') glue.

2: CHISELS (PLUS A MALLET)

3: CLAMPS (ONE OR MORE)

To hold pieces of wood while the glue dries.

4: CLOTHS, SPONGES AND RAGS

5: DRILL

6: FILLING-KNIFE (SMALL FLAT BLADED)

For applying wood stopper.

7: HAMMERS

8: HESSIAN (CANVAS) SACKING

For applying grain fillers and for liming.

9: PLANES

10: SCREWDRIVER

11: SOLDERING IRON

For melting shellac filler sticks and for removing

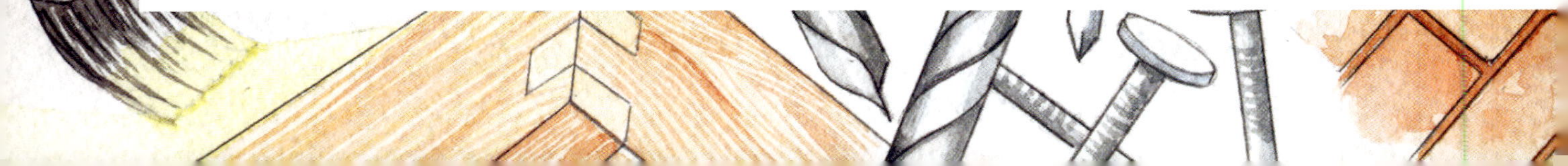

dents and hollows from wood surfaces.

12: SPOKESHAVE

A useful wood-shaping tool that can be set to remove very small amounts of wood. It can be used on curved surfaces such as chair legs.

13: TRIMMING-KNIFE

An essential tool, choose the type with a retractable blade so that you can maintain a sharp edge safely. For fine detailed work and for removing excess filler, an artist's scalpel is invaluable.

14: LAMBSWOOL COVER

Attached to an electric drill this will considerably speed up polishing.

ABRASIVES

Abrasive paper is one of the most useful types of abrasive. Two basic rules when using abrasives are:

1: WORK FROM COARSE TO MEDIUM TO FINE (COARSE GRADES ARE SELDOM USED).

2: WORK WITH THE GRAIN OF THE WOOD WHEREVER POSSIBLE.

There are many different types of abrasive:

GARNET PAPER

Used for final finishing and rubbing down between coats of, say, varnish.

GLASS PAPER ('SANDPAPER')

Useful for sanding down bare wood.

SILICONE CARBIDE

This can be used wet for finishing between coats of varnish (but not on untreated wood).

Abrasive paper can also be fitted to a powered sander but care should be taken to use the right abrasive with the right kind of power tool.

BELT SANDERS

These have the advantage that they remove material quickly and operate only in one direction.

ORBITAL SANDERS

Used for finishing, but they tend to leave tiny circles on the wood, even when used with the finest paper.

DISC SANDERS

Useful for rough finishing of surfaces, especially curved surfaces, they tend to leave swirl marks on timber, but the latest random orbital disc sanders are much better.

WIRE WOOL

This can actually polish the surface in its finest (0000) grade. Used with surface revivers and with various polishes and for removing the final traces of paint stripper. When working with wire wool, use a pair of scissors to cut a pad off the roll.

BRUSHES

You will need a good selection of brushes for working with stains and varnishes. The best quality brushes are made from animal hair – natural boar's bristle for paintbrushes and sable for artist's brushes which you can use for touching up and various other effects.

However, there are two types of finish for which you cannot use a natural brush. One is a water-based finish, which will cause the bristles to swell and the finish to drag; the other is bleach which will cause the bristles to fall out. Use a good-quality synthetic bristle brush for water-based finishes and a cheap nylon brush for bleaching (see page 116).

1: NATURAL BRISTLE

A good quality natural bristle is multi-purpose.

2: SQUIRREL

Used for fine finishes.

3: BADGER

A brush made with badger hair.

4: SQUIRREL

A soft, natural hair brush.

5: SYNTHETIC BRISTLE

For use with water-based mediums.

6: ARTIST'S BRUSHES

Fine sable hair (top) and synthetic (bottom) for detail work.

SCRAPERS

Scrapers have two uses in wood finishing – first to help strip the surface of an old finish and second to produce a really flat surface before applying the final finish.

To strip old paint or varnish off a surface, you need two types of scrapers – a flat-bladed one for normal surfaces and a shaped one which has a number of different curves on it for use on mouldings.

To produce a really smooth finish on a flat surface, you need a cabinet scraper.

1 This is a flat, rectangular, piece of steel with an edge that has been filed or ground square.

2 One of the ground edges is very slightly burred over by running a hard steel rod down it.

3 The T-shaped burr will remove a very thin sliver of wood and leave the surface absolutely flat and smooth.

4 To use the scraper, hold it upright in both hands, between the thumbs and forefingers. Press down on your thumbs to bend the scraper into a curved shape and angle the tool away from you before pushing it along the surface of the wood in the direction of the grain.

2

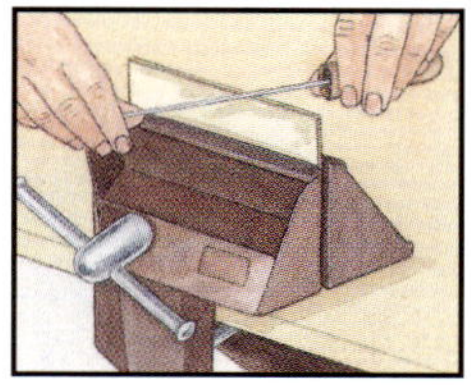

3

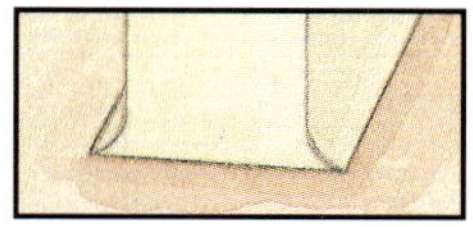

4

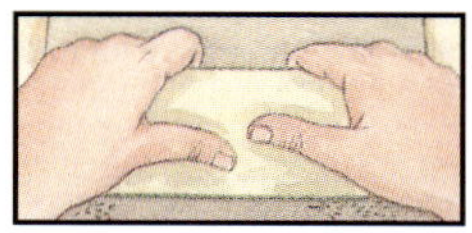

THE RIGHT WORKING ENVIRONMENT

It is best to have a separate finishing area which is well ventilated for applying stains and varnishes, away from the area where you sand and scrape wood. In the summer, working outside is an option but flying insects and airborne dust can be the death of a varnished finish.

A WOOD FINISHING WORKSHOP

You need to ensure that a workshop has adequate heating in winter and perhaps air-conditioning in summer and, more importantly, lighting, both natural light and good artificial light. If you are going to create dust or work with chemicals, fit an extractor fan and make sure you have a good quality vacuum cleaner.

You will need a good solid workbench and a woodworker's vice (or a workbench/vice) for holding timber.

Keep flammable materials isolated in a fireproof metal cupboard and poisonous chemicals out of reach of small children. Never decant chemicals into drinks bottles or food containers.

SAFETY PRECAUTIONS

1: Ensure that all woodworking tools are sharp. You are much more likely to injure yourself working with a blunt tool than with a sharp one.

2: Make sure that you have safety goggles to use when working with abrasives or toxic chemicals and face masks for working with volatile chemicals. With certain chemicals, such as caustic strippers and bleach, you will also need PVC gloves and protective clothing; when working with some powered machinery use ear protectors.

3: Always keep your working areas as clean as possible. Sawdust, wood shavings and chemical-covered rags are all fire risks. Have both fire extinguishers and fire blankets handy and do not smoke or use naked flames in the workshop.

4: Do not pour chemicals down the drain. When you have used wood-finishing and preparation chemicals, your local health and safety or environmental health authority should be able to advise you on how to dispose of them safely.

CHOOSING WOOD

TYPES OF WOOD

The finish you get will depend very much on the type of wood you work with.

All wood is classified as either hardwood or softwood. Hardwoods (such as oak, maple, teak and mahogany) come from broad-leaved trees while softwoods (such as pine, fir, redwood and spruce) come from coniferous trees with needle-like leaves.

In general hardwoods, are more durable than softwoods and have a much wider range of colour and texture. Sadly, some of the best-looking hardwoods, such as mahogany, rosewood, teak and afrormosia are fast becoming endangered species. On the other hand, hardwoods grown in Europe and North America are produced by 'sustainable' methods (which means that at least one tree is planted for every one felled) and many types of wood can be treated to produce the effect of the endangered species.

The effect of timber, especially hardwood, will also depend on which part of the tree has been used and the way the wood has been cut.

1: The 'heartwood' from the centre of the tree, for example, is usually darker and has a closely packed grain. Equally, it is more resistant to rot and woodworm attack and is less likely to shrink than the more porous sapwood.

1

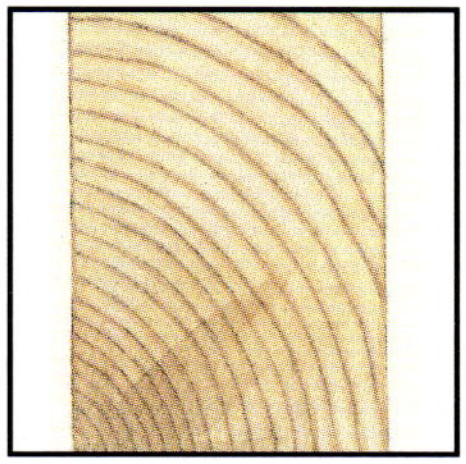

2: The 'sapwood' from the outside of the tree is usually lighter than the 'heartwood' and has a less closely-packed grain.

2

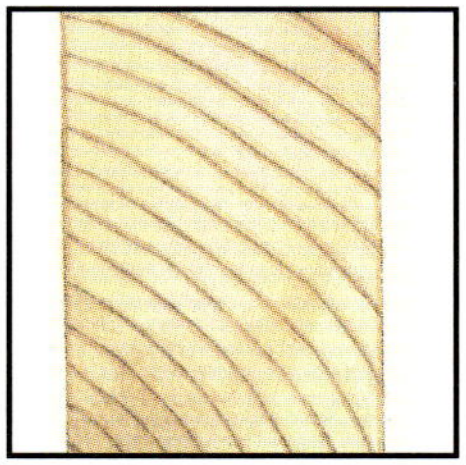

3: Quarter-sawn timber is where each quadrant of the circle forming the tree is cut into slices. It is less likely to warp than through-sawn timber.

3

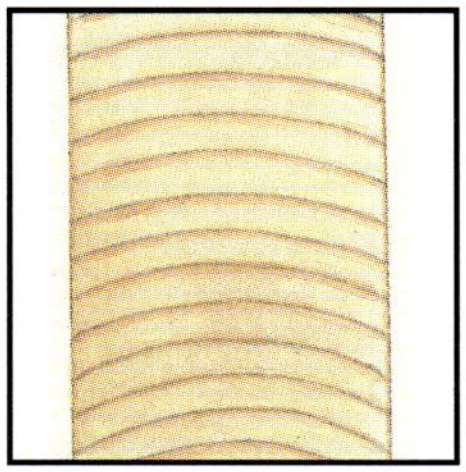

4: Through-sawn timber is where the whole tree is cut into slices disregarding the quadrant.

4

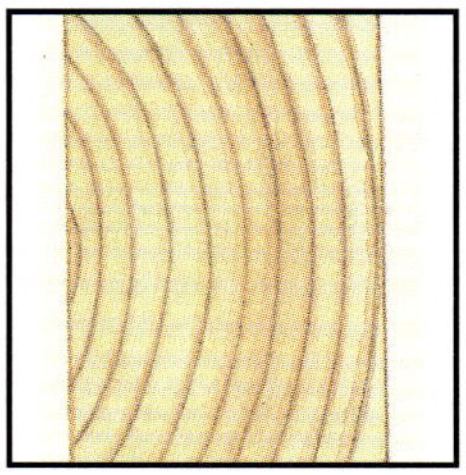

HARDWOODS

BEECH

A light-coloured durable wood, used widely for furniture. It has a straight, close grain and a fine, even texture.

BIRCH

A close-grained wood with the colour varying from yellow (sapwood) to reddish-brown (heartwood).

Steamed Beech

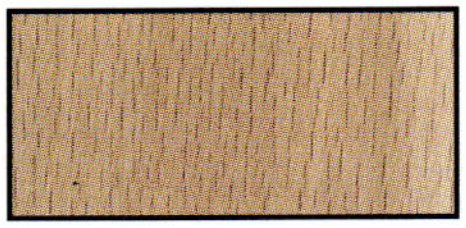

Brazilian Mahogany

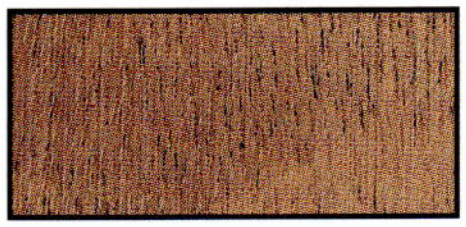

Maple

European Oak

Teak

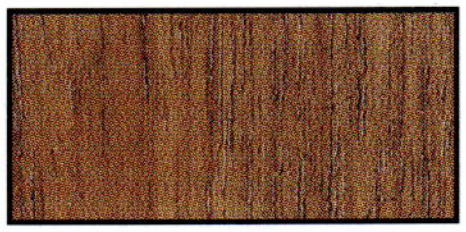

American Black Walnut

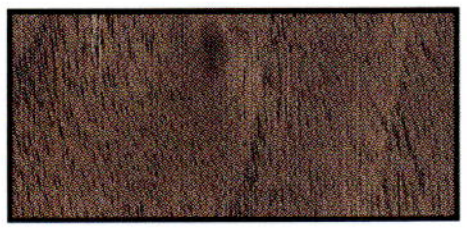

Southern Yellow Pine

It is used widely for veneers (especially on plywood) and can be stained and polished well.

ELM

A coarse-textured, light-brown coloured wood, now in short supply because of Dutch Elm disease. It takes stains and polishes well.

MAHOGANY

A medium-textured, red-to-reddish-brown wood. It stains well and can be polished to a fine finish but sadly mahogany is now an endangered species.

MAPLE

A nicely grained hardwood. Two of the grains are called curly and birds-eye.

OAK

One of the hardest, most durable woods. White and red oak are just two of the kinds available. Oak has a coarse grain and can be stained or polished. It lends itself to liming and is often waxed.

ROSEWOOD

A hard and heavy wood with a prominent dark grain structure. It is hard to work and generally requires grain filling before oiling, waxing or polishing. Used in furniture and for veneer. Now endangered.

TEAK

An oily wood with a coarse uneven texture, with a golden brown colour. It is used for joinery and can be stained, varnished or polished or treated with oil. Now endangered.

WALNUT

A coarse, dark-coloured wood with a marked grain. It is used for fine furniture and veneers and is generally polished with wax or oil rather than using stains or varnishes.

SOFTWOODS

PINE

This is the most common softwood and can be white, red or yellow. It has a straight, prominent grain and is an easy wood to work with, taking stains and varnishes well.

SPRUCE AND FIR

These are both similar in characteristics to pine, but not all types take stain well.

PREPARING WOOD

A new clean piece of wood needs preparation. If not prepared properly the stain and/or the varnish will 'raise the grain' of the wood with the result that the surface is no longer even. Any dust or dirt on the surface will also ruin the finish.

When you are working on old wood, there will be considerably more preparation to do.

CLEANING AND STRIPPING

If you are working on an old piece of furniture, the first thing to do is remove the layers of dirt, grease, and old polish.

1 Soap and water will remove surface dirt, but to remove ingrained dirt, use white spirit on a cloth rag. This will not damage whatever surface finish is underneath even if you rub quite hard.

2 Speed things up by using fine (000) grade wire wool, but do not rub this too hard or you could damage the finish underneath.

3 When all the dirt has been removed, use a clean cloth to wipe the surface clean.

Once the surface is clean, you will be able to see whether the finish is damaged, and to what extent.

If the finish is merely dull, it can be 'revived', using a proprietary reviver or burnishing cream, or by using liquid metal polish applied using a soft cloth. You can also apply an extra coat of the original finish, but it is not always easy to identify what it is. French polish will come off on a rag dipped in methylated spirit, while cellulose varnish will come off with cellulose thinners. Lacquer and polyurethane varnish will be impossible to remove except with a paint-stripping chemical.

The most effective way of stripping a finish off existing timber is to use a chemical stripper. Any method using hot air or a naked flame is out because of the possibility of scorching the wood; using abrasives is time-consuming and requires considerable care to avoid damaging the surface, though it is useful for small areas.

Buy strippers which are specifically designed for use with varnish and other hard surfaces; these are applied with a brush, allowed to work for a few minutes, and then scraped off with a scraper. Remaining patches of paint or varnish can be removed with a second coat, this time

1

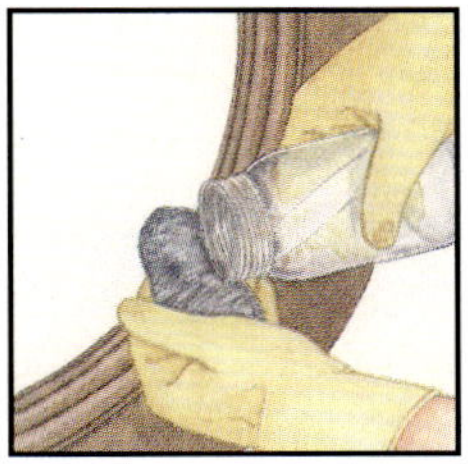

2

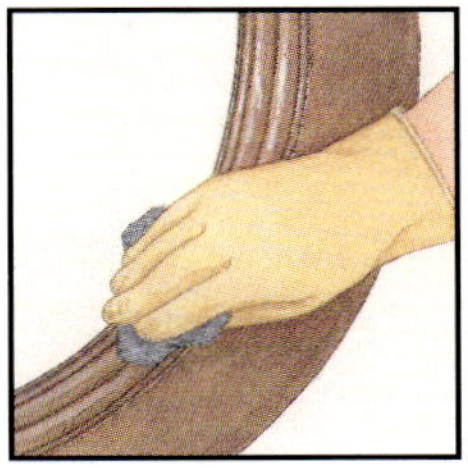

3

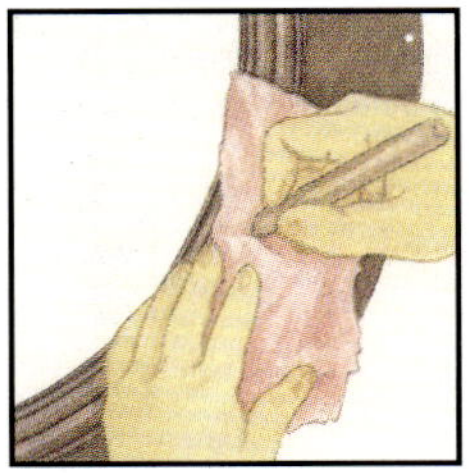

1 (bleaching wood)

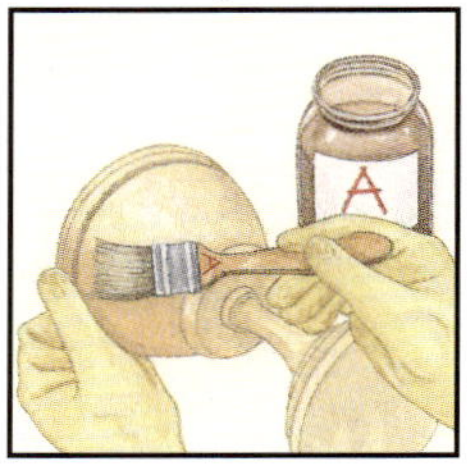

2

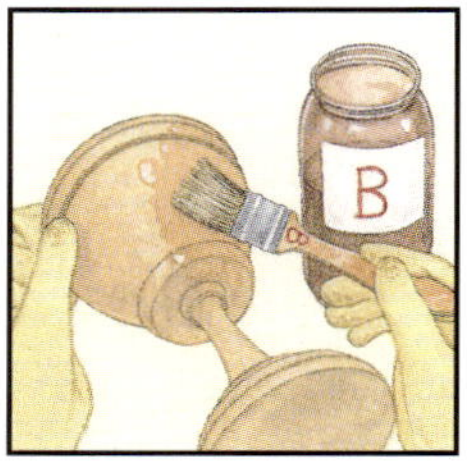

3

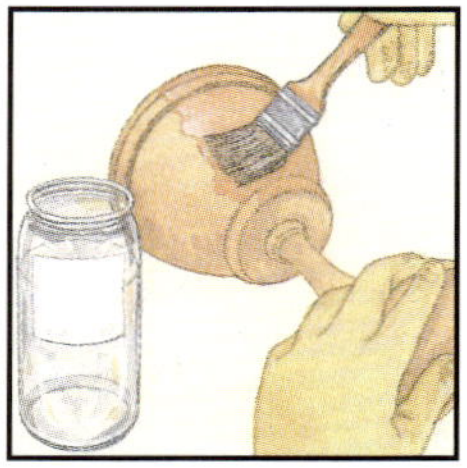

using (00 grade) wire wool to work it well into the surface and perhaps a cabinet scraper to achieve a smooth surface. Clean off residual stripper with white spirit.

If there are several coats of paint or varnish on a surface or you are working with a carved or moulded surface, you can buy paste strippers which are applied to the surface with a filling-knife, covered with a plastic sheet, and left for several hours. The stripper is then peeled off the surface, taking all the paint or varnish with it. This type of stripper is caustic in action, so be very careful how you use it. It may darken the wood and the water used for final cleaning will raise the grain of the timber, meaning the surface will need to be sanded down before re-finishing.

Some commercial firms strip painted or varnished items for you by dipping them in caustic soda. This is a good idea for pine doors, but not for furniture with glued joints or with veneer – the joints will loosen and the veneer may lift. Commercial dipping will tend to leave the wood looking rough, will certainly raise the grain, and may darken the colour.

DEALING WITH MARKS AND STAINS

On older furniture you may find ink stains, wine stains, water stains, or heat marks. The answer to all of these is to try a liquid metal polish or a proprietary stain remover on a clean cloth. For an ink stain, you could try using methylated spirit, but this will remove any French polish.

If the stain has gone deep into the wood, you will have to remove the finish in the area of the stain and use bleach on it. Apply the bleach as described below using a small brush.

BLEACHING WOOD

Bleaching is a way of lightening the colour of wood.

You can buy 'wood lighteners' or make up your own mild bleach using oxalic acid crystals dissolved in water. This is applied by brush, left for 30 minutes and washed off with plenty of water.

Commercial bleaches for treating wood can be brought in two parts which produce a chemical reaction to form a peroxide bleach.

1 Bleach can be applied with a nylon or fibre brush (do not use a bristle brush or the bristles will fall out) and left for about 20 minutes.

2 The second solution is then applied and left on one side for a few hours.

3 Clean the surface with a rag soaked in a dilute solution of vinegar (acetic acid) in water to neutralise the bleaching action on the wood.

REPAIRING HOLES, SCRATCHES AND CRACKS

There is a good choice of fillers for repairing scratches holes and cracks. It is most important that the colour of the filler matches that of the surrounding wood.

WAX

Wax can be used for small holes and cracks, using a knife to work it into the crack and then smooth it down, before buffing with a cloth.

WOOD STOPPER

This is a flexible filler for holes and cracks. 'Undercut' deep cracks and holes making the bottom of the hole wider than the top. After filling, rub down with fine abrasive when it is hard and apply a stain to match the surrounding wood surface.

PLASTIC WOOD

This sets really hard quickly so it can be shaped with a sharp chisel and sanded down with abrasive paper.

When filling deep holes with plastic wood or stopper, more than one layer may be necessary.

A useful filler for cracks along joints is a mixture of colour-matched sawdust with woodworking adhesive.

SHELLAC STICKS

These are a natural product of the lac insect that sets very hard. You can buy shellac sticks in a choice of colours from specialist stores.

1 To use shellac sticks you need a small soldering iron which you hold against the end of a shellac stick while holding the stick over the repair.

2 Shellac will harden very quickly, so you need to press it immediately into the wood, leaving it slightly raised above the surface.

3 Trim away the excess shellac with a sharp chisel, craft or trimming-knife.

4 Sand down the surface of the repair with a fine grade abrasive paper.

1

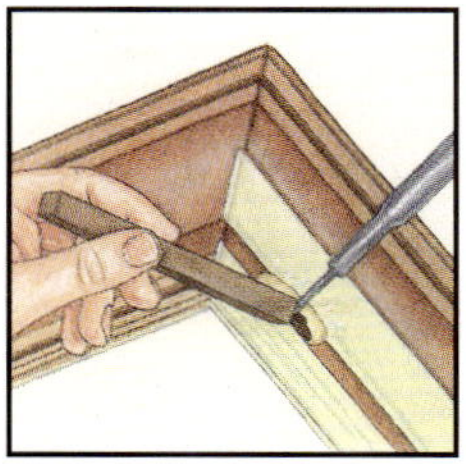

2

3

4

1 (dents and hollows)

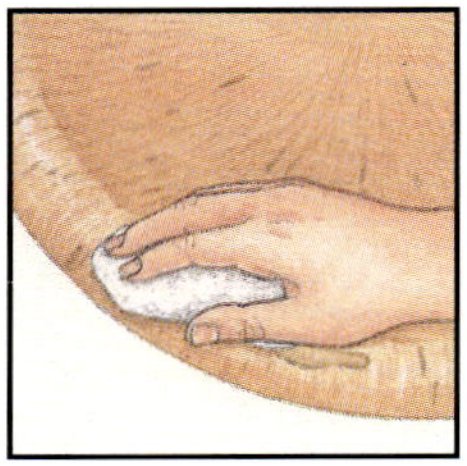

2

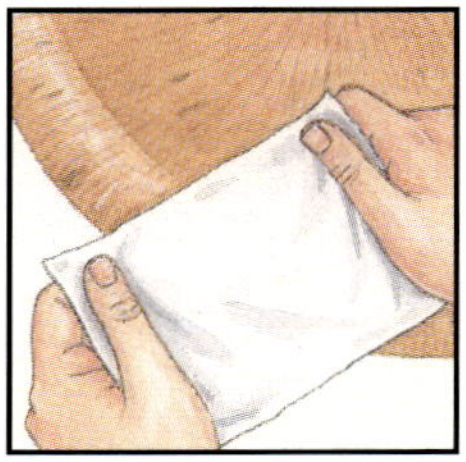

3

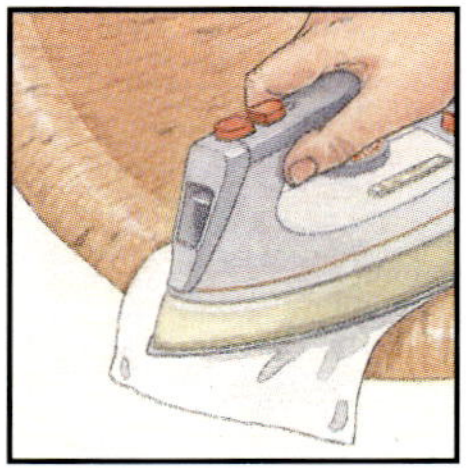

4

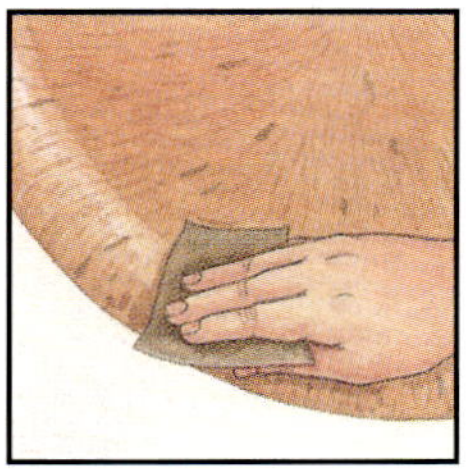

REPAIRING DENTS AND HOLLOWS

The difference between a scratch, hole or crack, and a dent or hollow is that the former actually have gaps or wood missing while the latter usually involve only the fibres being crushed.

It is possible to repair dents and hollows without using any filler by using a combination of water and heat, which will cause the fibres of the wood to swell.

1 Use a clean cloth and water to dampen the surface around the dent.

2 Lay a damp, clean cloth on the surface to protect the wood from further damage or bruising.

3 Apply heat through the cloth either with a soldering iron or with a domestic iron, depending on the size of the dent or hollow.

4 Check frequently to see how you are getting on (and that the cloth stays damp) and when the surface is restored, leave it to dry. Sand the surface smooth with fine abrasive paper.

You cannot use this technique for really deep hollows, which will need to be filled as for a hole.

REPAIRING BURNS

Cigarette burns are common and the first thing to try using is a reviver to see if you can remedy the burn.

If this is not successful, cut out any charred wood with a trimming-knife and fill the hole with wood stopper or, if it is on an edge, with plastic wood.

REPAIRING VENEERS

A veneer is a thin finishing surface layer of good-quality wood (usually a hardwood) glued to a solid wood backing in the manufacture of furniture.

A dent in a veneer can be removed in the same way as described for repairing dents and hollows in solid wood, with the application of heat and water. Care needs to be taken to prevent the glue from softening and the veneer lifting. Once the surface is level, clamp it in place, or apply weights until it has dried.

Blisters in veneer are caused by air trapped beneath the surface, usually because of missing or dried-out sections of glue.

REPAIRING A VENEER BLISTER

1 Slit the blister with an artist's scalpel – along the grain so the cut will not show.

2 Use a hot domestic iron on top of a damp cloth to re-heat the glue and press the veneer back into place.

3 If necessary, squeeze more polyvinyl acetate wood-working adhesive into the blister with the knife blade.

4 Force the veneer down with a wallpaper seam roller. Carefully wipe off excess adhesive with a damp cloth.

5 Clamp the repair while the glue dries, using paper under a piece of wood to protect the surface from the grip of the clamp.

REPAIRING DAMAGED VENEER

1 Tape a matching piece of veneer over the damaged area so that the grain and colour of the new veneer match the surrounding material.

2 Use a scalpel to cut through both the taped down layer and the underlying veneer.

3 Remove the cut portion with care – as it is very fragile – then remove the damaged veneer underneath with a sharp chisel, from within the newly cut shape.

4 Remove old glue from the surface and glue the new veneer shape into place.

5 If working near to the edge of the piece of wood, allow the veneer to overhang and trim it off afterward once the glue has dried.

STRUCTURAL REPAIRS

Many structural repairs require considerable skill and professional expertise but it is worth remembering that glues used in furniture-making are generally 'natural' glues (animal and 'Scotch' glues) which can be softened with the application of heat and water, allowing the furniture to be taken apart for repair. When re-assembling, you should use this type of glue again, rather than a polyvinyl acetate wood adhesive.

SANDING DOWN

It is essential that wood surfaces are flat and smooth before applying stains or varnishes. The slightest defect will show once the finish is in place. Before sanding, wipe the whole surface with a cloth dampened with water and allow the surface to dry. This will raise the grain which can then be

1 (damaged veneer)

2

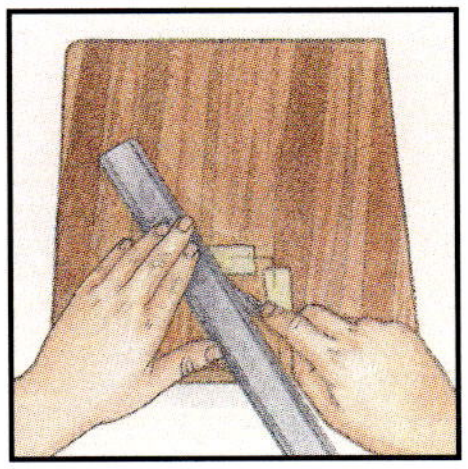

3

5

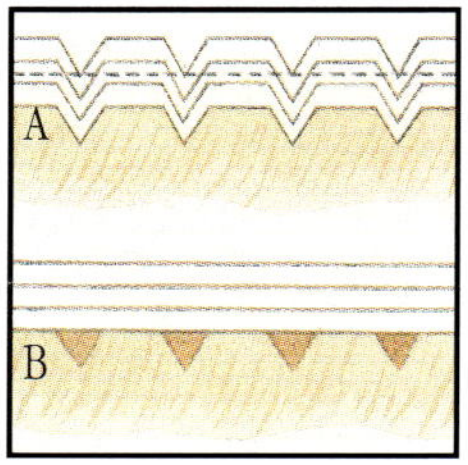

2

3

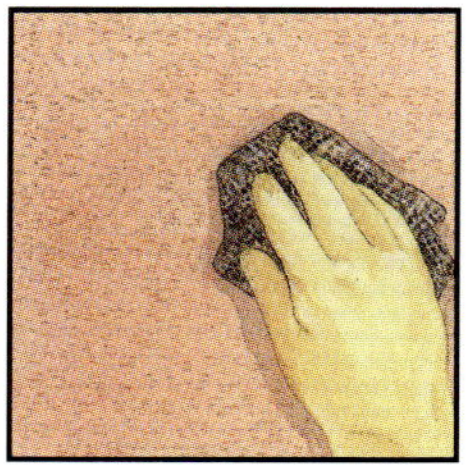

4

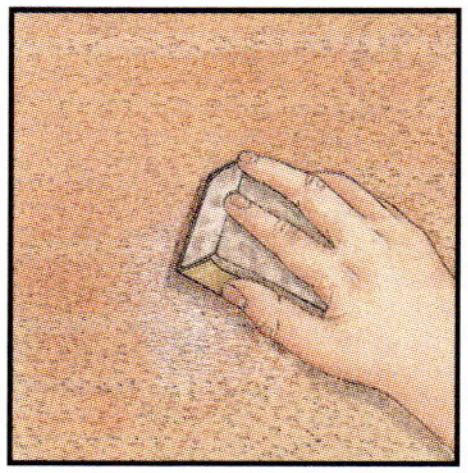

sanded flat: if you do not do this, the grain will be raised by water-based stains or varnishes and sanding at this stage will produce an uneven result.

HAND SANDING

Use a sanding block with a medium-grade glass paper wrapped around it. Always work in straight strokes in the direction of the grain. Follow with a finer grade of glass paper and finish with a fine garnet paper.

POWER SANDERS

These are useful if there is a lot of wood to be removed, but you should always finish sanding by hand to remove any marks left by the machine.

AFTER SANDING

Make sure all dust is removed with a soft brush. A hand-held vacuum cleaner is also useful. Use a cloth dampened with white spirit to remove dust before applying a solvent-based varnish.

FILLING THE GRAIN

Some woods, such as oak and teak, have an open grain structure (A). If you are using a finish such as French polish or varnish, it is best to fill the open grain (B) to achieve a high gloss finish.

The traditional method of filling the grain is with plaster of Paris, coloured with powdered pigment. This is not easy to do and the grain filler has a tendency to turn white in time. You can now buy, in many colours, proprietary oil-based grain filler. If necessary, you can add a stain to the filler in order to match the wood perfectly. If you are using a stain, this should be applied before the grain is filled.

1 Grain filler is applied with a coarse hessian cloth – a fine cloth would tend to pull it out again. It will normally need to be thinned with white spirit so that it has a creamy consistency.

2 Apply filler with circular motions of the cloth, making sure that the filler is pushed deep down into the wood.

3 When the whole surface is filled, use a clean piece of burlap to wipe off the excess, this time working across the grain.

4 Allow the filler to harden for several hours and then rub down lightly with abrasive paper before applying the final finish.

STAINS

A stain or dye is used to change the colour of the wood. A dye penetrates the wood, while a stain partly penetrates the wood but remains largely on the surface. Here the term 'stain' refers to both.

Most hardwoods already have a rich colour, so only need staining if you want to alter the shade. Softwoods can benefit enormously from the addition of a stain, sometimes to make them the colour of hardwoods, though it is difficult to match the grain structure.

Remember that you cannot make wood lighter with a stain, only darker. If you want to lighten wood, you will need to bleach it first (see page 116) before applying a stain which is lighter in colour than the original. Some woods vary in absorbency so it is always a good idea to try a stain out on an obscure part of the wood first to see the result.

Normally, you stain the wood before adding the final finish but one alternative is to use a coloured varnish which will produce the same effect. This has the advantage of ensuring that the colour of the wood will not vary with its absorbency. However, each successive coat makes the wood darker and surface scratches are also more obvious.

CHEMICAL-BASED STAINS

Chemicals are used to colour the wood by way of a chemical reaction so they are not strictly speaking a 'stain'. Most of the chemicals used are available from specialist suppliers.

AMMONIA

Diluted as a 10 percent solution in water, it is used to darken wood and is sometimes added to water stains to produce a warmer effect.

BICHROMATE OF POTASH

This can be used on mahogany to produce a really golden-brown effect (finished with French polish).

COPPER SULPHATE

This can be used on pale woods to produce a blue-grey effect. Apply it with a brush and wipe off any surplus with a cloth. When the wood has coloured sufficiently, use a cloth dampened with methylated spirits to stop the chemical reaction.

Above: A torchère made of light wood, finished with a base stain and a high gloss varnish.

SOLVENT-BASED STAINS

These are supplied ready-mixed in tins; the dye is dissolved in white spirit, naphtha or some other solvent.

SOLVENT-BASED DYES

These do not raise the grain and are named after different woods which indicates the intensity of colour not the wood on which they should be used. They should not be used directly under a wax finish: first apply a shellac sealer (French polish).

SOLVENT-BASED STAINS

These are applied in the same way as water stains (with a cloth). When staining the end-grain, a small amount of shellac sealer (French polish) should be applied first to reduce its absorbency.

Do not confuse solvent-based stains with spirit stains, which are based on methylated spirits and dry very quickly, making them difficult to use.

WATER-BASED STAINS

The most common water stains are based on Vandyke crystals or mahogany crystals, available from specialist suppliers. They are dissolved in boiling water and provide an economical way of staining wood.

You can vary the intensity of the colour by altering the proportion of crystals to water. Other effects can be achieved by using these stains with different finishes some of which are covered in the following pages.

When mixed, the stain should be tested out on a spare piece of wood first. It should be applied with a damp rag and worked into the timber, wiping off any excess as you go.

Two coats of a water stain are usually needed. The second coat will cover up any light areas left by the first coat. Water stains tend to raise the grain of the wood, so you will need to rub it down afterwards. To reduce the amount of raised grain, wet the wood first with clean water and rub down once the surface has dried.

VARNISH

A varnish is, in effect, a paint with no pigment. It provides a clear or stained finish which sits on the surface of the wood and protects it.

POLYURETHANE VARNISH

This wood finish has largely replaced French polishing as a way of finishing wood, mainly because it is exceptionally easy to apply and resists both stains and heat. Most polyurethane varnish is solvent-based, though there are some satin-finish water-based ones which emit very little odour while being used, dry quickly and do not yellow with age.

Polyurethane varnish is available in both clear and coloured versions – the colours imitate the colours of wood and can be thinned with white spirit if they are too strong. Two coloured varnishes can be combined to produce a different shade. Solvent-based varnishes are available in matt, gloss and satin finishes. Some polyurethane varnishes are free-flowing; others are 'non-drip' which usually only need one coat and dry quickly.

APPLYING A POLYURETHANE VARNISH

Polyurethane varnish is applied with a brush (a synthetic brush for water-based varnishes) and can be used with a spray gun (see page 128). It is easy to apply but avoid running by working on moulded sections first.

1 Begin applying the varnish in one direction, preferably along the grain. Apply the first coat with very light brush pressure. On large areas work in stages and keep the leading edge damp.

2 Then brush across the grain, at right angles, covering the same area again.

3 Again brush across the same area, diagonally – to cover the same area a third time.

4 Finish off with elongated, long, light strokes in the same direction as the grain for the finish.

5 Three coats of varnish are normally required for a high-gloss finish. Leave to dry before rubbing down between each coat with a fine abrasive paper or wire wool. Remove any dust using a damp rag soaked in white spirit.

When using coloured varnishes, switch to a clear varnish once you are happy with the colour – on highly absorbent woods, use a coat of clear varnish first, to prevent uneven absorption.

Good ventilation is essential as potentially harmful fumes are emitted during application.

1

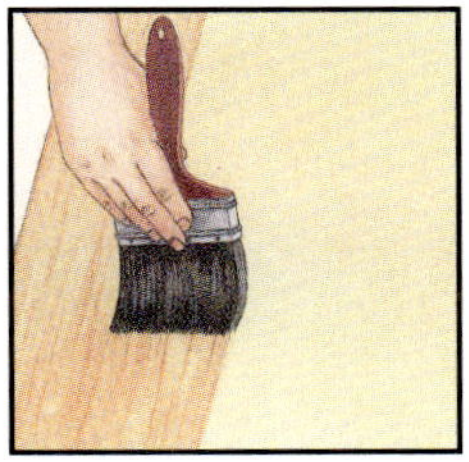

2

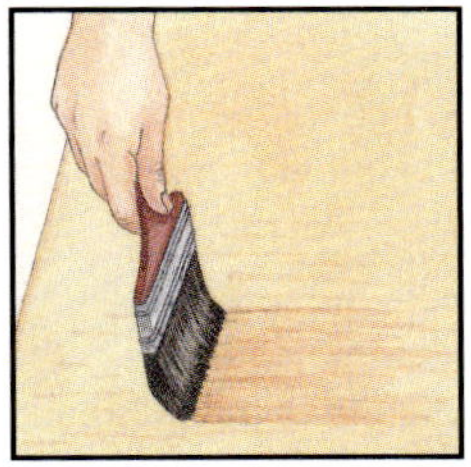

4

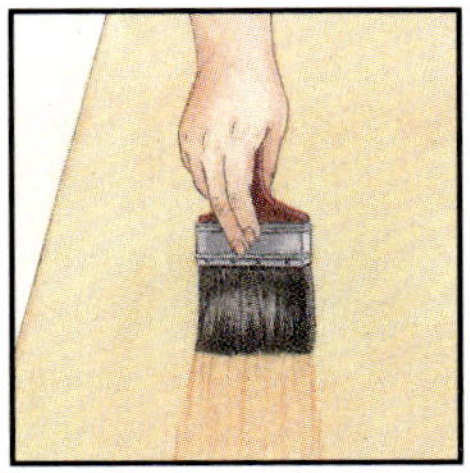

1 (applying)

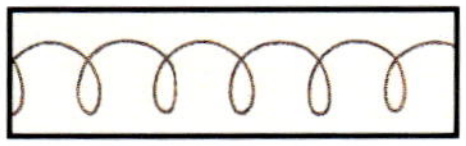

2

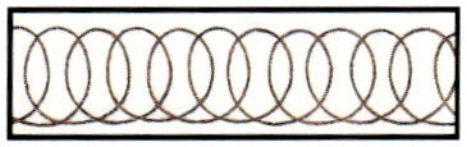

3

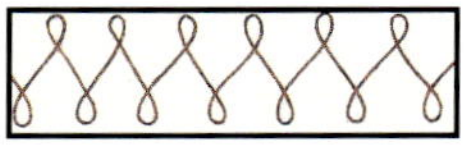

4

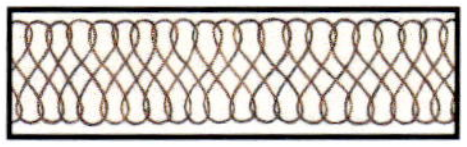

5

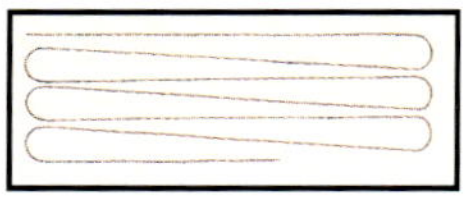

FRENCH POLISH

French polish is actually shellac dissolved in alcohol. It comes in three main colours: clear, white (light-coloured furniture), and red 'garnet' (dark woods such as mahogany). The purest form of shellac is called 'button' polish. Black French polish is useful for ebonising (see page 128).

French polishing requires considerable skill, but the result can be well worth the effort. Although French polish produces the finest looking finish available, it is not resistant to stains or heat (and can be removed with methylated spirit), so it should be reserved for the finest pieces of furniture and not those in everyday use.

The essential ingredients required for French polishing are the polish itself and a burnishing pad made from absorbent cotton wrapped in a clean cloth, linseed oil and methylated spirit.

MAKING A BURNISHING PAD

1 The burnishing pad is made by putting absorbent cotton in the centre of a large finely-woven, starch-free cloth, similar to a handkerchief.

2 Fold the edges over, then the corners in, repeating this progressively to make a large egg shape with no wrinkles on the side used for applying the polish.

3 Then unfold the centre of the cloth, and pour polish into the absorbent cotton until soaked but not overflowing.

4 Re-fold the pad, folding the side edges in, and apply a small amount of linseed oil – which acts as a lubricant – to the surface of the pad.

APPLYING A FRENCH POLISH

French polish is applied in two stages using a series of traditional tried-and-tested polishing movements.

THE FIRST STAGE

French polish is applied using a series of variable but consistently equal different strokes. The pad should never be allowed to rest on the surface and should be kept moving at all times.

1 Use systematically equal and even wide circles to spread the polish.

2 Then equal and even interlocking circles to produce a consistent and even coating.

3 Followed by interlocking wide sweeps that will, again, spread the residue.

4 Alternate with (3) above, with a figure-eight movement to build up the body.

5 Finally long, sweeping strokes along the direction of the grain to smooth the surface.

After 15 minutes, you can apply a second coat, and up to three more coats. Leave it to harden overnight and add more coats the following day. Store the pad in an airtight container to prevent it drying out.

Professional French polishers sometimes put on as many as 20 coats, but 10 should be plenty. 'Kits' that require only three coats are available from DIY and specialist stores and are a good way for an amateur to start.

If any marks, runs, or dust appear on the surface, use a fine silicone carbide paper or (000) grade wire wool to rub down the treated surface before applying further coats of French polish.

THE SECOND STAGE

Known as 'spiriting off', it involves the use of methylated spirits to remove any linseed oil from the surface and to provide a final burnishing.

To do this, pour some methylated spirits into a clean pad (unless the original pad is largely free from polish) and rub in long strokes along the direction of the grain.

If you want a less-than-glossy finish on your French polish, let it harden for a few days and then use fine (000) grade steel wool dipped in wax, using very light long strokes in the direction of the grain.

Below: An antique beech chair with a Rosewood grained effect and French polish finish.

COLD-CURED LACQUER

This finish is extremely hard and durable and can be burnished to a high gloss or rubbed down to a 'satin' or even a matt finish. Most lacquers are colourless, but you can get white or black lacquer.

The lacquer comes in two parts, which must be mixed together before application; once mixed, it should be used within 24 hours – or three days at the outside.

A cold-cured lacquer can be applied with a brush, roller or spray gun; when using a brush, apply generously but do not overbrush as it dries quickly. You can apply a second coat after around two hours, but leave for longer before applying subsequent coats.

For a high-gloss finish, rub down with very fine wet-and-dry silicone carbide paper and use a metal polish, burnishing cream or proprietary 'reviver' to achieve the high gloss. For a 'satin' or matt finish, use fine wire wool and finish with wax.

Do not use shellac filler under a cold-cured lacquer.

WAX FINISHES

Waxing produces a soft natural sheen which deepens with time. The problem is that the surface is soft and, when applied to bare wood, it can absorb dirt and is easily marked by heat, water and alcohol. It is best to seal the wood first with shellac or polyurethane varnish, especially if a solvent-based stain is used.

Ready-mixed furniture waxes are available in a choice of colours in a cream paste or stick form.

APPLYING WAX FINISHES

Apply wax to the prepared surface using a clean, lint-free cloth. It is first applied liberally with circular movements, making sure it is worked well into the grain, and then finished off with long strokes in the direction of the grain. After it has been left for around 15 minutes, further coats can be applied, this time using a very fine (0000) grade steel wool, rubbing with the grain and allowing several hours between each coat. To give a final gloss, use a clean cloth to polish the surface.

You can also buy brushing waxes that are semi liquid and that can be brushed on and buffed with a cloth when dry.

OIL FINISHES

An oil finish is very simple to apply and, when used on open-grained hardwoods, can considerably enhance the appearance of the wood, though the finish is not very heat-resistant, nor stain-resistant.

You can buy teak oil, 'Danish' oil or 'Scandinavian' oil, which are faster drying than traditional linseed oils, so pick up less dust and dirt in the drying process and are also more resistant to heat and solvent stains.

APPLYING OIL FINISHES

To apply an oil to wood, you need a clean, soft cloth with which to coat the surface liberally, wiping off any excess with a second cloth. Two or three coats are all that is required, with a light sanding using fine silicone carbide paper between coats. After the final coat, use very fine (0000) wire wool in the direction of the grain to burnish the surface and finish off with a clean cloth to remove any fine dust.

This section looks at some of the techniques used to decorate wood.

ANTIQUING

Antiquing or 'distressing' is a way of making new or reproduction furniture look old by deliberately trying to age it.

There are several different techniques you can use. Old furniture will have lots of dents in it and one way to imitate this is to hit the surface with a cloth bag filled with nuts and bolts. Follow this by applying a water stain across the whole area, worked well into the damaged areas to make them darker. Finally, apply a shellac sealer (French polish) on top.

Additional stains can be added. Make a water ring by filling a tin can with hot water or by applying a stain to the bottom of a cup and leaving it on the surface long enough to make the familiar mark.

You can also use stains to give an uneven appearance, using a technique known as 'rubbing'. Here a dark water stain is used first, followed by a dark solvent stain. When the stains have dried, fine (000) wire wool can be used to remove some of the stains to simulate the effect of sunlight and wear over the years. The effect is enhanced with a final polish.

1 (spray finishes)

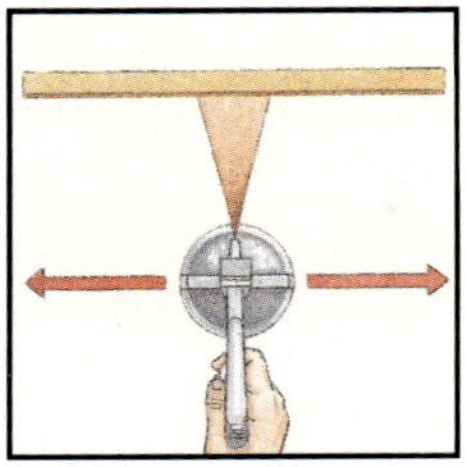

2

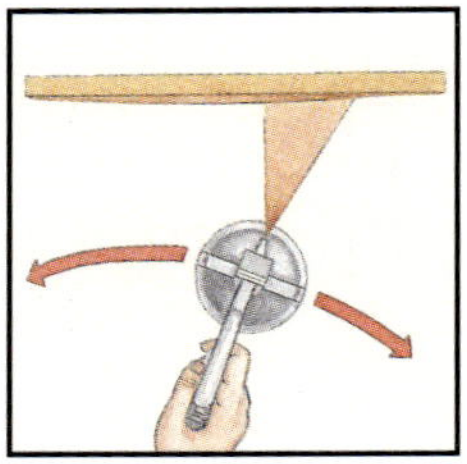

EBONISING

Ebony is a rare (and endangered) wood, almost pure black in colour. You can re-create this effect on other woods.

First, the surface is stained using a black (nigrosine) water stain rubbed well into the surface, followed by light sanding and a black grain filler. Then black French polish is applied (see page 124). You could make up your own black French polish, using normal French polish mixed with black aniline spirit dye.

If you want to completely obliterate the grain and to produce the high-gloss, jet-black finish associated with Chinese and some Victorian furniture, paint the wood with a black-board paint or black under-coat. Finish with a black French polish.

LIMING

Liming enhances the grain of wood and should only be used on woods which have a pronounced open grain. The grain can be opened up by scrubbing the surface with a wire brush.

Before liming, the wood should be stained to the colour required and a finish applied. When the finish has dried, liming paste is rubbed into the surface, using a coarse cloth or piece of burlap, working across the grain. When you are sure all the grain has been filled, remove excess paste with a clean cloth, dampened with white spirit. Leave the paste to dry overnight, rub well with a soft cloth, and apply a final coat of sealing polish.

Graining is another effect that can be used with varnishes and stains (see page 171 in painting effects for this technique).

SPRAY FINISHES

Using an aerosol or spray-gun to apply stains and varnishes produces a much more even coat than is possible with a paintbrush.

This is an ideal way to finish a piece of furniture which has a lot of carving or moulding, or for cane furniture where using a paint brush is difficult. Using a spray-gun is fast but, because each coat is very thin, more coats are needed.

Both aerosol and spray-guns are used in the same way.

1 Use straight parallel overlapping passes along the work, keeping the spray-gun or aerosol at a constant distance from the surface.

2 Do not pivot or swing the spray-gun from side to side. The result will be uneven distribution and subsequent runs or pools of the finish.

Spray-guns operate at a higher pressure than aerosols, so they need to be held further away from the wood – around 200mm/8in compared with 150mm/6in for an aerosol – and should be cleaned immediately after use with the solvent appropriate to the varnish or other finish being used.

WOOD EFFECTS

You can use a combination of stains and other finishes to achieve different effects on wood. Here, we give just three examples of what is possible.

ROSEWOOD EFFECT

Rosewood is a beautiful but endangered species. You can achieve the same effect using a wood such as beech or hickory.

The wood is first stained with a dark water-based stain, such as mahogany crystals, and left to dry. This is sanded with a very fine-grade abrasive paper and a coat of French polish is applied. Then the grain effect of the rosewood can be produced with an artist's paintbrush, using a black spirit stain and finished off with a varnish.

MAHOGANY EFFECT

Mahogany has become an endangered species, but it is possible to reproduce its beautiful patina by using beech or hickory. The wood is stained with mahogany crystals (a water-based stain) and then sanded and French polished. Spirit-based stain will need to be added to the French polish to achieve the mahogany effect.

JACOBEAN OAK EFFECT

This is applied to new oak to simulate old oak. The wood needs to be stained with a water-based stain (Vandyke) and left to dry. Then a dark solvent-based stain is used, making sure it gets well into the grain structure. The surface is then finished with a clear French polish, rubbed down with very fine abrasive paper and several coats of 'antique' wax polish.

Woodworking Joints

TIMBER BASICS

Few jobs require the skill and expertise needed to make a mitred dovetail joint or a stopped housing, but many require a simple butt joint or a lapped joint to join timber end to end or at right angles.

Few special tools are needed for making woodworking joints, whether traditional ones or modern 'knock-down' ones. What is needed, however, is the ability to mark out the wood or the board squarely and to cut it accurately. Various devices are at hand to help with both of these, but a good eye, sharp tools, attention to detail and a steady hand are all essentials.

All natural timber is categorised under two headings – either softwood or hardwood. See page 113 in Staining and Varnishing for more information.

BUYING TIMBER

The biggest problem in buying timber is understanding the sizing – the relationship between the European metric standard and the old imperial standard.

Although timber is, today, priced by the metre (or for bulk purchase by the 100m), it is actually sold in lengths which are multiples of 0.3m (300mm), which is nearly equal to the imperial foot – 300mm is actually 11.81in. This 'metric foot' may suit older carpenters, but can be a nightmare if you actually need a six-foot length but are supplied with a length that is just over an inch less. If you are familiar only with the metric system and naturally used to dealing in multiples of 5 or 10, then the supply of multiples of 0.3m can be confusing.

The sizing of timber becomes even more complicated when specifying widths and thicknesses. The direct conversion to metric sizes from the old imperial sizes has led to odd amounts such as 12mm/½in, 19mm/¾in, 22mm/⅞in, 38mm/1½in and so on, but most other sizes – 25mm, 50mm, 75mm, 100mm – are a little more intelligible because 25mm is roughly one inch.

The real problem comes in the fact that wood is sold in two ways – 'sawn' and 'planed'.

SAWN TIMBER

This has rough surfaces and it is the size it says it is – so 100mm x 50mm sawn timber is actually 100mm wide by 50mm thick.

PLANED TIMBER

This has smooth surfaces. It is described as 100mm x 50mm, but is a finished size of 97mm x 47mm, the missing 3mm being the amount taken off by the planing machine.

Sawn timber is used in basic house construction where it is out of sight – roofing timbers, floor and ceiling joists, stud partition walls and so on. Planed timber, usually known as PAR (planed all round), is used in exposed joinery – doors, windows and their frames, floorboards, shelving, cupboards and so on.

Timber is sold in builder's merchants, do-it-yourself stores and at specialist timber merchants. The best selection and prices are generally obtainable at timber merchants – and there is an additional bonus in that the timber will be well seasoned and properly stored.

'Seasoning' (drying out) is important for timber. If you buy wood which has not been properly seasoned, it can warp or split once it has been used.

Recently, some of the larger do-it-yourself superstores have improved their sources of supply for timber and it is now possible to buy good timber in these large shops, which is convenient as you will probably be buying other supplies there at the same time.

When buying timber from any source, however, it is vital that you inspect it to make sure it is straight, true and free of faults, such as splits or dead knots, particularly if you are having timber delivered by a timber merchant, when you should also check that you have got the lengths you asked for, if this is critical.

MAN-MADE BOARDS

Man-made boards are cheaper than timber and are supplied in a larger size than the real thing – 2440mm x 1220mm/8ft x 4ft is a standard sheet size. They can also be stronger than real timber by virtue of the fact that the different layers of the board use wood with the grain running in different directions.

1: BLOCKBOARD

This has one grain direction for the central strips and the opposite grain direction for the surface veneers. Wood bends more, but breaks less along the grain than across it.

2: CHIPBOARD

One of the cheapest man-made boards which consists of wood chippings held together with glue. It is widely used in kitchen units and cheaper furniture construction. Although not very strong, it is a versatile and popular material. Its biggest disadvantages are that it weakens considerably if subjected to moisture and is hard work to cut because of the glue. It does not take ordinary wood-screws well.

3: MEDIUM-DENSITY FIBREBOARD

This is a recent development. Made from wood fibres bonded together, it has several advantages over chipboard. For a start, it is easier to cut and has a smoother surface, it takes paint well and will take ordinary wood-screws without splitting.

4: PLYWOOD

This has attractive facing veneers, and consists of several thin sheets with the grain running at right angles in alternate layers.

MOULDINGS

You can now buy a wide variety of mouldings where a square-edged piece of timber has a profile shaped by a machine.

Apart from the huge range of specialist mouldings available for picture framing, most of the mouldings you will come across are used for constructional detailing in and around the home and you will find a good selection of all styles to meet your personal requirements at most DIY stores and timber merchants.

ADHESIVES AND FILLERS

The type of adhesive you should use depends on the components being jointed and where they are to be used.

POLYVINYL ACETATE ADHESIVE (PVA)

This is applied to both surfaces to be joined and must be clamped while it sets. Excess adhesive can be removed with a damp cloth before it dries or, once set, it can be picked off with a sharp knife. If a PVA adhesive is used, the joint is made for life.

NATURAL GLUES

For furniture restoration, natural glues, mainly fish and animal glues or 'Scotch' glue are used. These have to be heated, but they can be softened by applying wet heat, allowing the furniture to be taken apart.

Using screws for joining wood can leave the screw heads exposed or some joints may not be perfect leaving exposed gaps. A filler is useful to solve these problems.

DECORATOR'S FILLER

This can be used if the surface is to be painted, but for large cracks it will not expand and contract with the natural movement of the wood.

WOOD STOPPERS

Used if the surface is to be stained or varnished or left looking 'natural'. They are available in a range of natural wood colours that can be mixed together with a small amount of stain, to ensure a perfect match with the wood you are working on. Waterproof versions are available for outside use.

Below: A selection of ready-made cladding and mouldings.

1

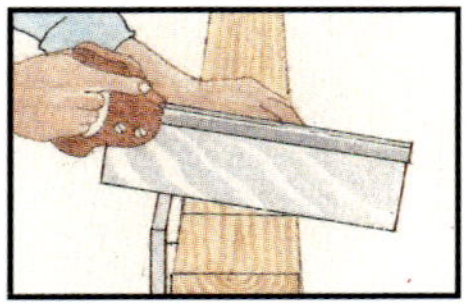

2

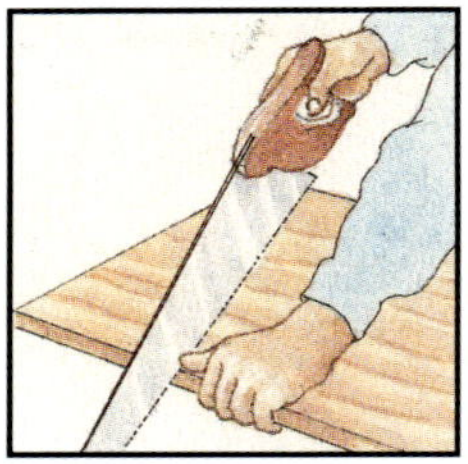

4

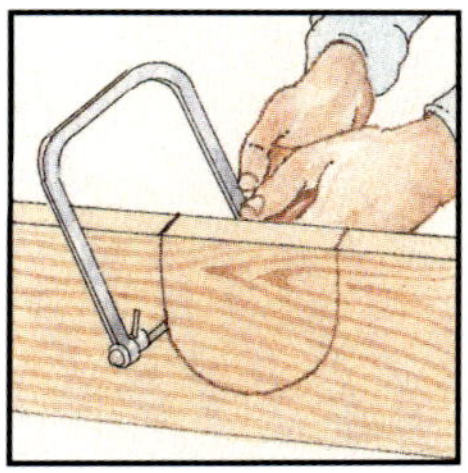

5

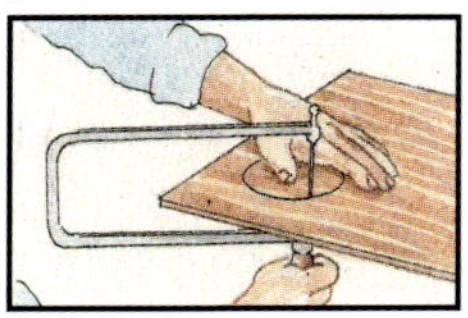

7

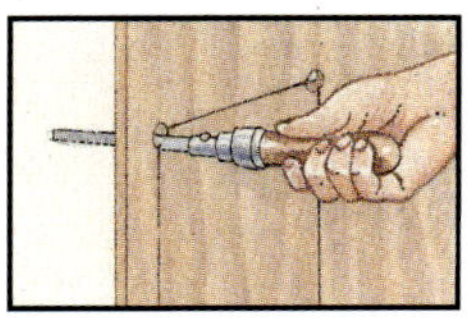

USING A SAW

The golden rule when using any saw is to cut on the waste side of the line that you have marked on the wood.

PANEL SAW OR TENON SAW

1 Point your index finger down the blade and use the full length of the blade.

2 Start the cut by drawing the blade back towards you held against the side of your thumb for accuracy.

3 If you wander off line with a panel saw, twist the blade to bring it back to line. With a tenon saw which is used at a less steep angle, start the cut again if you wander off line.

COPING SAW OR FRET SAW

4 A coping saw is used with the wood held vertically. The handle, being screwed, is adjustable for both tension and position of the hooped back frame during cutting.

5 A fret saw should be held vertically with the handle below the timber pulling down on the cutting stroke, with the work positioned horizontally. This way you can see the line you should be following more clearly and you have more control.

PADSAW OR KEYHOLE SAW

6 Mark the outline of the shape you want to cut, then drill holes on the perimeter where the direction changes.

7 Keeping the handle horizontal, place the blade through one hole and cut on the push stroke.

SHAPING WOOD

To shape wood you will need a selection of chisels.

BEVEL-EDGE CHISEL

Available in a range of sizes from 6mm/¼in to 38mm/1½in, but what makes it useful is that it has sloping sides (bevels) on the top of the blade which allow the tool to be used for undercutting (cleaning out a corner of less than 90°) – essential when making dovetail joints.

FIRMER CHISEL

This has a rectangular cross-section and is stronger than a bevel-edge chisel, making it more suitable for use when making mortice joints where the chisel is used to lever out the waste wood from a deep slot. You probably need only one or two sizes – say 6mm/¼in and 12mm/½in.

GOUGE

This is a chisel with a curved blade and comes in two types (scribing and firmer), depending on whether it is being used on the concave inside surface of a curve or the convex outside surface.

USING A CHISEL

A chisel is used in four ways – for undercutting, for paring, for chopping and for morticing.

1: UNDERCUTTING

This is cleaning out a corner with an angle of less than 90°, such as when making dovetail joints.

2: PARING

This is removing thin slivers of wood. It is best to use the chisel downwards using only enough hand pressure to slide it across the surface of the wood removing a thin sliver. Place the workpiece on a block of scrap wood so that you do not damage the work surface. Keep the flat side of the blade towards the work.

3: CHOPPING

This is removing larger amounts of wood. Hit the end of the chisel handle with a mallet to force it through the wood. Face the flat side of the blade away from the work with the front bevel facing the work – this will prevent the chisel digging in and help to keep it on line.

4: MORTICING

Cutting a slot for a mortice-and-tenon joint. First, the chisel is used for chopping (A) and then used as a lever (B) to remove the cut wood from the slot. The slot may already have been made using a drill (see page 148).

SMOOTHING WOOD

For giving cut surfaces a smooth finish you need a plane.

1: BLOCK PLANE

A small tool, with the plane blade set at a low angle, used for trimming across the end grain of wood.

2: SMOOTHING PLANE

Used for giving smooth surfaces to lengths of timber. If you are making joints, you will also be involved in woodworking so a smoothing plane which is around 200–250mm/8–10in long will be useful to have.

1 Using a chisel

2

3

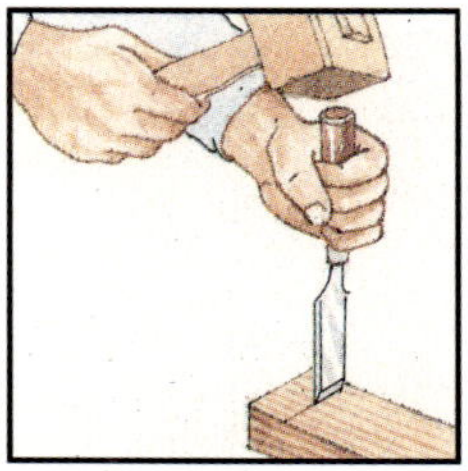

4

3

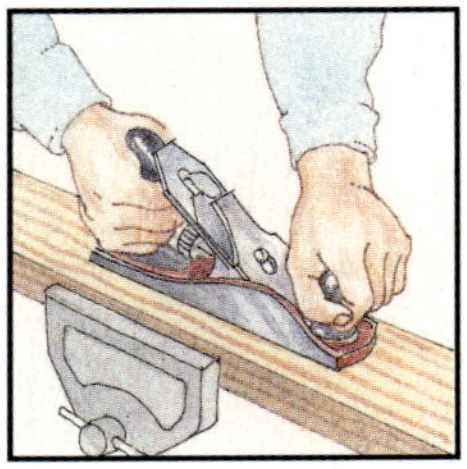

4

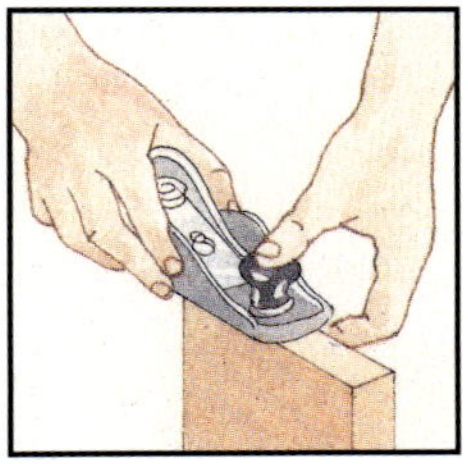

3: ELECTRICAL PLANES

These make removing wood quicker and easier especially when dressing (smoothing) lengths of timber to face-side and face-edge (squaring the surfaces) for stock. They are difficult to control and are not suitable for accurate work.

USING A PLANE

It is vital that a plane blade is properly sharpened and is properly set – that is with just a small amount showing beneath the sole plate and with the blade parallel to the sole plate.

1 Set the projection of the blade to equal the depth of cut – the smaller the projection, the finer the finish.

2 The workpiece must be held securely in a bench or vice and the plane held firmly with both hands.

USING A SMOOTHING PLANE

3 Try to work along the workpiece in a single stroke – at the start of the stroke have most weight on the hand holding the front of the plane (the left hand for right-handers) and gradually transfer the weight to the other hand.

USING A BLOCK PLANE

4 Used in its own unique way with the blade set to give a very fine cut. Always work from the outer edges of the work towards the centre – working towards the edge will split the wood – use small strokes rather like using a chisel.

DRILLING WOOD

For making small holes in wood up to around 9mm/⅜in, an electric or a hand drill can be used with twist drill bits.

When using an electric drill it is much better to mount it in a drill stand with the work supported underneath to ensure that you get the hole drilled straight and can control the depth, especially if the drill stand is fitted with a depth stop.

For making larger holes, 'spade' bits can be used with the electric drill or 'auger' bits with a hand-operated brace. A brace-and-bit will give a more accurate hole, which may be essential when using large dowelling rod. Neither spade bits nor auger bits can be used to enlarge an existing hole. If a hole is too small, use a round file or a gouge to make it bigger.

For smaller dowelling, special drill bits

are available which have a pronounced point and are easier to position. They come in three common dowel sizes – 6mm/¼in, 8mm/5/16in and 10mm/3/8in – and have rubber ring depth stops.

CUTTING MITRES AND ANGLES

Use a mitre-box – a three-sided U-shaped box with slots cut in the long sides – to ensure accuracy. One degree out will cause a gap at either the inner or outer corner of the mitre, and if the cut is not straight the two mouldings will not meet along their length.

1 Place the moulding inside the U resting on a scrap piece of wood. Put a saw into a pair of slots to guide the saw at the correct angle through the wood.

Most mitre-boxes have three sets of slots – one for each 45° angle and one to cut through the moulding at 90°. A mitre block has only two sides and one slot to guide the saw.

It is worth investing in a mitre saw for cutting a lot of mitres for picture framing. This has a saw with a thin blade, which is held at an angle over a machined bed on which the moulding sits. It will accurately cut 45° and 90° angles, and can also be used for other angles.

WORKBENCH, VICES AND CLAMPS

When cutting or shaping wood, it is important that it is held securely.

A workbench is essential to rest the workpiece on: a vice can be used to secure wood when planing, chiselling, sawing or drilling. Make sure it is a wood-working vice with large protected jaws; the serrated jaws of a metalworking vice will damage the surface of the wood.

A selection of clamps are needed for holding joints together while adhesive dries. Traditional G-clamps are the most useful, but larger sash clamps – or tape clamps – are needed for working on doors, windows and bookshelves.

1 A particularly useful clamp is a corner clamp which holds two pieces of wood at right angles without forcing them together. Some corner clamps have a slot which can be used for cutting a mitre.

1 (mitres and angles)

1 (vices and clamps)

MAKING JOINTS

1 (L-box joint)

5

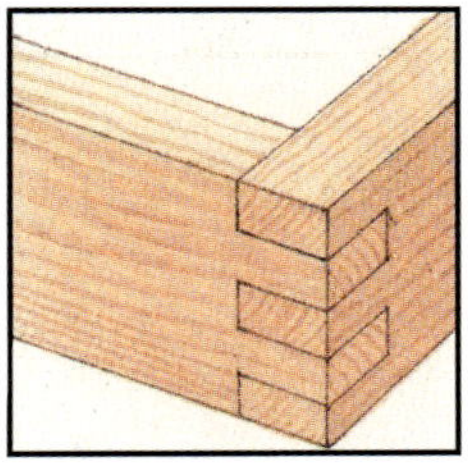

BOX JOINTS

A box or comb joint is used in furniture-making for the corners of wide frames, boxes and drawers.

The two pieces of wood to be joined must be the same width and, preferably, the same thickness.

This joint performs much the same function as a dovetail joint, but is easier to make. It provides a greater gluing area than many other joints and, if well made, looks good.

A CORNER L-BOX JOINT

1 Measure the width of wood being joined and divide it into an odd number to give alternate tenons and recesses of equal sizes. The tenons in one piece will fit into the recesses of the other.

The minimum width of a tenon is normally 10mm/⅜in – any less than this and the joint will be weakened.

2 Mark out all the tenons to the 'depth line' (the thickness of the wood) and use a pencil to cross-hatch the recesses so that you remember to cut on the waste side of each line.

3 Hold the wood vertically in the vice to cut down the lines with a tenon saw.

4 Use a chisel to chip out the waste wood, working from both sides towards the centre.

5 Use adhesive to assemble the joint, wipe off excess adhesive with a damp cloth and clamp the two pieces of wood at right angles while the glue sets.

TO MAKE A T-BOX JOINT

This is, in effect, a mortice-and-tenon joint with more than one tenon. To conceal the joint when making cabinets, for example, cut the tenons to half the thickness of the wood and make the mortices to half the depth to provide a 'stopped' joint.

1 Cut the tenons on the end of one piece of wood in the same way as above.

2 Cut the recesses (mortices) to marked positions on the other piece by drilling holes right through the wood.

3 Chop out the drilled holes to the edges of the marked positions using a chisel.

BRIDLE JOINTS

A bridle joint is used for joining pieces of wood of the same thickness and is useful when joining one long piece to the tops of several vertical pieces.

It is a strong joint, similar in many ways to the mortice-and-tenon joint. The rule for making a bridle joint is that the tenon should not be less than one-quarter nor more than one-third of the thickness of the timber in which it is cut.

A CORNER BRIDLE JOINT

1 Mark out the tenon and the tongues which form the slot using a mortice gauge. Make the depth of the slot and the length of the tenon both slightly longer than the width of the wood.

2 Use a tenon saw to cut out the waste wood either side of the tenon and down the inner sides of the slot.

3 For the tenon, make two further cuts at the marked depth for the slot, and chip out the waste wood using a narrow chisel working from both sides towards the centre.

4 Assemble the joint using adhesive and use a block plane to remove the ends of the tongues and the end of the tenon when it has dried.

A T-BRIDLE JOINT

5 Mark out the tenon and the tongues which fill the slot as described above in 1 and 2.

6 Cut down to the marked lines on either side of the tenon then chisel out the waste.

You will find it easier to make several more cuts down to the marked line before using a wide chisel, working from both outer sides to the centre.

Make sure the gap you leave is exactly the width of the wood being used.

7 When the joint is assembled and the glue has dried, carefully plane off the ends of the protruding tongues.

2

4

5

7

1 (dovetail joint)

4

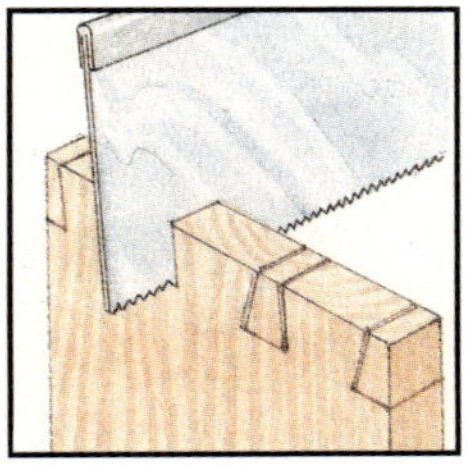

5

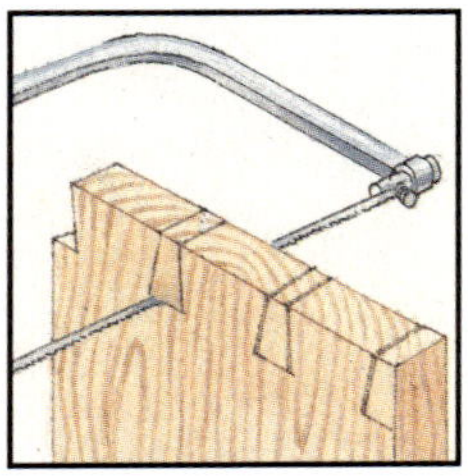

BUTT JOINTS

This is the simplest of all woodworking joints and only involves cutting the two pieces of wood to be joined so that they are the correct length and are square to each other on the ends.

Butt joints can be T-joints or L-joints and are used in making frames, such as those used in partition walls.

1 Check both pieces of wood to be joined. Make sure that they are the correct length and depth, and that the ends have been accurately cut square.

2 Make sure that the two surfaces to be joined are clean and free of grease. Apply glue to both surfaces.

3 Butt the pieces of wood together and secure them into position using the following options for reinforcement.

REINFORCEMENT OPTIONS

4 Screws are normally put through the joint; when using nails – angle them for greater strength (skew nailing).

5 T-shaped or L-shaped metal bracket can be unsightly – or use shaped blocks glued and pinned into the corners of the joint.

6 Sometimes a better option is to use a triangular shaped piece of plywood screwed over the face of the joint.

7 For very light frames, corrugated fasteners or timber connectors can be used.

DOVETAIL JOINT

The dovetail joint comes in many guises, the most common being the through dovetail joint, used at the corners of boxes and drawers in a similar way to an L-box joint.

The strength of the dovetail joint comes from angled pins fitted into similarly angled recesses between larger tails. The pins are typically angled at 80° (1:6) for hardwood and 83° (1:8) for softwood and at their widest point are normally two-thirds the width of the tail at its narrowest point, but should not normally be less than 10mm/⅜in wide.

A dovetail joint can be used to join wood of different thicknesses – the pins should be in the thicker piece and the tails in the thinner piece.

MARK OUT THE TAILS

1 Decide how many tails you are going to have and divide the width of the wood by that number. Divide this answer by five to give an answer X. The tails are then 3X at their narrowest point (the shoulder) and the recesses for the pins are 2X at their widest point – the half recesses at either edge are X wide.

2 Butt the two pieces of wood together and mark lines on each piece to represent the thickness of the other.

3 Mark out the tails on one of the two pieces (the thinner one if they are unequal).

You can use a sliding bevel set to 80° or 83° to mark the angles of the dovetails (mark half the lines before turning it over) You could make yourself a small mortice gauge out of a piece of thin metal sheet.

4 Once the tails have all been marked (with the recesses for the pins cross-hatched), cut down the waste sides of the lines using a tenon saw.

5 Use a coping saw, carefully insert the blade to cut along the bottom of the recess.

6 Use a bevel-edge chisel to clean out the corners. If you are making four repeat corners for a box, align the two opposite sides, then nail them together before clamping them in a vice. Cut the tails in both pieces at the same time.

TO MARK OUT THE PINS

7 Use the cut tails as an accurate guide for marking out the pins – use a marking knife to mark precise cut-lines.

8 Cut out the pins in the same way as for the tails and try the joint for fit.

The joint should be a tight fit, needing a mallet (or hammer and scrap wood) to drive it home. If it is too tight, use a chisel to remove some slivers of wood – if it is too loose, use some slivers as packing.

9 Apply woodworking adhesive to the joint surfaces, re-assemble and clamp it up square while the adhesive sets.

The two pieces of wood cannot be pulled apart once the joint is made.

When making a box or a drawer, assemble all the corners at the same time.

6

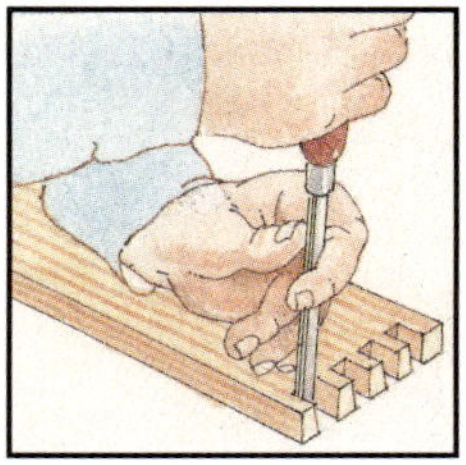

7

9

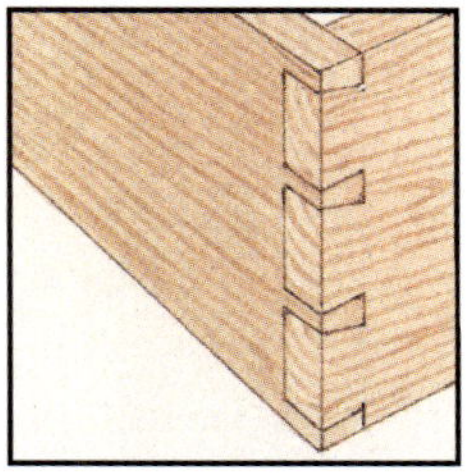

1

2

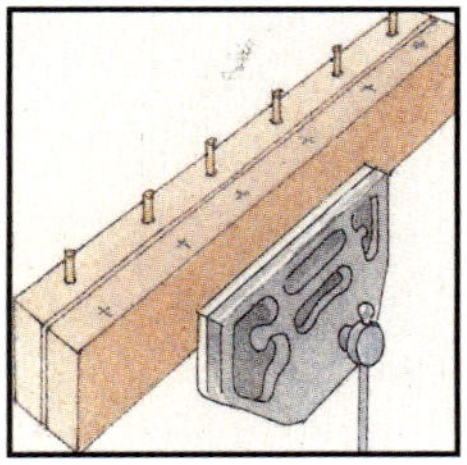

3

7

DOWEL JOINTS

A dowel joint is basically a butt joint reinforced with 6mm, 8mm or 10mm dowels.

Both the pieces of wood to be joined have drilled holes into which the dowels fit. The secret of making this joint is to ensure the holes line up and that the two wood surfaces mate accurately.

A proper dowelling drill bit should be used – this has a sharp centre point making it easier to position and comes with a rubber ring to use as a depth gauge.

SECRET DOWEL JOINTS

These are extremely good for joining pieces of wood end to end or edge to edge. The dowels are completely hidden but this form of joint is difficult to make. There are three options for ensuring the holes are in the correct place:

1 Mark out the holes with both bits of wood clamped together, making sure they are exactly in the middle of the thickness, and then drill them out making sure the drill is square to the dowelled edge.

2 Make the holes in one piece, then fit 'centre points' into the holes and use these to mark the position of the holes in the other piece – drill these out as before.

3 Use a dowelling 'jig' which will also help to guide the drill bit square into the wood.

4 Once the holes have been made, put a little adhesive into each and tap the dowels into place.

If you use dowel cut from a rod, make one or more grooves along the length so that the glue can escape from the hole – pre-cut dowels are fluted to allow this.

A THROUGH DOWEL JOINT (USED AT CORNERS)

5 Cut the two pieces to be joined to the correct size and then clamp in their final position.

6 Use a dowel bit to drill holes right through one piece of wood into the other.

7 Apply wood adhesive to the holes and insert the dowel. Leave a bit of the dowel protruding so that it can be cut flush with the wood once the adhesive has dried.

HALVING JOINTS

The halving or half-lap joint is useful for making frames and other carpentry jobs.

It is made by cutting out each piece of wood to half its thickness (it is used only when joining two bits of wood of the same thickness) and joining them together.

A CORNER HALVING JOINT

1 Slightly overlap the two pieces of wood to be joined and mark the width and position on each piece.

2 Cut down the grain at an angle from both sides before finishing by cutting square.

3 Cut accurately across the grain to remove the waste part of the joint.

4 Repeat the process for the second piece of wood. Apply adhesive and clamp into position until set.

VARIATIONS

5 T-Halving – made in a similar way, except that for one of the pieces of wood you need to chisel out the recess.

6 Dovetail Halving – the joint is shaped like a dovetail, thus preventing the two pieces being pulled apart.

7 Cross Halving – two bits of wood cross over without increasing the thickness of the frame. Both recesses need to be cut and chiselled out of both pieces of wood.

8 Lap Joint – used on wood of different thicknesses. It is used in much the same way as a halving joint, but the recess in one piece of wood is cut to a depth equal to the whole thickness of the inset piece.

1

2

3

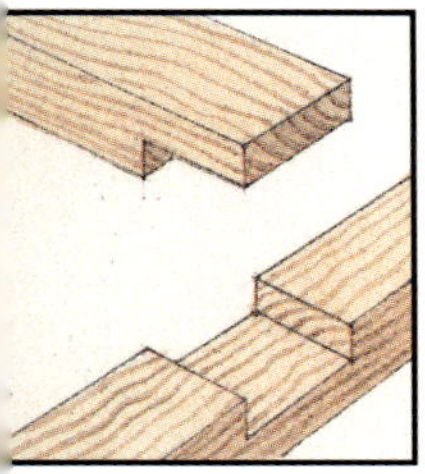

6

7

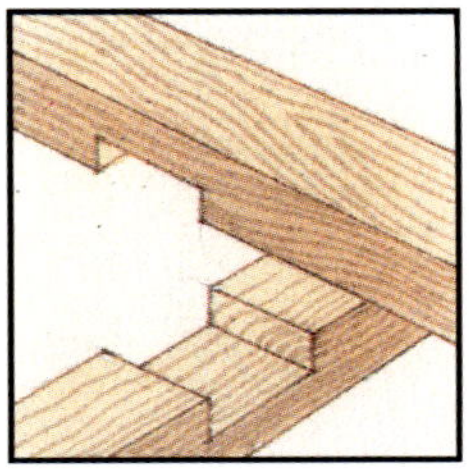

8

4

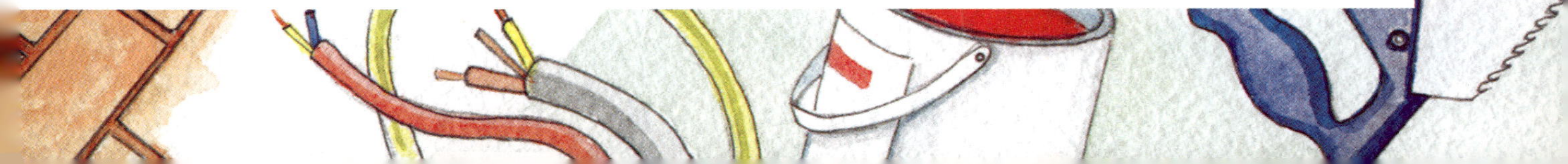

1

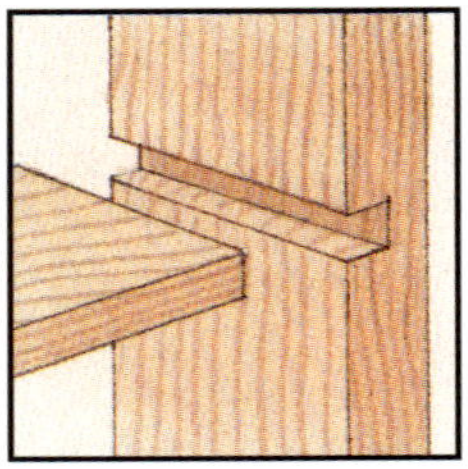

3

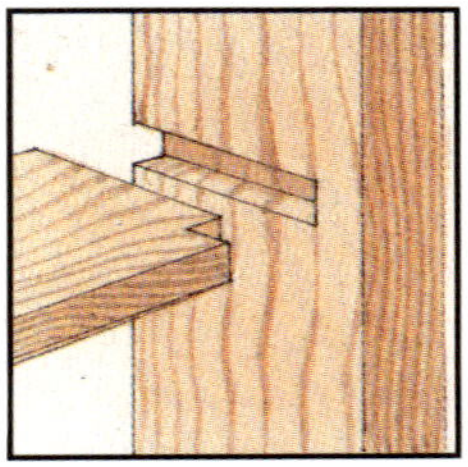

5

6

HOUSING JOINTS

A housing joint is used for making bookcases where the shelves are supported by side uprights.

A slot is cut out of the uprights and a shelf is fitted into it. Where the bookcase is free-standing, the joint needs to be reinforced with adhesive; where the uprights are restrained (as in an alcove), the joint can be left unglued if you want to be able to remove the shelves.

A THROUGH HOUSING JOINT

1 Mark the thickness of the cross member – make sure that it is in the correct position and square on the upright.

2 Use a tenon saw to cut to the depth of the recess, then remove the waste with a chisel.

A router, guided along a timber batten clamped to the workpiece, can be used to cut the slot. The router can be set to give a slot of exactly the correct depth – no more than half the thickness of the upright. One or two passes can be made depending on the thickness of cutter used relative to the width of slot required.

A STOPPED HOUSING JOINT

3 Mark the thickness of the cross member – make sure that it is in the correct position and square-on to the upright.

4 Mark off 20mm/¾in of the slot short of the front edge on the upright – do not remove this.

5 Use a tenon saw to carefully cut on the waste side to the depth of the recess.

6 Then remove the waste from the recess with a chisel and square off the front stop of the housing.

If a router is used, you will need to square off the stopped end of the slot with a chisel.

7 Cut a matching 20mm/¾in piece from the front edge of the cross member so that the final effect is that of a simple butt joint.

LAP JOINTS – SEE HALVING JOINTS.

MITRE JOINT

This joint has two main uses. The first is specifically for making picture frames, the second is for neat corners when fitting architrave moulding around door frames.

Although the joint looks good – because no end grain is exposed – it is very weak unless reinforced in some way.

1 Mark the cutting angle of 45° on the top edges of both the pieces to be joined. When put together, they should make an exact right angle.

2 Use a try square to mark the saw guide lines on either side of each of the pieces of wood.

3 Using a tenon saw cut the mitres on both pieces of wood – the mitre can be cut freehand; using either a mitre block or box; or using a mitre saw (see page 139).

4 Either nail from the outside of the corner through the mitre and into the width of the timber, or apply adhesive to both surfaces and then cramp into position. Remove excess adhesive, and leave to dry.

MORTICE-AND-TENON-JOINT

A mortice-and-tenon joint is one of the strongest used by woodworkers. It is used widely in doors and windows and in making frames.

A mortice-and-tenon joint can be used either at a corner where a top or bottom rail meets a side rail or to make a T-joint, where a centre rail meets a side rail.

In all cases, the joint consists of a tongue (the tenon) which fits into a matching hole (the mortice).

The joint can either be 'stopped' – the tenon cannot be seen – or 'through' – the mortice passes through the wood.

TO CUT THE TENON

For a stopped joint, the tenon should be a little shorter than the depth of the hole; for a through joint, it should be a little longer than the width of the wood, so it can be trimmed off.

1 Mark up the piece of wood so that the tenon is the full width of the wood but only one-third of the thickness.

1 (mitre joint)

2

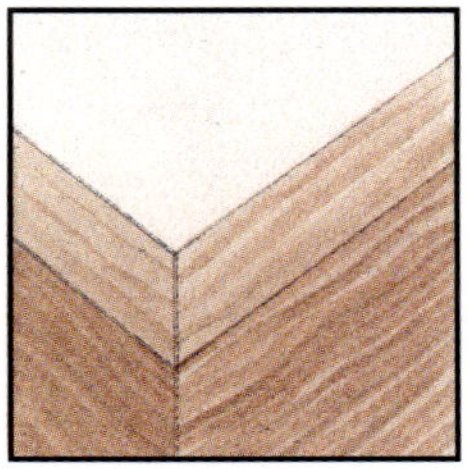

2 (mortice and tenon)

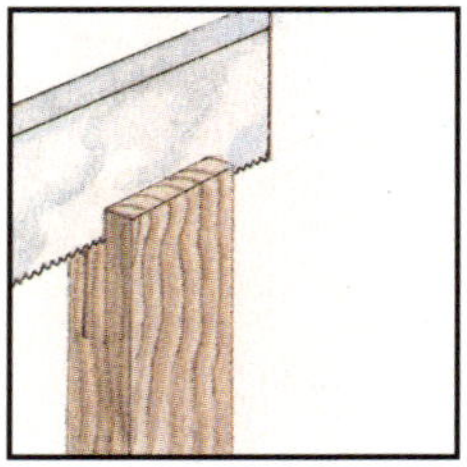

4

5

6

2 First use a tenon saw to cut down the grain, then across the grain to remove both the outside thirds of the wood.

TO CUT THE MORTICE

3 Accurately mark up the mortice in the correct position for the centre one-third of the thickness of the wood.

4 Use a firmer or mortice chisel to dig out the wood and square off the edges. The joint needs to be a tight fit, so you should check the fit regularly at this stage.

To speed things up, use a drill to remove the centre waste.

5 Apply adhesive to both mortice and tenon – cramp the assembly, remove excess glue and leave to set.

6 Strengthen the joint using dowels at right angles through the tongue (a good way of reinforcing old loose joints).

7 Or use wedges driven-in from the end either side of the tenon. With a through joint, the edges of the mortice need to be tapered to allow for these. With a stopped joint, the wedges are inserted into saw cuts on the tenon.

TONGUE-AND-GROOVE JOINT

Tongue-and-groove joints are used mainly on timber cladding and on flooring where one piece of timber is put in place right up against another.

Both the tongues and the grooves are already cut – the tongue on one side and the groove on the other. All you have to do is to assemble the boards correctly so that the tongue on one piece fits neatly into the groove on the next.

FOR CLADDING

The tongues are not pushed fully home into the groove – a small gap should be left for expansion.

FOR FLOORING

It is essential that the boards are pulled as tight together as possible. Sheet chipboard flooring and timber floor covering have tongue-and-groove on the ends of the board as well as along the edge.

It is all very well knowing what all the joints are called and how to make them. In practice, as with all jobs around the home, it is knowing which is the best joint to use for which job.

MAKING A DRAWER

If you are making replacement drawers to fit into an old and, perhaps, valuable piece of furniture, you will want to make the joints in the same way as the original.

1 They will either be dovetail joints (see page 142) or box joints (see page 140). With both of these, the drawer front will usually be an integral part of the drawer and be jointed to the sides; sometimes, the drawer front will be fitted separately onto the front of a square-sided box.

2 When using dovetail joints to make a drawer, make sure the tails are on the side pieces facing forwards, to prevent the drawer being pulled apart as it is yanked in and out. A lapped dovetail is often used for the front corners of the drawer so that the tails do not show. Here, the tails on the side pieces, and the recesses to take them, are cut to less than the thickness of the drawer front.

3 A very important part of the drawer is its base. In wooden furniture, this will usually be plywood, normally fitted into slots routed out of the front and sides and overlapping the back, so that it can be slid into place once the drawer is made and then secured by nailing up through the base into the back. Sometimes, the base will be supported by L-shaped pieces of timber glued to the sides.

With modern kitchen cupboards, do not use wooden drawers. Not only are they hard to make accurately, but they will get dirty rapidly and will tend to swell as the humidity in the kitchen varies.

4 Instead, you can buy drawer-making kits, which consist of lengths of pre-moulded plastic channelling which are joined together at the corners by plastic connectors. The base of the tray is melamine-faced hardboard, slid into a groove in the sides and back – note that this usually has to be put into place before the drawer is finally assembled. As with wooden drawers, there is a choice of having the drawer front as part of the drawer or of screwing it on to the front of a box structure. When replacing broken drawers, re-use the old drawer fronts.

1

2

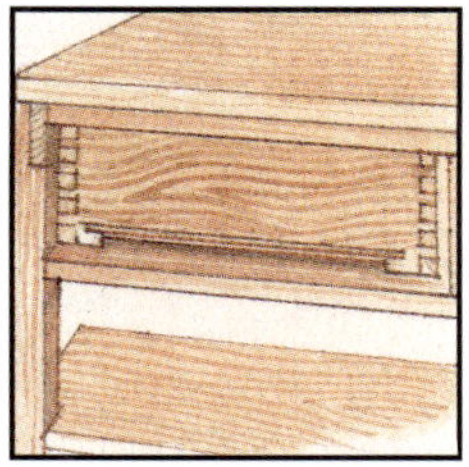

3

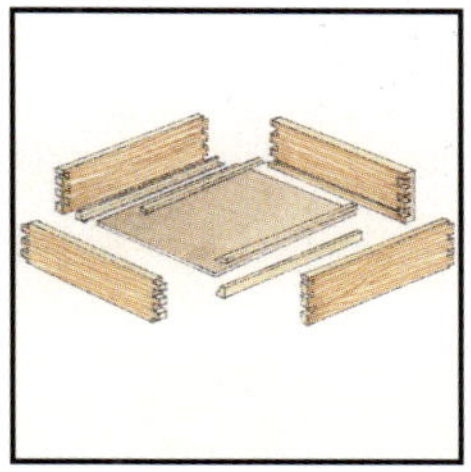

4

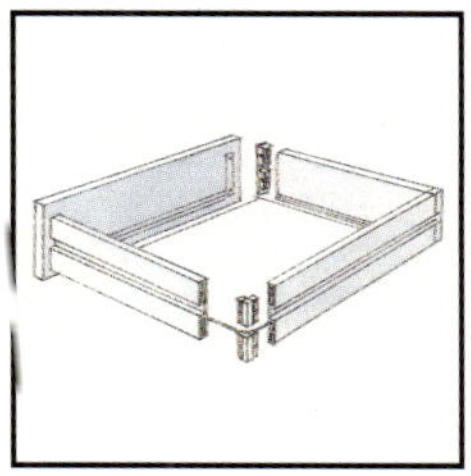

1

2

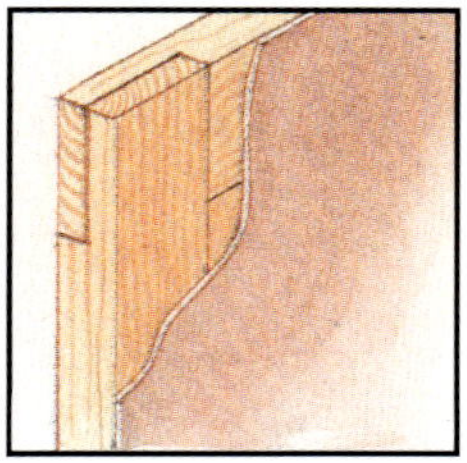

3

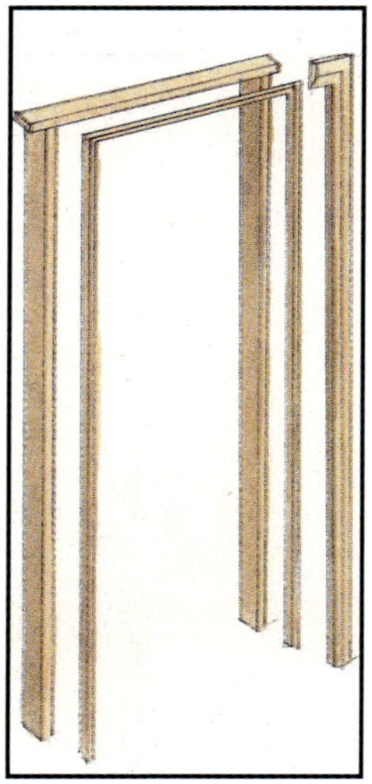

MAKING A FRAME

The type of joint(s) you should use when making up frames depends on what the frame is to be used for, and where it is.

1: PARTITION WALL

The framework for a partition wall is made from 100mm x 50mm/4in x 2in rough-sawn timber. Simple butt joints (see page 142), reinforced with skew nails, can be used where the uprights (studs) meet the top and bottom rails of the frame and where the horizontal noggins meet the uprights. The frame itself will be secured in position (by nailing the sole plate and head plate to the floor and ceiling and screwing the end studs to the side walls), so there is little trying to pull the frame apart.

2: FLUSH DOOR

To make a lightweight flush door to fit a particular size of hole, the framework can be made using simple halving joints (see page 145) secured with adhesive. The frame will be secured in place (and prevented from twisting) by the hardboard or other covering which you nail to both sides of the door frame. A stronger result would be achieved using bridle joints at the corners and where any horizontal frame members meet the side uprights.

3: DOOR FRAMES

An internal door frame usually consists simply of three pieces of wood butt jointed together and screwed to the wall.

Once the frame is in place, a door stop is fitted and architrave added. For standard sizes of external doors, with a sill, you can buy the door frame parts already fitted with mortice-and-tenon joints. All you need to do is to fit them into the opening.

But if you need to make up a new frame for a non-standard door size, cut mortices at either end of the frame head and the sill to take tenons on the two side uprights (jambs) and assemble the frame before fitting it into the opening.

MAKING A BOOKCASE

For a free-standing bookcase, you will want the joints between the shelves and the uprights to look as neat as possible.

1 The simplest way to make a bookcase is to cut the shelves and the uprights to length and then to drill holes in the uprights and butt joint (see page 142) them to the uprights with reinforcing screws through the uprights into the ends of the shelves. This has the disadvantage that the screw heads will show, but you could conceal them by drilling the hole a little deeper (counterboring) so that the screw heads are below the surface and then use decorator's filler if painting the bookcase or wood stopper if varnishing or staining it. An even neater result can be obtained by using a combination drill bit (which drills the pilot hole, clearance hole and counterbore for the screw in one go), plus a 'plug cutter' on a waste piece of the same wood to cut out a circular plug of exactly the correct size to go into the hole. Careful choice of whereabouts in the scrap wood you cut the hole and how you fit it into the hole can mean that you can very nearly match up the grain size and direction.

2 Another way to make a bookcase is to use dowelled joints (see page 144) – stopped dowels will look neater than through dowels – but these are really suitable only for bookcases taking a light load as heavy books could break the dowels.

3 A stronger answer, but one which requires more skill and the use of a router, is to use a housing joint (see page 146) where the shelves fit into slots cut out of the uprights, either glued or screwed in place to strengthen the joint. For a neater result, use a stopped housing which looks like a butt joint, but is much stronger.

1

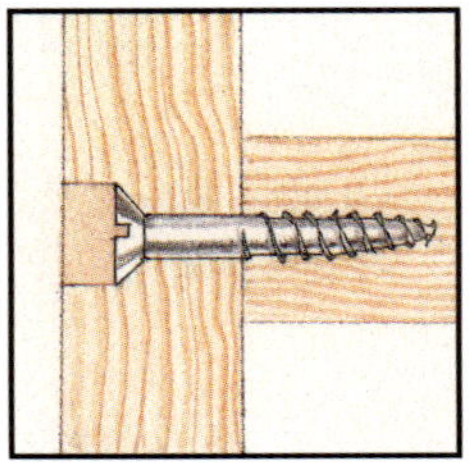

2

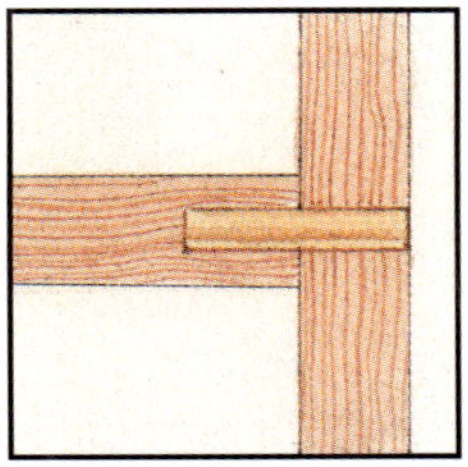

3

1

3

4

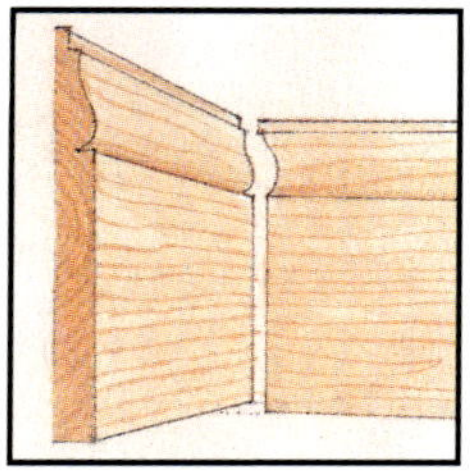

DOORS AND WINDOWS

Although it is unlikely that you will want to make your own doors and windows, it is possible that you will need to make repairs where the glue in the joints has dried out and/or the wood has shrunk.

Most door and window joints are mortice-and-tenon joints (see page 147). It may be possible to squeeze adhesive into the joint and simply clamp it up while it sets. But normally the joint will need reinforcing in some way. If the joints have wedges, new and perhaps larger wedges can be cut from scrap timber and hammered into the joints along with some new adhesive, clamping up the joints while the adhesive dries and trimming off the excess wedge afterwards.

Joints without wedges can be reinforced using dowels fitted across the joint – ie through holes drilled so that they pass right through the tenon. It is essential that the dowels are a good tight fit, so it is better to use dowelling rod to effect the repair and choose a drill bit size so that the rod has to be tapped into the hole – experiment on scrap timber beforehand.

SKIRTINGS, CORNICES AND ARCHITRAVES

All these mouldings have a dual purpose – to cover up a gap in the house construction and to look decorative.

1 An architrave is fitted around internal door frames and, in older houses, around window openings. The moulding is in three pieces – two for the sides and one across the top – joined with mitre joints (see page 147).

It is important that mitres are cut in straight lines, but they will rarely be 45°. Cut one half of the mitre at slightly more or slightly less than 45° as the door frame will not be exactly square. Cut the two side pieces first, then use these to mark the cutting lines for the top piece.

The architrave itself, which covers the gap between the door frame and the wall plaster, is nailed to the door frame. It is not necessary to glue the corners of an architrave, but nails are usually driven in downwards through the top piece into the side members to secure them in place.

2 Constructional mouldings such as skirtings and cornices, picture and dado rails are fitted around a room. Skirtings to cover the gap between wall and floor and cornices to cover gaps between wall and ceiling. Where skirtings and dado rails meet a door frame, they are cut square to butt up against the edge of the door frame. Where any of these mouldings meets another length of the same moulding – at the corner of a room – they make a joint.

Square-edge skirtings are the easiest – cut them square to make a butt joint (see page 142), fit one piece into the corner and overlap it with the second. Use the same technique on external corners.

3 For moulded skirtings, dado and picture rails, you will have to use a different technique. At external corners, use a mitre joint (see page 147) and cut the skirting to go past the corner by the thickness of the board.

4 Using a mitre joint at internal corners is tricky if the room is not absolutely square and causes problems getting the final piece of moulding into place. A solution is to make a shaped butt joint where the end of one piece of moulding is cut to the profile of the other (3). The first piece is cut square and put into the corner, the second piece is shaped and then fitted over it.

Right: A dado rail and high skirting board fitted around a room.

PAINTING EFFECTS

PAINTS AND PAINTING TOOLS

Painting walls and doors is one of the first jobs new home owners tackle and most of us feel confident that we are going to achieve a good result.

Decorative paint effects, though, are a different matter. Patience and planning will take you nine-tenths of the way. The final tenth will come with practise and that can only be gained once you have overcome your lack of confidence.

You may already own many of the materials you will need to get started, but you will need to seek out specialist paints and tools to have a go at some of the more advanced techniques.

PAINTS AND GLAZES

Many of the standard paints can be used to create paint effects, but in addition there are a large number of specialist glazes which are now available in most DIY stores.

Which type of paint or glaze you use will largely depend on the effect you are trying to achieve, but within each 'look' there are dearer and cheaper options.

Most paint effects are achieved by manipulating a surface glaze that has been applied over a dry base coat of a different hue. The surface glaze you use will determine the type of base coat:

EMULSION GLAZE

Applied over an emulsion base coat.

OIL GLAZE

Applied over a vinyl silk or 'eggshell' base coat.

Emulsion, vinyl silk and eggshell paints can all be bought from DIY stores and are relatively inexpensive. The range of colours sold is vast and in many large stores you can actually mix your own to create shades not available off the shelf.

Some of the most popular effects – sponging on, ragging on and colour washing – can all be achieved using a glaze made by mixing standard emulsion paint with tap water.

Professional decorators and keen amateurs, however, prefer to use an oil glaze in most, if not all, of their designs.

The presence of oil in a glaze gives the finished effect a more striking appearance

– lines will be crisper, colours brighter and the whole piece will appear to glow.

But the oil has a practical benefit too; it keeps the glaze wet longer enabling you to work on the effect for longer to get the finish you require.

There are two distinct types of oil glaze:

TRANSPARENT OIL GLAZE ('SCUMBLE')

This is the more versatile of the two. It stays wet longer and can be used in more projects but is also more laborious to prepare. It is mixed with artist's oil paint and thinned with white spirit.

How much white spirit you add to the mix will depend on the make of scumble you buy so check the manufacturer's instructions carefully. Do not assume that the more white spirit you add, the more workable the glaze will be – too much, and the glaze will start to separate out and be ruined.

To make the glaze, transfer a small amount of the artist's oil paint into a mixing bowl and pour in just enough white spirit to form a solution.

Add a little of this solution to the scumble in a separate bowl and mix. If the colour is not strong enough, add a little more of the solution and mix again. Should you find that the colour is too strong, you can tone it down using a dilute solution of oil-based white undercoat in white spirit.

When you are happy with the colour, dilute the mixture with the rest of the white spirit (following the manufacturer's instructions as to quantity) and combine the two thoroughly to form your glaze.

Make sure that you mix enough glaze to complete the task you have set yourself in one go. You will not have time to mix more if you run out half way through, and you would struggle to achieve a good colour match between the two batches.

OIL PAINT GLAZE

This is a lot quicker to mix up. The paint used here is a standard oil-based product you can buy in any DIY store. Simply dilute the paint with the same volume of white spirit and mix it well.

Any glaze you make up will look a lot darker in the mixing bowl than it will when it has been spread over a wall or door. It is always a good idea to test the colour on a piece of scrap board first.

When you are working with either of these glazes, always remember to open doors and windows to ventilate the room and allow the fumes to disperse.

PREPARING SURFACES

Uneven, crumbling or dirty surfaces can all make your job harder. All need to be prepared correctly to give you a firm, smooth base on which to paint.

Cracks or dents in unpainted bare wood should be treated with a wood filler. Knots should be painted with a knotting solution to prevent resin oozing out and spoiling the finish. The entire surface of the wood should be sanded down using coarse, medium and fine-grade glasspaper and then coated with a primer.

Wood that has previously been painted may need to be stripped if the old paint is peeling badly. If the paintwork is in good condition, simply wash it down with a sugar soap solution to remove any grease and rub it over lightly with glasspaper to provide a 'key' for the new paint to grip.

New plaster on walls and ceilings will need to be left to dry out before decorating. When the plaster has dried out it will need to be primed before you can apply a decorative finish.

Old plaster that has started to crumble and come away from the wall or ceiling will need to be repaired using filler then sanded flat and primed. It may be easier and quicker to have a badly cracked wall skim-coated with a thin layer of plaster. Bare stone or brickwork should be sealed to prevent any loose material flaking off.

Old wallcoverings can be painted over provided they have a smooth surface. Stick down any lifting edges or seams and coat the surface with a primer. Vinyl wallcoverings will need to have their top layer peeled off as this will not provide a good 'key' for paint. You can then paint over their backing paper after it has been painted with a dilute coat of emulsion.

If you are planning to decorate a radiator, you will need to clean and rub down the surface first. Bare metal surfaces will need coating with metal primer.

PROTECTING SURFACES

Before you start it is important to protect all the surrounding furniture and floor coverings against accidental spills. Use old sheets or newspapers to cover the work area thoroughly before opening any of the tins of paint. Some techniques can send flecks of paint flying off several feet from the work surface, so play it safe and cover as much of the room as possible.

WORKING WITH COLOUR

Most paint effects involve the use of more than one colour. This can mean using two shades of the same colour in tandem but it can also mean using two completely different colours.

Photographs in books and manufacturers' brochures are a good source of ideas if you are unsure which colours work well together, but it is always a good idea to experiment at home on a square of hardboard or plywood first. Many paints are available in tiny sample sizes so this need not be an expensive exercise.

A colour wheel is a handy aid which will help you to build up complementary colour schemes, not only for walls and ceilings but also for curtains and carpets.

The wheel shows the three primary colours – red, blue and yellow – interspersed with the shades you can create by combining them – hence green appears between yellow and blue. As a general rule, any two colours that sit directly opposite each other on the wheel will complement each other. For example, a green carpet will work well in a room with warm red walls.

the colour wheel

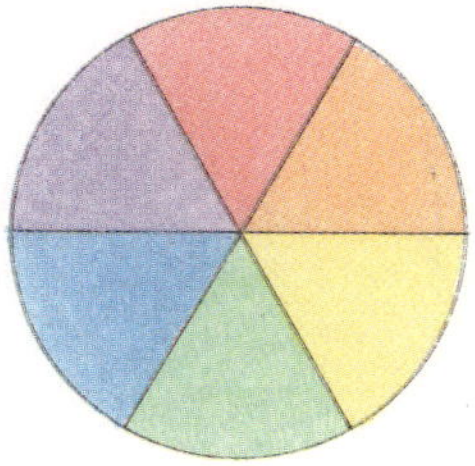

WHICH FINISH WHERE?

Not all effects work equally well on all surfaces. Consideration should be given to the type of surface and the style of finish. The table below is a guide to which surfaces work best with which techniques.

SURFACE	SUITABLE FINISH
Painted Woodwork	stencils, sponging, ragging
Bare Woodwork	stencils, sponging, ragging, stippling, dragging, rag-rolling
Metalwork	all finishes
Fresh Plaster	all finishes
Old Plaster	stencils, ragging, sponging, colour washing
Brickwork/Stone	ragging, sponging, colour washing

2

3

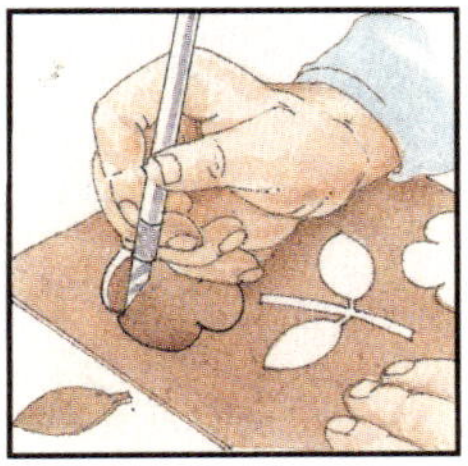

4

6

STENCILS

Stencilling is probably the easiest paint effect to master.

A number of manufacturers make stencil kits which include designs and sometimes both brushes and paints. If you can not find a design that you like, it is very easy to create your own stencils by tracing shapes from wallpaper samples, pieces of fabric and similar items.

It is a good idea to stencil your design onto a piece of board first to check that it works and to make sure you are happy with the colours you have chosen.

Any object that you wish to stencil will need to be clean, smooth and flat. Clean paintwork using warm soapy water and fine grade wet and dry glasspaper. Leave the surface to dry then wipe it over with a lint-free cloth soaked in methylated spirit.

TOOLS FOR THE JOB

tracing paper
piece of manilla card
pencil and rubber
sharp craft knife
cutting board or mat
stencil paint
stencil brush
masking tape or spray-mount adhesive

1 Start by tracing the pattern you have chosen on to your tracing paper.

2 Attach your sheet of tracing paper to the manilla card using masking tape or a light coat of spray-mount and transfer the design onto the card. Remove the tracing paper.

3 Cut out the sections of the pattern you are going to paint using a sharp craft knife.

4 Apply the paint one colour at a time with a stencil brush or piece of foam.

5 Use the paint sparingly, dabbing at the surface to build the colour up gradually.

6 Take care when removing the stencil not to smudge the paint.

Below: A simple stencil on a drawer front.

PAINT ROLLING

Paint rolling makes use of the humble paint roller. In addition to the normal plain roller sleeve, you will need to buy a sleeve with a bark pattern.

This paint effect can be applied to walls and ceilings. The only skill required is the ability to work up and down the surface in straight lines.

TOOLS FOR THE JOB

paint tray
paint roller
two roller sleeves – plain and bark pattern
masking tape
plumb bob and line
pencil

1 Fit the plain sleeve to the roller and cover the walls with a base coat of white or off-white vinyl silk emulsion. Two coats may be needed if painting over a strongly patterned wallpaper.

2 When this has dried, use your plumb bob and line to establish a true vertical line from the ceiling to the floor and mark this lightly on the wall with a pencil. Fix a strip of masking tape down the wall along one side of this line.

3 Fix your roller with the bark pattern sleeve and load this with the top coat paint. Do not overload the roller – it is important to apply an even coat of paint in one go as over-painting later will prove awkward.

4 To achieve an even distribution of paint, press lightly at the top of the wall and gradually increase the pressure as you work your way down to the bottom.

Drag the roller down the wall, following the masking tape. Repeat the process, overlapping the edge of the first pass with the second. Continue in this way around the room until your last pass meets up with your first.

Do not try to use your roller in the corners of the room – you will smudge the paint. Use a 1in paint brush instead.

1

3

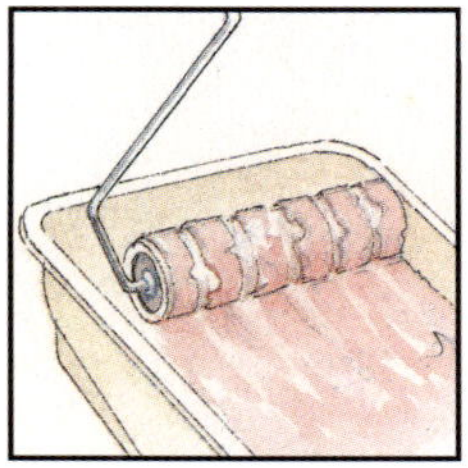

4

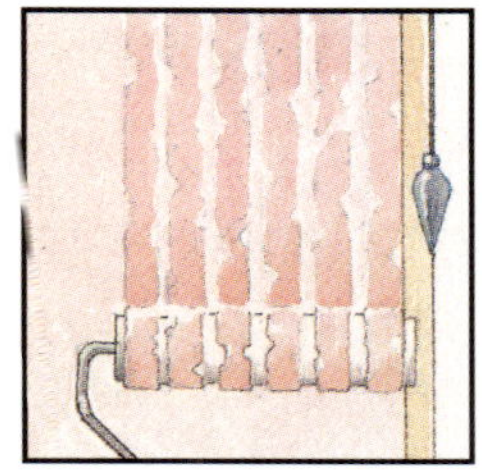

3

4

Below: A wild spattering of paint looks great in a modern environment.

SPATTERING

A fine spray of paint droplets can give an unusual finish to a piece of furniture. A bolder application can turn a kids' bedroom into a fun place for them to work and play.

This treatment can be applied to uneven surfaces as well as smooth ones as the brush will not come into contact with the object or wall that is being decorated.

Use two complementary shades such as cream and yellow for the spattered top coat. The base coat should be a contrasting colour such as blue. Use matt emulsion on walls; eggshell or satin finish on woodwork. Cover the surrounding area before you start work.

TOOLS FOR THE JOB

dish washing brush
mixing bowl or paint kettle
water or white spirit

1 Apply the base coat using either a roller or a paint brush and leave to dry.

2 Pour some of the first spattering colour into a mixing bowl or paint kettle and dilute it with a little water (emulsion) or white spirit (oil-based paints). Mix thoroughly.

3 Dip your brush into the paint – take care not to overload it. You need a small amount of paint on the tips of the bristles only,.

4 Hold the brush 150mm/6in away from the surface and run your fingers over the tips of the bristles. As they flex and spring back, the paint will be splashed onto the surface.

5 Leave the paint to dry and then apply the second top coat in the same way.

A very fine spray pattern can be achieved with a metal grid – a piece of fine wire mesh, for example. Hold the grid 50mm/2in from the object you want to spatter, load an ordinary paint brush and run this over the back of the grid.

COLOUR WASHING

Colour washing creates subtly different tones and shades by applying multiple layers of a nearly transparent glaze over an emulsion base coat.

The glaze can be made using oil or water-based paints. The glaze is a mixture of paint and a thinner (white spirit for oil-based paints, water for water-based ones). The glaze needs to be thin enough to allow the base colour to show through clearly even after two or three coats.

TOOLS FOR THE JOB

large flat paint brush
sponge or soft brush
mixing bowl or paint kettle
mixing spoon

1 Paint the wall with the base coat of emulsion using a large flat brush and leave to dry.

2 Mix up the glaze in a mixing bowl or paint kettle. If you are using emulsion paint, add no more than two or three tablespoons of emulsion to every litre/pint of water. You can add a small amount of PVA adhesive to give it a bit of 'body'.

3 Apply the wash boldly with a large, flat brush – do not worry about achieving an even coat. Use a sponge or soft brush to blend in any runs. Leave to dry.

4 Apply a second coat of glaze in the same way as above, but this time taking care to give the wall a more even coat. Leave to dry.

5 If you are happy with the effect, give the wall a light coat of clear acrylic varnish to seal the colour and protect the wall against dirt.

If you feel that it is not quite right, add one more coat of the wash. Every coat you add will darken the surface and even out the finish. How many coats you choose to add will depend on the effect you wish to achieve.

3

4

Below: colourwash.

SPONGING AND STIPPLING

THE PRINCIPLES OF SPONGING

Sponging is an easy paint effect to master. It can be used to cover walls quickly with dramatic and striking colour blends – or just as easily with soft and subtle tones.

A natural sponge is preferable to an artificial one because of its irregular structure which makes a much more pleasing pattern. You can emphasise this by twisting and turning the sponge in your hand as you work.

Sponging is an ideal paint effect to apply to an uneven wall. The surface will still need to be clean and stable (see page 158), but does not need to be perfectly smooth. You can sponge successfully over a wall covered with a woodchip wallpaper. You can also sponge over unplastered stone or brickwork, provided it has been painted first with a suitable base coat.

There are two basic ways to sponge – sponging-on and sponging-off. Either can be practised using solvent-based or water-based glazes. Whichever technique you choose, a natural sea sponge needs to be lubricated before it can be used effectively. If you are working with a water-based glaze, soak the sponge in water and then squeeze it partly dry. If you are going to use an oil-based glaze, pre-soak it in white spirit and then remove the excess.

SPONGING-ON

This involves applying a wet glaze using a natural sponge to a dry base coat.

FOR A WATER-BASED GLAZE

Use four parts of water to every one part of emulsion. A water-based glaze should be applied over a vinyl silk or eggshell paint base coat.

FOR AN OIL-BASED GLAZE

Mix white spirit and oil paint in equal proportions. An oil-based glaze should be applied over an oil base coat.

In both cases, the base coat should be left to dry completely before applying the glaze top coat.

You have the option when sponging-on paint to apply more than one coloured glaze but you must allow the first glaze to dry before applying the second.

TOOLS FOR THE JOB

natural sea sponge
paint roller
roller tray
mixing bowl or paint kettle
mixing spoon or stick

1 Cover the floor with dustsheets or newspaper below the wall you are going to decorate. Apply the base coat to the wall using a roller and leave to dry. You may need to apply two coats to obliterate a strong background colour if the walls have been painted before.

2 Mix up the glaze, either water or oil-based, and pour some of the glaze into the roller tray.

3 Once the sponge is prepared using water or white spirit (see page 164), dip one side of it lightly into the glaze, wiping off any drips or heavy concentrations of paint on the edge of the tray.

4 Dab the sponge lightly over the surface of the wall. Twist and turn your hand to ensure that different parts come in contact with the surface. The aim is to produce a random pattern that still allows the base coat to show through clearly.

5 Cover the entire surface of the wall with one light coat of paint and allow this to dry .

6 If you think that you have applied rather too much of the top colour and that the overall effect is too dark, clean out your sponge, moisten it again with water or white spirit and then use it to dab some of the undiluted base coat over the glaze to break it up slightly.

7 If you think that you have not applied enough glaze the first time, apply a second coat. Alternatively, you may choose to use a second glaze colour on top of the first.

SPONGING-OFF

This involves the partial removal of a wet surface glaze with a natural sponge.

You apply the base coat just as you would if you were sponging-on. The entire wall surface is then brushed with surface glaze. The finished effect is achieved by dabbing at this glaze while it is still wet with a clean sponge.

There is more time-pressure with this technique as you need to work across the whole wall with the sponge before the glaze begins to dry. For this reason a (slow-drying) oil-based glaze is better than a (quick-drying) water-based glaze.

2

3

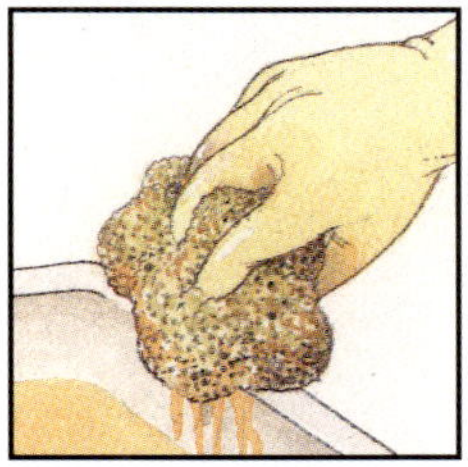

5

3

4

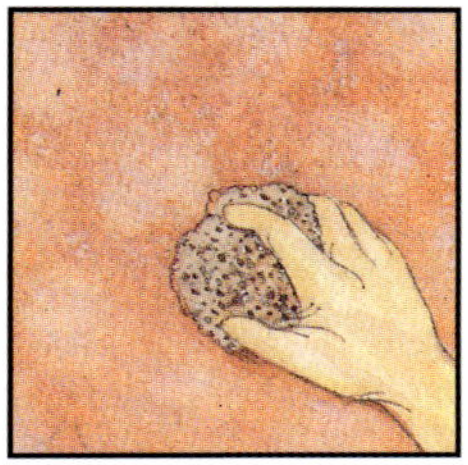

TOOLS FOR THE JOB

natural sea sponge
paint roller
roller tray
mixing bowl or paint kettle
mixing spoon or stick
large, flat paint brush

Below: Sponging on three different coloured glazes over a lighter base colour can add another dimension to an entrance hall.

1 Start by painting the wall with the base coat using a roller. More than one coat may be necessary to obliterate a strong background colour. Leave to dry.

2 Mix up the glaze in a mixing bowl or paint kettle using the proportions detailed on page 164.

3 Brush the glaze evenly across the wall using a large, flat brush. This needs to be done fairly quickly to give yourself as much time as possible to sponge it off before the glaze begins to dry.

4 Moisten your sponge using water or white spirit as appropriate to the glaze being used. Then start to distress the glaze, dabbing at random over the surface.

Work quickly and lightly at first over the entire surface, then go back and dab more intensively over any areas you may have missed. Do not spend a huge amount of time on one end of the wall only to find the glaze has dried before you are ready to tackle the other end.

Hold the sponge lightly and dab it over the surface of the wall – do not smear it or you will smudge the design.

STIPPLING

The pattern you are aiming to achieve here is a series of colour dots and flecks. It is much finer than a sponged pattern and you will need to use bolder colour combinations to make a real impact. Most people achieve this by applying a pale glaze over a dark base coat, but you can achieve good results working 'in reverse'.

Both water-based and oil-based glazes can be used in stippling. You can achieve greater clarity and definition of pattern using an oil-glaze. You will also have longer to go back over your work and touch-up any areas you are unhappy with before the glaze dries out. Water-based glazes offer a softer, flatter finish which can work well in older, traditional settings.

Stippling brushes are expensive for a one-off job and you will find that a (clean!) shoe brush will do the same job.

TOOLS FOR THE JOB

stippling brush
paint roller
roller tray
mixing bowl or paint kettle
mixing spoon or stick
large, flat paint brush

1 Apply the base coat to the wall using a paint roller and allow this to dry out completely.

2 Mix up the glaze and apply this quickly and roughly to the wall with a large, flat brush.

It is not necessary to achieve an even covering as long as there is some glaze on all parts of the wall. Apply the glaze in one metre/yard wide vertical strips from floor to ceiling. Stipple each strip with your brush (see below) before applying the next area of glaze. This ensures that the glaze does not start to dry out.

3 Tap your stippling brush lightly against the wall to create the pattern, taking care not to smear the glaze. Try to keep the flecks even.

4 If you have missed a small area of the wall, dip your stippling brush into a little of the glaze, wipe any excess off on the side of the tray and then tap the brush over the bare patch.

Wipe your brush regularly on a clean cloth to remove excess glaze. Otherwise the bristles will become clogged and the pattern blurred.

2

3

RAGGING AND DRAGGING

THE PRINCIPLES OF RAGGING

Ragging is generally considered a step-up from sponging in terms of difficulty.

The technique is broadly the same but there are four variations on the basic theme – ragging-on, ragging-off, rag-rolling on and rag-rolling off.

A pale base coat is often teamed with a darker surface glaze, but this combination can be reversed. Experiment with different colours on a piece of board until you are happy with the effect.

Below: Yellow ragging adds a touch of sunshine to any room.

RAGGING-ON

You can use both water and oil-based glazes to rag-on. The size of rag you use will determine how bold the pattern is. The larger the rag, the bolder the pattern will be. Most people prefer smaller, more delicate patterns in small rooms, for decorating doors and for pieces of furniture.

TOOLS FOR THE JOB

lint-free rags
paint roller or flat brush and roller tray
mixing bowl or paint kettle
mixing spoon or stick

1 Apply the base coat with a paint roller or flat brush and leave to dry.

2 Mix up either an oil-based or water-based glaze and pour it into a clean roller tray.

3 Roll up the rag into a ball and soak it in the glaze. Squeeze out any excess – the rag should be loaded but not dripping with glaze.

4 Dab the rag at random over the surface of the wall, taking care not to smear the pattern – use a pecking action not a rubbing one.

5 Each time you recharge your rag, undo and re-roll it to vary the pattern outline on the wall.

If a rag becomes completely clogged with paint, put it to one side and carry on with a fresh one.

RAGGING-OFF

This technique works best with an oil-based glaze, which will stay wet longer.

An extra pair of hands also comes in useful if you can find a willing partner.

The glaze is applied over the entire surface and then removed in places by dabbing at it with a rag over the entire surface before the glaze dries.

TOOLS FOR THE JOB

lint-free rags
paint roller or flat brush and roller tray
mixing bowl or paint kettle
mixing spoon or stick

1 Cover the surface evenly with the base coat using a roller or flat brush and leave to dry.

2 Paint a one metre/yard vertical section of the wall with the glaze.

3 Screw a piece of rag up into a ball and start to 'peck' at the surface, altering the angle of attack each time to create a random pattern.

There is no need to moisten the rag with white spirit before you start but some people believe this gives them a better finish.

4 Paint the next metre/yard vertical section of wall with glaze and repeat the process. Work your way around the surface until it has been covered with glaze and ragged.

Leave used rags to dry off and allow the white spirit fumes to evaporate before disposal. Do not burn them – throw them in the bin.

RAG-ROLLING

Rag-rolling uses the same materials as basic ragging-on and off except that the rag is rolled into a sausage shape, then rolled over the surface of the wall or door.

The aim is to keep the rag in constant contact with the surface while you are working on it, so the surface you are decorating needs to be reasonably flat.

RAG-ROLLING ON

The key to successful rag rolling is to maintain an even pressure on the surface.

It is essential that you do not press too

1

3

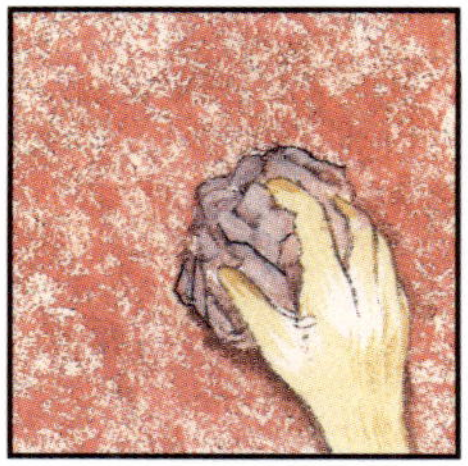

4

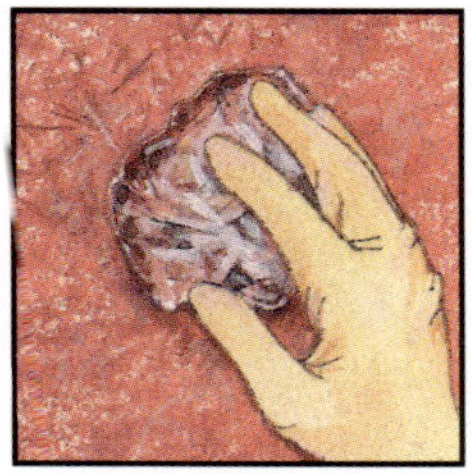

1 (rag-rolling on)

2

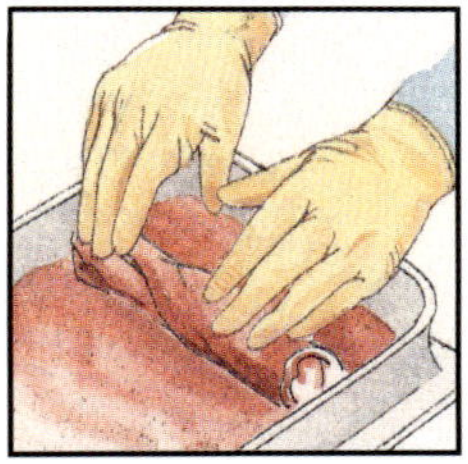

3

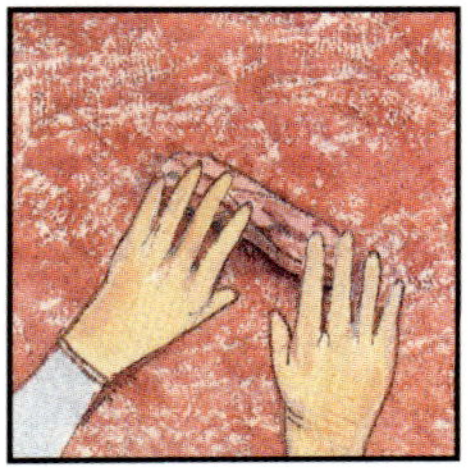

hard and smear the paint. The definition of the pattern must be maintained right across the surface.

Either water-based or oil-based glazes can be used.

TOOLS FOR THE JOB

lint-free rags
paint roller or flat brush and roller tray
mixing bowl or paint kettle
mixing spoon or stick

1 Start by applying the base coat with a roller or flat brush. Leave this to dry out thoroughly.

2 Mix the glaze and pour it into the roller tray, then roll the rag into a sausage shape and roll it in the glaze, squeezing out the excess.

3 Roll the rag lightly over the surface of the wall, changing direction at frequent intervals to create a random surface finish.

4 If you think you have not applied enough glaze, leave the first coat to dry and then take a clean rag and repeat the process.

If you think you have applied too much glaze, leave the first coat to dry and then using a fresh rag, roll on some of the base coat.

RAG-ROLLING OFF

Rag-rolling off is a technique that needs to be tackled at speed. The working time is controlled by the speed at which the paint dries. An oil-based glaze will give you a lot more working time.

TOOLS FOR THE JOB

lint-free rags
paint roller or flat brush and roller tray
mixing bowl or paint kettle
mixing spoon or stick

1 Start by applying the base coat using a roller or flat brush. Leave this to dry.

2 Mix up the glaze and pour it into the roller tray. Then paint a one metre/yard-wide vertical strip of wall with the glaze.

3 Roll a clean rag into a sausage shape and then roll this lightly over the surface of the wet glaze. Adjust the angle at which you are rolling the rag at frequent intervals to create a random finish.

4 Apply fresh glaze to the next vertical section of the wall and repeat the process.

Wearing thin plastic gloves over your hands will save you a lot of scrubbing after the job!

DRAGGING

Dragging imitates the natural grain of a piece of wood. It requires a steady hand and the ability to draw reasonably straight lines. It works best on doors, but can also be used to decorate other large pieces of furniture. Before starting, you will need to study the timber you are trying to imitate so that you know what the finished grain should look like

Any surface that is going to be dragged must be flat as the glaze is distressed with a flat brush in straight lines.

An oil-based glaze is preferable to a water-based one because this is a finish that cannot be rushed.

Soft, neutral colours work far better with this technique than bright primary ones.

TOOLS FOR THE JOB

mini paint roller or flat brush
flogger brush
roller tray
mixing bowl or paint kettle
mixing spoon or stick
cleaning rag

1 Apply the base coat with a mini paint roller or flat brush and leave it to dry.

2 Mix up the glaze and pour it into the roller tray. Apply the glaze to the entire surface using a brush or mini roller.

3 Take a clean flogger and drag it carefully through the glaze following the wood grain.

1

3

Keep a cleaning cloth handy to wipe any build-up of glaze from the tips of the bristles as you work.

Below: Effective use of dragging can transform tired kitchen units.

WALLPAPERING

TYPES OF WALLPAPER

Finding the most suitable wallcovering can be a daunting task, given the array of patterns and colours available to the home decorator today. You will find inspiration in magazines and shops and there is usually someone in your local DIY store to advise if you are not sure.

Colour will probably be your first consideration. All too often we opt for neutral beiges, creams and off-whites because we are afraid of making mistakes with stronger shades. As a result we end up with uninspiring interiors.

Few people want to decorate an entire room with a strong primary colour, of course, and this is where a colour wheel can be used to good effect (see page 159).

Patterns can make a big difference in a room. Be careful not to choose too large a pattern for a small room as this can make the room seem even smaller. The array of designs on the market is endless so take the time to find something that you really like and are going to feel comfortable looking at day after day.

WHICH WALLPAPER TO USE?

Some papers are easier to hang than others and there are substantial price differences between the mass market designs and the more unusual papers offered by home decor specialists.

LINING PAPER

This is used to cover slightly uneven walls and ceilings prior to hanging a decorative wallcovering. Various thicknesses are available, but none of them will disguise a badly damaged surface

STANDARD WALLPAPER

This consists of a single sheet of paper with a design printed on the face. The cheapest are thin and more prone to tearing when they are wet with paste. They cannot be cleaned easily, so do not use them in the kitchen or bathroom.

WOODCHIP

This consists of two layers of paper with tiny fragments of wood trapped between them. It is a cheap wallcovering that is invariably painted with emulsion after hanging.

RELIEF WALLCOVERINGS

These have a three-dimensional surface pattern and are intended to be painted with emulsion after hanging. Some have a vinyl surface, making them easy to clean and suitable for kitchens and bathrooms. Others, known as 'blown' wallcoverings, have a raised surface pattern that feels spongy.

HIGH RELIEF WALLCOVERINGS

These are much more expensive than any other type of sculpted paper. They are sold in stiff sheets rather than rolls and are far more durable than conventional wallcoverings. The backing paper needs to be soaked prior to pasting.

FABRIC WALLCOVERINGS

Silk, hessian, oriental grass, sisal and suede finishes are all available if you are prepared to seek them out in specialist interior design shops. They are generally much more expensive than other papers, and hard to hang without leaving visible joins.

VINYL WALLCOVERINGS

These are designed for use mainly in wet areas like kitchens and bathrooms. They can be wiped clean if food splashes over them. A PVC coating is applied over the paper backing material during manufacture to create this hardy hybrid, which is probably the easiest wallcovering of all to hang.

FLOCK WALLCOVERINGS

These have a velvet overlay bonded to them, are relatively expensive and too fragile for busy areas.

WHICH ADHESIVE TO USE?

Most pastes and adhesives are starch-based and are sold in powder form for mixing with cold water, though ready-mixed pastes are available.

If you are hanging lining paper or standard wallpaper, a cheap paste will do, but heavier papers like relief wallcoverings and flocks need a thicker adhesive. There are a number of adhesives formulated for this purpose. If in doubt, opt for an all-purpose paste which can be mixed with the required amount of water to achieve the recommended strength.

Vinyl wallcoverings should always be hung using a paste that contains a fungicide to prevent mould growth on the wall behind them. It is essential to wash your hands after handling this type of adhesive and keep it away from children and pets.

HOW MUCH PAPER WILL I NEED?

Take the time to make an accurate estimate of the number of rolls of wallpaper you are going to need before you start. By purchasing your wallpaper all at the same time, you can ensure that all the rolls come from the same manufacturing batch. Rolls made at different times can vary in colour so look for a sticker on the packaging of each roll to find the batch number.

Measure the height of the room from the skirting boards up to the coving or to the ceiling itself. Then measure the distance around the four walls to arrive at a total for the circumference of the room. Include in your measurements all doors and windows except ones which stretch from floor to ceiling. Although you will save some paper at these points, you will still need to paper the walls above and below the openings. It is far better to buy slightly too much paper than to run short.

The table will enable you to work out how many rolls of paper you will need for each room. It is based on the standard UK roll size of 10m long x 530mm/33ft x 21in wide. If this is the first time you have hung wallpaper, it would be as well to add an extra roll to allow for cutting mistakes, tears and creases. If you are working with a patterned paper, you will obviously have to waste some in the matching process. Allow one extra roll per room for a paper with a small pattern, two extra rolls for one with a large pattern.

WALLPAPER CALCULATOR

	LENGTH OF WALLS							
HEIGHT OF WALLS	10M	12M	14M	16M	18M	20M	22M	24M
2.0M – 2.2M	4	5	6	7	8	9	10	11
2.2M – 2.3M	5	6	7	8	9	10	10	11
2.3M – 2.5M	5	6	7	8	9	10	11	12
2.5M – 2.7M	5	6	7	9	10	11	12	13
2.7M – 2.8M	6	7	8	9	10	11	12	13

ESSENTIAL TOOLS

WALLPAPERING TOOLS

1: CUTTING GUIDE

A metal tool which can be used as a straight edge when cutting paper with a trimming-knife.

2: PAPER-HANGING BRUSH

To smooth out any folds and work out air bubbles trapped behind the paper as you hang it. It is vital that the brush is clean and dry to avoid marking the face of the paper.

3: PASTE BRUSH

A wide-headed brush with synthetic bristles is needed to apply paste to the paper and/or walls.

4: PASTE BUCKET

A plastic bucket is needed for mixing the paste. Tie a length of string across the top of the bucket, attaching the ends to the handle. This is used to wipe excess paste off the brush as you work.

5: PASTING TABLE

It is worth investing a few pounds in a folding table that is solely used for wallpapering. A purpose-made pasting table will be light enough to carry around from room to room and can be calibrated along its edges for easy measuring.

6: PLUMB BOB

An essential tool if you want to hang your paper vertically. A bob is a metal weight attached to a length of string and is used to make a vertical line on the wall prior to hanging your first length of paper.

7: SEAM ROLLER

Used to smooth down edges that are lifting immediately after the paper has been hung. Never use a seam roller on embossed or blown vinyl wallpapers, which have a sculpted surface pattern.

8: SPONGE

A clean sponge to wipe any excess adhesive off the face of the paper before it has a chance to dry.

9: STEPLADDER

To reach the ceiling and tops of walls comfortably.

10: TRIMMING KNIFE

A sharp knife for trimming the paper at the top and bottom once it has been positioned on the wall. The blade must be sharp to prevent tearing or 'chewing' of the paper.

11: WALLPAPER SCISSORS

A sharp pair of scissors with long blades (around 250mm/10in) is needed to cut the paper without tearing it. The longer the blades, the easier it is to cut the paper in a straight line.

WALLPAPER PASTER

For large-scale papering projects, it is worth considering investing in a pasting machine. These can paste lengths of paper in a fraction of the time it takes to do the job by hand and in this respect do away with the need for a pasting table. What they do not provide you with is a clean work surface on which to measure and cut paper. A paster should be regarded as an extra rather than an essential piece of equipment.

12: WATER TROUGH

A trough that you can fill with cold water is an essential piece of equipment for hanging ready-pasted wallpapers that need to be soaked to soften the adhesive. The trough needs to be long enough to take a full width of paper without folding.

Right: A selection of wallpapering tools designed to make the decorator's life much easier.

PREPARING THE WALLS FOR PAPERING

All walls must be prepared before you attempt to hang a new covering.

PAPERED SURFACES

In most instances, the first stage in the preparation process will be to strip off existing wallcovering. This can be done in one of two ways:

1 The traditional way is to soften the adhesive holding the old paper in place using a sponge and a bowl of warm water and then strip it off with a scraper. This is slow and tedious but adding a little washing-up liquid to the water helps.

2 The modern alternative is to hire or buy a steam stripper which is a hot water kettle that feeds steam to a hand-plate. The plate is pressed to the wall and softens the adhesive in seconds, allowing you to peel off large sections of the wallcovering in one go.

Paper that has been painted should be scored with a trimming knife to allow the water or steam to penetrate the surface.

The top layer of vinyl wallcoverings can be stripped off dry, leaving the backing paper in place. The backing can remain where it is to be used as a lining paper for the new wallcovering.

It is not essential to strip off the old wallcovering. If it is still firmly attached to the wall, you can paper over the top, provided that the old wallcovering does not have a raised surface design.

PAINTED SURFACES

Walls that have been previously painted with emulsion need only a wipe over with sugar soap or warm, soapy water. If there is any paint flaking, rub over with coarse grade abrasive paper.

Walls that have been coated with a gloss need to be rubbed all over with abrasive paper to roughen them slightly.

Textured paint should be stripped completely. Special chemical solutions are available for this purpose, but a steam stripper can also be effective.

BARE SURFACES

Bare plaster and plasterboard walls need to be 'sized' before they can be papered. This is done by brushing a diluted solution of wallpaper adhesive over their surface and then leaving it to dry. Sizing reduces the capacity of both surfaces to absorb

2

1

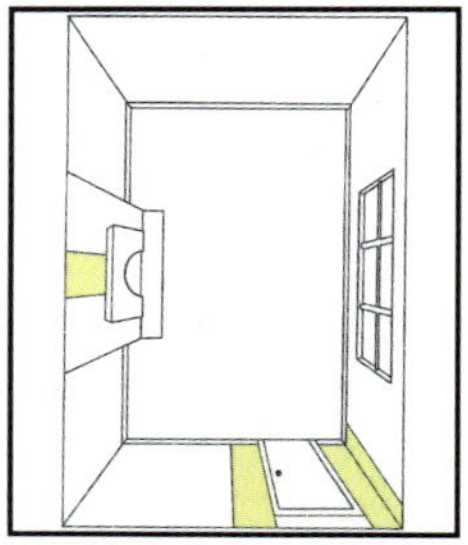

3

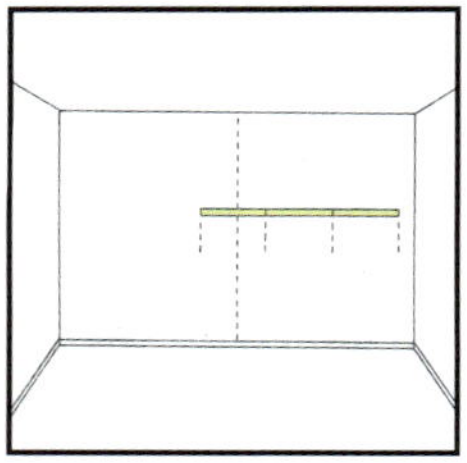

moisture and makes it easier to slide lengths of paper into position once they are on the wall.

DAMAGED SURFACES

Any cracks or crumbling plaster must be filled and made sound before proceeding further.

Small repairs can be made using filler (available both ready-mixed in tubes and in a powder form to which water is added), but large-scale damage demands the attention of a professional plasterer. Leave repairs to dry out thoroughly and then sand down rough spots before sizing and papering.

Below: Careful preparation puts you well on the way to a professional finish.

WHERE TO START

The joints between each length of paper and its neighbours should be invisible, so where you start is relatively unimportant.

1 Having said that, if you are hanging a wallcovering with a bold pattern, it makes sense to centre it on the focal point of the room – a chimney breast or the middle of the main wall.

2 The other point to bear in mind is the distance from your starting point to the first pair of internal corners (external on a chimney breast) you are going to encounter. To avoid creasing, it is essential that you do not attempt to turn more than 25mm/1in of paper on to the adjoining wall (see page 184). This will mean trimming the paper vertically at almost every corner. While this will not be particularly noticeable if you are only cutting 50mm–75mm /2in–3in off each length, it will if one of the lengths is only 50mm–75mm/2in–3in wide!

3 To guard against this, mark your intended starting point in pencil on the wall and then use a roll of wallpaper as a measuring guide to divide up the space between this point and each of the corners. If this indicates that you are going to be forced to hang a very thin strip of paper in either corner, adjust your starting point accordingly.

HANGING PAPER ON PLAIN WALLS

When you have prepared the surface and settled on your starting point, your next step is to draw a vertical line on the wall. Use a plumb bob to find true vertical and – if you can – get a friend to help draw the line while you hold the bob.

1 It is essential that you hang the wallcovering vertically. Failure to do so will make accurate pattern matching impossible and will leave you with an awkward strip to cut at an angle off the last piece of paper to butt it up against the first.

2 Do not assume that the walls and ceiling of the room you are working in are perfectly square. Few are – hence the need for a plumb bob to give you an independent verdict.

MIXING PASTE

Unless you are using a ready-mixed adhesive or a ready-pasted wallcovering, you will need to mix the paste in a plastic bucket before you hang the first length.

1 Pour the cold water in first then add the powdered adhesive, following the manufacturer's instructions with care so that the correct consistency is achieved. Stir the mixture with a clean wooden spoon and then let it stand while it thickens.

2 While the paste is thickening, clear the room of furniture and cover the floor with newspaper or dust sheets to catch any drips or scraps of sticky paper. You are now ready to erect your pasting table and assemble your toolkit (see page 177).

MEASURING AND CUTTING

1 Unwrap your first roll of paper and lay it face up on your pasting table. Decide which way you want the pattern to run if you have a choice and measure the distance between the top of the skirting and the edge of the ceiling or cornice.

2 Add an extra 100mm/4in to this figure so that the paper will overlap the wall top and bottom when it is initially hung. This overlap can then be trimmed to fit the skirting and ceiling profile.

This may appear wasteful, but if you do not allow any overlap you will inevitably be left with ugly gaps where the ceiling or skirting is uneven and be forced to bin whole lengths of paper.

3 You may decide that you want a particular motif or portion of the design to sit just below the cornice or just above the skirting. If so, turn the wallcovering over and trim your first length accordingly.

4 (measuring & cutting)

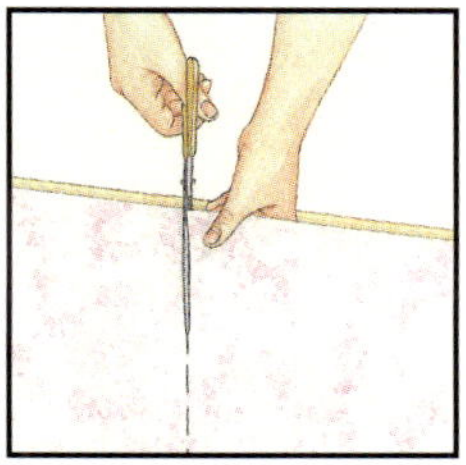

5

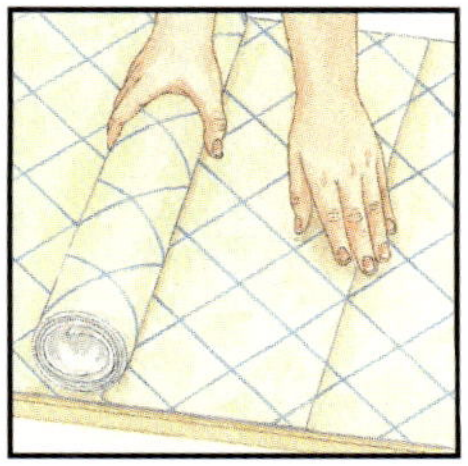

2 (pasting paper)

3

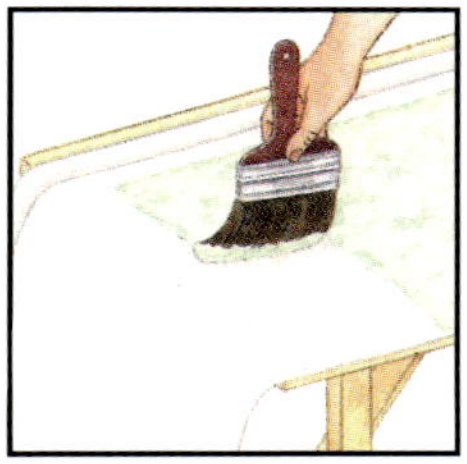

4

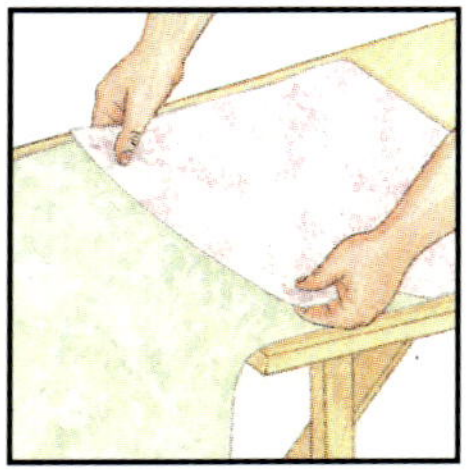

7

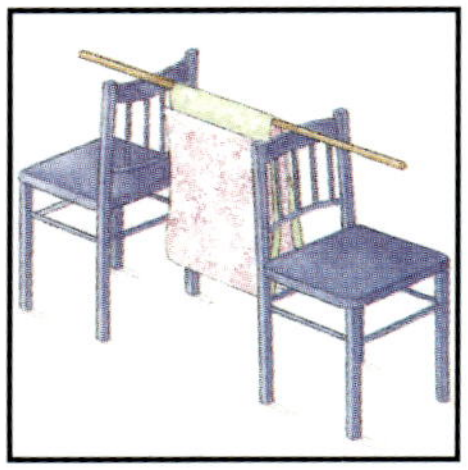

4 Cutting should always be done with the wallcovering face downwards on the pasting table. This allows you to lightly draw a cutting line in pencil across the back. Always use a metal straight edge to guide your pencil. Use a pair of long-bladed scissors to make the cut.

5 If you have a pattern to match, cut several lengths of the wallcovering to size before pasting any of them to the wall. This allows you to match the pattern 'dry'.

6 To do this, turn your first length of paper face upwards on the table and unroll a second length beside it. Align the pattern on the two lengths and then mark the second lightly on the face to indicate where it should be cut. Then turn it over and mark and cut it to size.

7 Repeat the process with a third and fourth length and then number them on the back before commencing pasting. Before hanging Number Four, dry-match and cut another couple of lengths, and continue this process as you work your way around the room.

PASTING PAPER

1 Lay the first length face down on the table with the bottom hanging down towards the floor and the top overlapping the table by 10mm/½in.

2 Load your brush with paste and apply the solution thickly along the centre of the paper.

3 Use the brush to spread it out from here to the edges, making sure that the entire surface is pasted. If you work with your back to the light, any dry areas should be clearly visible. Take care at the end that it is only just overlapping the table – this overlap is designed to stop paste getting on to the work surface, whilst allowing you to coat right up to the edge of the paper.

4 When you have pasted the top half of the paper, fold the end in (pasted side to pasted side) far enough to allow the unpasted portion to lie flat on the table.

5 Paste this portion in the same way and again fold the end in towards the middle. It is important not to crease the paper when folding it.

6 Carefully lift the wallcovering off the table, holding it in the middle with the two loops hanging down either side. Most need to be left for a few minutes while the paste soaks in, so you will need a clean space on which to place them.

7 You can suspend them from a broom handle laid across the backs of two chairs.

HANGING THE FIRST LENGTH

1 Pick up the first length of paper, hold it in the middle to avoid creasing the folds. Climb up to ceiling height and carefully unpeel the top fold.

2 Press the top portion of the paper on to the wall, sliding it across the surface until it is perfectly aligned with your pencil mark. The top edge should overlap the ceiling or cornice by about 50mm/2in. If there are any folds in the paper which are threatening to crease, ease the paper back away from the wall and re-position it.

3 Brush out any air bubbles or folds in the top half of the paper, working from the centre outwards. Only when you are happy with the position of the top half of the paper should you unfold the bottom half.

4 If you have positioned the top half correctly, the bottom half should fall naturally into place, its edge butting up neatly against your pencil line. Smooth down all the edges.

5 The bottom edge should overlap the skirting by about 50mm/2in. Crease it in the angle formed by the wall and skirting and the same between the wall and ceiling.

6 Trim away any excess paper straight away – if you leave it until you have hung three or four lengths, the adhesive will have started to dry out. The quickest – and neatest – way to do this is to peel the paper back from the wall and cut along the creases with your long-bladed scissors. If you lack the confidence to do this, you can cut most wallcoverings while they are still pressed against the wall using a sharp trimming knife. A useful tool called a trimming guide is available to help guide your hand.

7 Hang the second and third lengths in the same way, butting each up against the other. Do not allow the edges to overlap, because the ridges this creates will be very obvious when the paste has dried. A seam roller will come in handy to press down all the edges, but do not press too hard or you risk damaging the paper. Never use a roller on a wallcovering with a relief pattern.

8 Patience is important here – wet paper tears easily. An hour spent hanging the first two or three lengths is time well spent if they are hung vertically and the pattern is carefully matched. Improvised tools often work as well as, if not better than, those available in the shops. The tip of a rounded teaspoon handle, for example, is ideal for closing up and smoothing over joints between two lengths of paper.

2

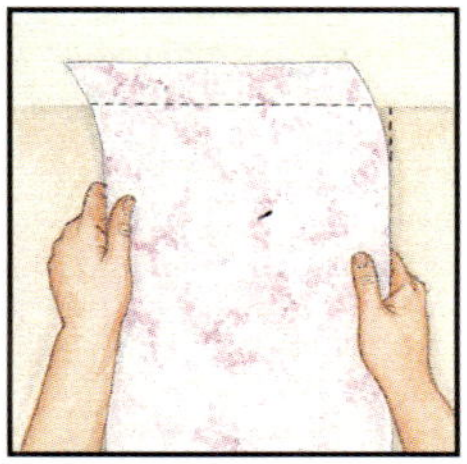

3

6

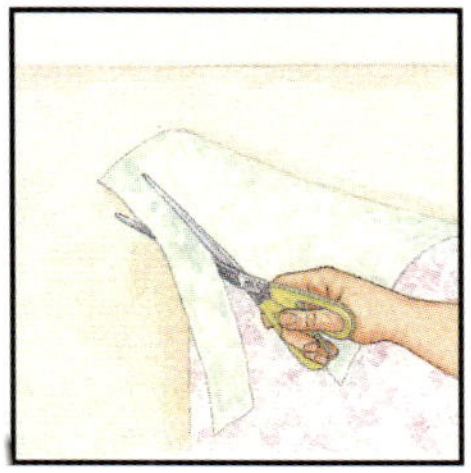

1

4

5

6

TACKLING CORNERS

Few corners in a room are perfectly square – house builders simply do not work to the same standards of accuracy as engineers. As a result, wallpaper will always start to crease and twist out of true vertical when it is wrapped around a turn.

To overcome this problem, trim your wallcovering vertically so that you are not turning more than 25mm/1in around the angle of the corner.

To avoid hanging very narrow strips of paper at the corners – which can look odd as well as being wasteful – you must plan for corners when deciding on your starting point (see page 180). Assuming that you have avoided this potential pitfall, this is how to tackle internal corners:

1 Measure the gap between the edge of the last full width of covering that you have hung and the corner. Measure this gap at several heights as the walls may slope slightly and note the widest measurement. Add 12mm/½in to this figure unless the wall slopes by more than this amount, in which case you will need to turn 25mm/1in.

2 Place a length of paper face down on your pasting table and mark a line in pencil vertically where it is to be cut.

3 Cut along this line using long-bladed scissors and put the strip of excess paper to one side. Do not throw it away.

4 Paste the trimmed paper and leave it to soak in the normal way, then hang it, matching one edge to the last piece you hung then brush the other gently into the corner.

5 If the corner is fairly square, the strip of wallcovering that you have turned around the corner should lie flat. If it is creasing, make a series of horizontal cuts at intervals along the edge with your scissors to correct this problem.

6 Now measure the width of the excess paper you cut in (3). Mark a vertical line with your plumb bob this distance along the return wall. Paste and hang the excess strip on the return wall, using this line as a guide. You may have to overlap the edge of the last length of paper in order to follow this line, but it is essential that you do so.

External corners are tackled in exactly the same way, except that you can generally turn slightly more paper around the angle without it creasing.

PAPERING AROUND A DOORWAY

At first sight, this looks like a job that is going to involve a lot of detailed measurement in order to pre-cut the paper to fit around the door frame. In fact, there is no need for any of this work.

1 Paste the first length of paper you are going to hang around the doorway as if it were to be hung on a plain section of wall.

2 Position it on the wall above the doorway in the normal way, allowing it to hang loosely over the frame.

3 Use a pair of long-bladed scissors to roughly cut the excess paper around the frame, leaving about 25mm/1in of an overlap all the way around.

4 At the corner, at the top of the frame, make a short diagonal cut in the overlap to allow the paper to lie flat.

5 Now brush the entire length of paper flat, pressing the overlap into the angle between the frame and the wall.

6 Carefully peel the overlapping paper back from the door frame and cut it off using your long-bladed scissors.

7 Repeat the process on the other side of the doorway.

PAPERING AROUND A LIGHT SWITCH

You should always switch off the electricity supply at the mains before papering around a light switch. Different techniques are used for papering around either a square or a round switch plate.

A SQUARE PLATE:

1 Hang the length of wallcovering in the normal way, brushing it flat at the top and pressing it gently over the switch plate to mark its outline on the back of the paper. Do not brush it on to the wall below the switch at this stage.

2 Pierce the wallcovering near the centre of the plate and make four diagonal cuts outwards from this point to the four corners of the plate.

3 Fold back the four triangular flaps of paper this has created. Trim the flaps back so that they only overlap the sides of the plate by 2mm-3mm/⅛in.

4 Unscrew the plate and pull it about 6mm/¼in away from the wall. Carefully pull the plate through the hole you have cut in the wallcovering, then press the paper flat against the wall.

5 Tuck the flaps behind the plate and then brush the bottom half of the length into position. Screw the switch plate back into place.

1 (a doorway)

4

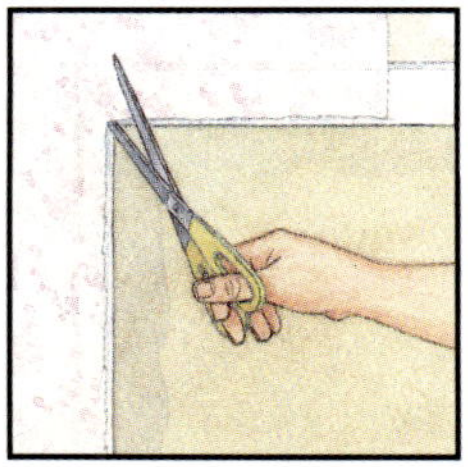

2 (a light switch)

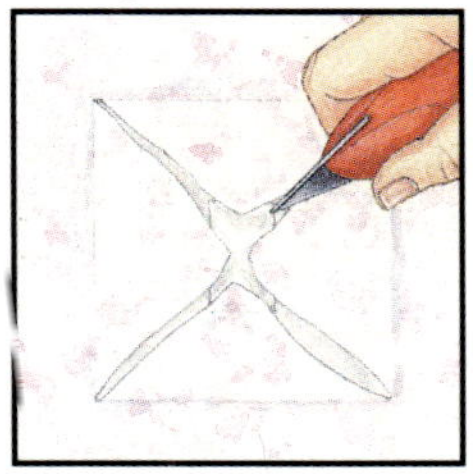

4

2

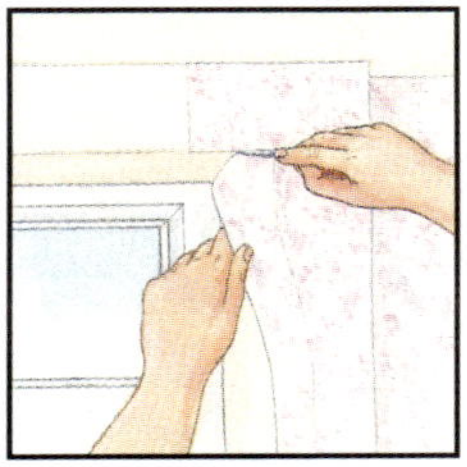

4

Below: a perfectly papered window.

A CIRCULAR SWITCH PLATE:

1 Hang the length of paper in the normal way, brushing it into place along the top of the wall and pressing it over the switch to mark its position on the back of the paper.

2 Pierce the wallcovering over the centre of the switch and make about 8–10 diagonal cuts out from this point to the edges of the plate.

3 Crease the triangular flaps of excess paper that this has left against the edges of the plate where it joins the wall.

4 Cut the flaps along the crease marks, allowing 1mm/$\frac{1}{32}$in overlap of wallcovering on the edges of the switch plate.

5 Brush the wallcovering flat around the plate.

PAPERING AROUND A WINDOW

A flush window can be treated like a doorway. Simply hang the lengths of paper on the wall above the window and trim them to fit around the frame as described on page 185. A recessed window needs to be treated in a slightly different way, but again there is no need to measure and pre-cut the wallcovering.

1 Paste the first length of paper that will overlap the window and position it on the wall above the opening. Let it hang loosely over the window soffit and reveal.

2 Press the paper against the edge of the soffit and cut along this line with a trimming knife, taking care not to tear the wallcovering.

3 This will allow you to wrap the paper below the cut around the angle of the wall and cover the reveal. Trim this paper where it overlaps the window frame.

4 Cut a small rectangle of wallcovering just large enough to overlap the reveal and soffit edges and fit this into the soffit end.

5 Brush the paper on the wall above, and to the side of this offcut, over the edges.

PAPERING AROUND A FIREPLACE

Paper around a fireplace is tackled in much the same way as a window or door frame. Position a full length of wallcovering on the chimney breast above the opening and allow this to overhang the mantlepiece before making any cuts.

1 Lightly crease the wallcovering along the right-angled joint where the back of the mantlepiece butts up against the chimney breast.

2 Carefully peel the paper back from the mantlepiece and trim the waste paper below this crease with a pair of long-bladed scissors. Do not cut the full length of the crease at this stage – leave an inch overhanging the mantlepiece, to allow for any slight adjustments on either side.

3 Press the paper at either side of the fireplace against the uprights that support the mantlepiece, again lightly creasing it to indicate where it should be cut.

4 Peel the paper away and trim the excess off to within an inch or two of these creases.

5 Use a pair of short-bladed scissors to finish trimming around any mouldings or tight corners. Long-bladed scissors will give you a better edge along the back of the mantlepiece.

PAPERING AN ARCHWAY

Papering an archway between two rooms presents you with a similar problem to papering an external corner only worse – the wallcovering will crease horribly if you attempt to turn more than an inch or so around its edges.

1 Hang each length of paper that overlaps the archway as normal, brush it flat along its top edge but let it hang loosely over the opening.

2 Press it against the archway to mark the outline on the reverse of the wallcovering, and trim off the excess to within 25mm/1in of this mark.

3 Cut a series of triangles out of the remaining strip of excess wallcovering so that it will lie flat on the face of the arch. Paste the overlap on to the face of the arch. Repeat this process all the way around the arch.

4 Now measure the width of the face of the arch and cut a strip of wallcovering long enough to cover it from the floor to its apex. Cut a longer strip if you have a pattern to match. Paste this length into position and then repeat the process, working from the other side of the archway.

1 (a fireplace)

2

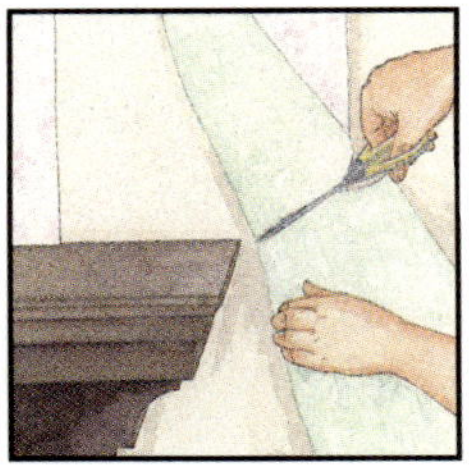

3 (an archway)

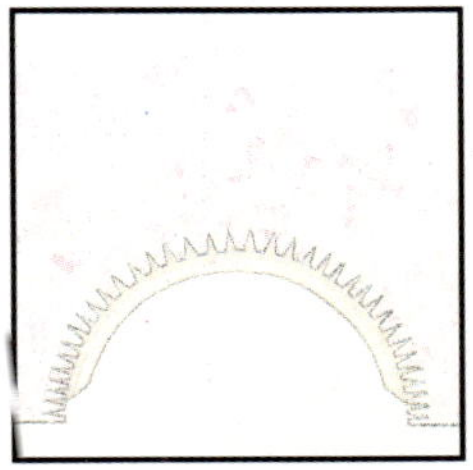

4

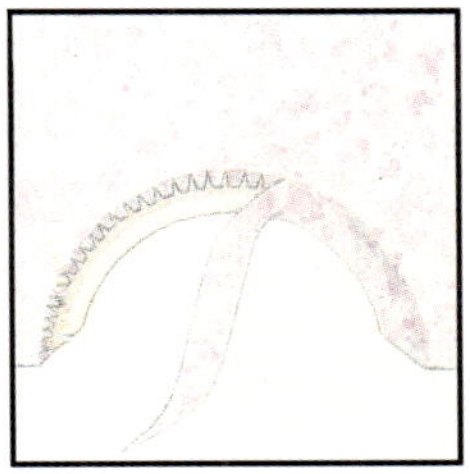

4

6

PAPERING BEHIND A RADIATOR

If a radiator is situated under a window sill it makes more sense to hang strips of wallcovering below the sill and above the skirting board, each finishing a couple of inches behind the radiator.

A radiator that is fixed to a plain wall will need to be papered behind it completely. However it is perfectly possible to do the job with the radiator left in place.

1 Paste only the top half of a length of wallcovering that is going to hang behind a radiator.

2 Position this on the wall and brush it flat in the normal way, with the bottom half hanging loosely over the top of the radiator.

3 Carefully feed the bottom edge of the paper behind the radiator from above, pushing it down just far enough to crease it against the radiator bracket(s).

4 Pull the paper back up from behind the radiator and make a vertical cut up through the paper along the line initiated by this crease. This cut should run from the top of the skirting to the top of the radiator bracket, where two small diagonal cuts need to be made to ease the paper around the bracket.

5 Fold the wallcovering gently back up the wall so as to paste the lower half, taking care not to make any splashes.

6 When the paste has soaked in, feed the paper back down behind the radiator, using a long-handled paint roller to press it flat against the wall.

PAPERING OVERHEAD

A ceiling is papered in much the same way as a plain wall.

It is important that you cover the floor and any furniture that you cannot move out of the room with dust sheets.

It also makes sense to protect your eyes from flying debris when working overhead, so equip yourself with a pair of plastic goggles.

It is both safer and more convenient to stand on a work platform than a single stepladder when you are papering ceilings. You can create your own working platform from two trestles or a pair of step ladders with a scaffold board hung between them. Arrange the platform so that you paper the full length of the ceiling in one go – if you can. You will probably need to use two boards, one placed on top of the other, if the distance between the platform ends is much more than 1.8m/6ft. You can hire working platforms cheaply from tool hire shops.

Arrange the platform so that you have just enough room to stand up straight on it without hitting your head on the ceiling.

PREPARING THE CEILING

Papering a ceiling is not going to disguise serious cracks, lumps or bumps. Textured paint would be a better choice if you want to cover-up imperfections of this kind.

If the ceiling has been papered before, strip off the old covering, sand down any rough spots and smooth all the cracks and hollows out using filler.

Then give the entire surface a coat of 'size' (watered down wallcovering paste) to reduce its absorbency. This will make it easier for you to slide lengths of paper across the ceiling to adjust their position slightly.

WHERE TO START

Before you start, use a roll of paper as a measuring stick to work out on the floor how many widths of paper you are going to have to hang. This exercise will indicate if you are going to be left with a very thin strip of paper to cut for the gap between the last full width of paper and the top of the far wall. If so, trim 50mm–100mm/ 2in–4in off your first length to prevent this.

1 If the room has windows on only one wall, start papering immediately above this wall, hanging lengths parallel to it. This way, if there are any overlapping joints, they will not cast shadows on the ceiling.

2 If the room has windows on more than one wall, hang the paper across rather than along the ceiling. The shorter the lengths of paper you have to cope with, the easier the job will be.

1

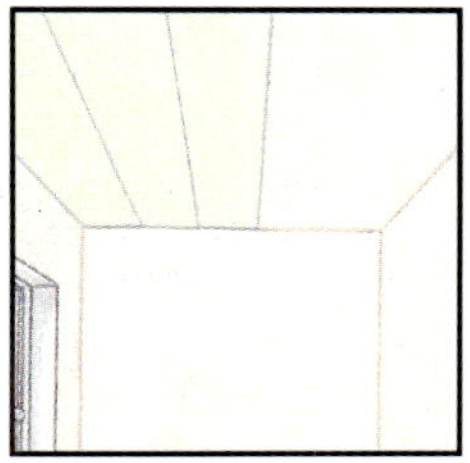

2

1

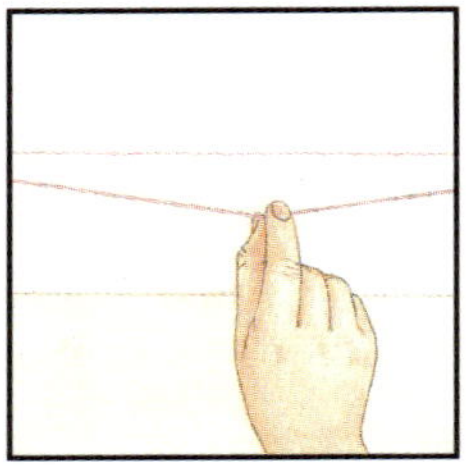

2

5

8

PAPERING THE CEILING

The angles between the walls and ceiling of the room you are decorating are unlikely to be perfectly smooth, so it makes sense to hang your first length of paper against a chalk mark and then trim it to fit.

1 Measure the width of your paper and then mark the ceiling this distance minus 25mm/1in from the top of the wall you are using as your starting point. Press a drawing pin into the ceiling at this point and do the same at the far end of the room. Attach household string rubbed with chalk to these two pins and snap it against the ceiling to create your marking line.

2 Measure the length of the ceiling and add on 25mm/1in for an overlap at either end. Cut this much paper from your roll, lay it on the pasting table and paste it. Paste the entire length of paper in one go, folding it in to a concertina-style stack (paste side to paste side) as you go along. Make a fairly loose fold every 600mm/2ft, taking care not to crease the paper.

3 When the entire length has been pasted and the correct soaking time elapsed, pick up the concertina stack and climb on to one end of your work platform.

4 Unpeel the top edge of the paper and position it against your chalk mark, so that 25mm/1in overlaps the end wall and a similar amount overlaps the side (window) wall.

5 Brush this first section of paper smooth against the ceiling before unpeeling the second fold and repeating the process. You may find that an extra pair of hands to hold the concertina stack comes in useful here.

6 Align the second section of paper against your chalk mark and again brush it smooth before unpeeling any more paper. In this way, you should never have more than 600mm/2ft of paper to handle at any one time. The rest will be either in your hand or firmly attached to the ceiling

7 If the paper refuses to stick to the ceiling, you have probably made the paste too watery. Fold the paper back into a concertina stack, strengthen the mix and apply this to the ceiling. Then slide the paper back into place.

8 When you have hung the first length, trim its edges to fit the angle between the ceiling and the tops of the walls.

9 Hang the second and each successive length in exactly the same way until you reach the far side of the room.

INDEX